The Richard C. Kessler
Reformation Collection

An Annotated Bibliography

Emory Texts and Studies in Ecclesial Life

General Editor
Channing R. Jeschke

Number 6

The Richard C. Kessler

Reformation Collection

An Annotated Bibliography

1999

The Richard C. Kessler
Reformation Collection
An Annotated Bibliography

Volume 4
Printed Works, 1550–1582

Compiled by
Fred A. Grater

Edited by
Wm. Bradford Smith

SCHOLARS PRESS
Atlanta, Georgia

EMORY TEXTS *AND* STUDIES
IN ECCLESIAL LIFE

The Richard C. Kessler Reformation Collection

An Annotated Bibliography
Pitts Theology Library, Emory University
Volume 4
Printed Works, 1550–1582

Compiled by Fred A. Grater
Edited by Wm. Bradford Smith

Copyright © 1999 by Emory University

Library of Congress Cataloging-in-Publication Data
Pitts Theology Library. Richard C. Kessler Reformation Collection.
    The Richard C. Kessler Reformation Collection : An annotated bibliography
Pitts Theology Library, Emory University / compiled by Fred A. Grater : edited
by Wm. Bradford Smith.
        p.   cm. — (Emory University texts and studies in ecclesial life ; nos. 3, 4, 5, 6)
    Contents: v. 1. Manuscripts and printed works, 1470–1522. ISBN 0-7885-0487-8
(alk. paper)—v. 2. Printed works, 1523–1531. ISBN 0-7885-0548-3 (alk. paper)—v. 3.
Printed works, 1532–1549. ISBN 0-7885-0549-1 (alk. paper)—v. 4. Printed works,
1550-1582. ISBN 0-7885-0550-5 (alk. paper).
    1. Reformation—Bibliography—Catalogs. 2. Theology—
History—16th century—Bibliography—Catalogs. 3. Pitts Theology
Library. Richard C. Kessler Reformation Collection—Catalogs.
I. Grater, Fred A.   II. Smith, Wm. Bradford (William Bradford)
III. Title. IV. Series: Texts and Studies in Ecclesial Life ; no. 3.
Z7830.P58   1998
[BR305.2]
0.16.2706—dc21   98-26151

            08 07 06 05 04 03 02 01 00 99   5 4 3 2 1

Published by Scholars Press
for
Emory University

Table of Contents

1550

Amsdorff, Nicolaus von, 1483-1565.

CONFESSIO ET APOLOGIA PASTOrum & reliquorum ministrorum Ecclesiae Magdeburgensis.

Impressum Magdeburgi per Michaelem Lottherum. (Anno 1550. Idibus Aprilis.)

[79] p. ; 21 cm. (4to) Signatures: A-K^4; [A] unsigned, K4b blank.

This is the sixteenth item bound with Gallus' *Der Theologen bedencken* ... Gedruckt zu Magdeburgk durch Michel Lotther 1550.

There are manuscript notations on the title page, as well as manuscript marginalia in the text.

BM STC German, p. 585; Kolb, p. 261, no. C (between B and D); VD 16, A 2332; OCLC: 18622630.

N. von Amsdorff fled to Magdeburg as a result of the enforcement of the Interim of Leipzig. There he became a forceful propagandist against the Interim as an associate of Flacius. He held firmly to a strong Gnesio-Lutheran position. (A large woodcut printers device on the title page, incorporates the coat of arms of Magdeburg.)

1550
Gall: 16

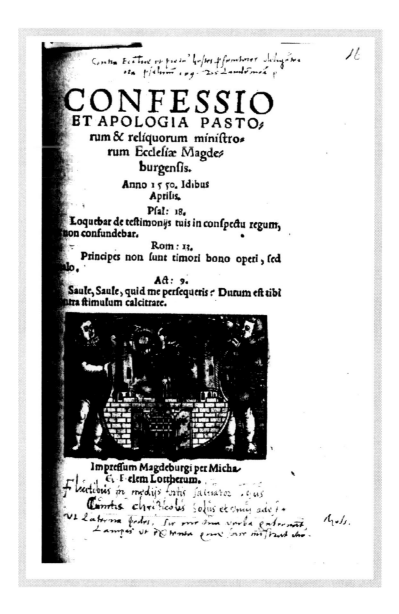

Bekentnis Vnterricht vnd vermanung, der Pfarrhern vnd Prediger, der Christlichen Kirchen zu Magdeburgk.

(Gedruckt zu Magdeburgk durch Michel Lotther), Anno 1550. Den 13. Aprilis.

[127] p. ; 19 cm. (4to) Signatures: A-Q^4; [A] unsigned, Q4b blank.

This volume was formerly in the Stewart collection, #7933.

VD 16, A 2333;   OCLC: 22771233.

The Magdeburg preachers wrote to defend their rebellion against the Empire, justifying it on the grounds that when the Emperor tried to usurp the free exercise of conscience or take away the Word of God, they had no choice but to take up arms against the usurpation. N. von Amsdorff, the exiled Lutheran Bishop of Naumburg, is listed as the first signer because he was the chief author of the tract. It was published in Latin and German versions.

1550
Pfar

Brenz, Johannes, 1499-1570.

ESAIAS PROPHETA, COMMENTARIIS EXPLICATVS.

FRANCOFORTI EX OFFICINA TYPOGRAPHICA PETRI BRVBACHII, ANNO DOMINI MILLESIMO QVINGENTESIMO QVINQVAGESIMO, MENSE VERO SEPT.

1079, [26] p. ; 32 cm. (fol. in 6s) Signatures: pi, A-Z, a-z, AA-ZZ, aa-xx, $^2a^6$, $^2b^7$; [pi]1 unsigned, [pi]6 blank, e, e2, e3 missigned "[epsilon]", "[epsilon]2", "[epsilon]3" respectively.

This volume is bound in blind-stamped pigskin over wooden boards and dated, "1551." The clasps are intact.

On the inside, upper pastedown is an embossed library bookplate of a former owner, A. Randle Elliott. On the title page is the manuscript inscription of a former owner, Georg Ludwig Oeder, a nineteenth century German theologian. There are manuscript marginalia in the text.

Adams, B-2783; VD 16, B 7775; OCLC: 14251423.

J. Brenz was one of the foremost Biblical commentators of his day. This commentary on the Prophet Isaiah is one of his major achievements, published twenty years before his death. During his lifetime, Luther valued Brenz's commentaries highly and often wrote commendatory prefaces for them. This is the first printing of the work.

1550
Bren

Brunus, Conradus, 1491?-1563.

DE SEDITIONIBVS LIBRI SEX, RATIONIBVS ET EXEMPLIS EX OMNI DOC-
TRINARVM ET AVTHORVM genere locupletati.

Moguntiae apud S. Victorem EX OFFICINA FRANCISCI BEHEM Typographi, M.D.L.

[20], 355, [1] p. ; 31 cm. (2o in 6s) Signatures: [pi]^2, b[clover]^4, a[clover]2-5, A-Z^6, a-f^6, g^4; I4, N4, c4 unsigned.

This volume is bound in vellum.

Adams, B 2961; BM STC German, p. 158; Spahn, p. 371, no. 197; V 16, B 7209; OCLC: *10202684.*

Conrad Brun dedicated this treatise on sedition and heresy to Ferdinand I, King of the Romans and later Emperor. He urged the king to take up the battle of virtue against vice. Cochlaeus edited this work.

1550
Brun

Canones Concilij PROVINCIALIS COLONIENSIS ANNO CELEBRATI
M.D.XXXVI.

PARISIIS Apud Guillielmum Cauellat in via D. Ioannis Lateranensis, e regione Collegij, 1550.

3 parts bd. as 1 v. ; 18 cm. (8vo) Signatures: Canones: $*^8$, a-m^8; [*] unsigned. Decreta Concilii: aa-dd8, ee2; [aa] unsigned. Enchiridion: [paragraph]^8, 2[paragraph]^{10}, A-Z^8, AA-RR^8, Ss^4; [paragraph] unsigned, C3 missigned "C2", II3 missigned "II2."

This volume was formerly in the Stewart collection, #2805.

OCLC: 24934676.

In 1547, Charles V forced Hermann V von Wied to abdicate as Archbishop and Elector of Cologne on account of his Protestant sympathies. This volume contains the proceedings and decrees of the reform synods held by his successors, in an effort to remedy abuses and extirpate heresy.

1550
Colo

Civilius, pseudonym.

Eine freidige vermanung, zu klarem vnd öffentlichem bekentnis Jhesu Christi, wider die Adiaphoristische, Dauidianische, vnd Epicurische klugheit, des heuchelns vnd meuchelns, sehr nützlich zu lesen. Gestelt durch Ciuilium einen Italiener.

Gedruckt zu Magdeburgk durch Michel Lotther, den 4. Octobris. Anno 1550.

[24] p. ; 21 cm. (4to) Signatures: A-C⁴; [A], C4 unsigned.

This is the eighteenth item bound with Gallus' *Der Theologen bedencken* ... Gedruckt zu Magdeburgk durch Michel Lotther 1550.

Preger, II, p. 546;   VD 16, C 3966-3967 (under Civile, Marco);   OCLC: 18585930.

The Magdeburg presses poured out reams of anti-adiaphorist polemic. This pamphlet issued pseudonymously by one "Civilius, an Italian" was translated from the Italian with a preface by M. Flacius Illyricus.

1550
Gall: 18

DEr Von Magdeburgk Ausschreiben an alle Christen.

Gedruckt zu Magdeburgk Durch Hans Walther. Anno M.D.L. den XXIIII. Marcii.

[15] p. ; 21 cm. (4to) Signatures: A-B⁴; [A], A2 unsigned, B4b blank.

This is the fifteenth item bound with Gallus' *Der Theologen bedencken ...* Gedruckt zu Magdeburgk durch Michel Lotther 1550.

There are manuscript marginalia in the text as well as a manuscript note on the verso of the last printed page. A large woodcut printers device on the title page incorporates the coat of arms of the town of Magdeburg.

BM STC German, p. 585; Pegg, Swiss, 3840; VD 16, M 127; OCLC: 18586128.

This is a further defense of the Magdeburg city council's decision to oppose the Interim.

1550
Gall: 15

EPISTOLARVM MIscellanearu[m] ad Fridericum Nauseam Blancicampianum, Epis-copum Viennensem, &c. singularium personarum, Libri X.

BASILEAE, EX OFFICINA IOANnis Oporini, Anno Salutis humanae M.D.L. Mense Martio.

[8], 501, [3] p. ; 31 cm. (fol. in 4s) Signatures: [alpha]^4, A-2Z^4, AA-RR^4; [alpha], 2T3, RR3, unsigned, 2X missigned "X", FF3 missigned "Ff3", RR4a blank.

This volume is bound in limp vellum.

This volume was formerly in the Stewart collection, #4660.

Adams, N-84; BM STC German, p. 635; VD 16, E 1736; OCLC: 20153504.

F. Nausea became Bishop of Vienna in 1541. At the Council of Trent he argued in favor of communion in both kinds, and for clerical marriage. This volume in ten parts includes the correspondence addressed to Nausea throughout his lifetime.

1550
Epis

EPISTOLARVM MI-
fcellanearū ad Fridericum Nau
fcam Blancicampianum, Epifco
pum Viennenfem,&c.fingu-
larium perfonarum,
Libri x.

Harum uerò editionis rationem atcp ufum in
Præfatione reperies.

ADDITVS EST SVB FINEM OPE-
ris, eiufdem Epifcopi Viennenfis lucubrationum
Catalogus.

Cum Cæf. & Regiæ Maieft.gratia & priuilegio ad quinquennium.

BASILEAE, M. D. L.
Menfe Martio.

Flacius Illyricus, Matthias, 1520-1575.

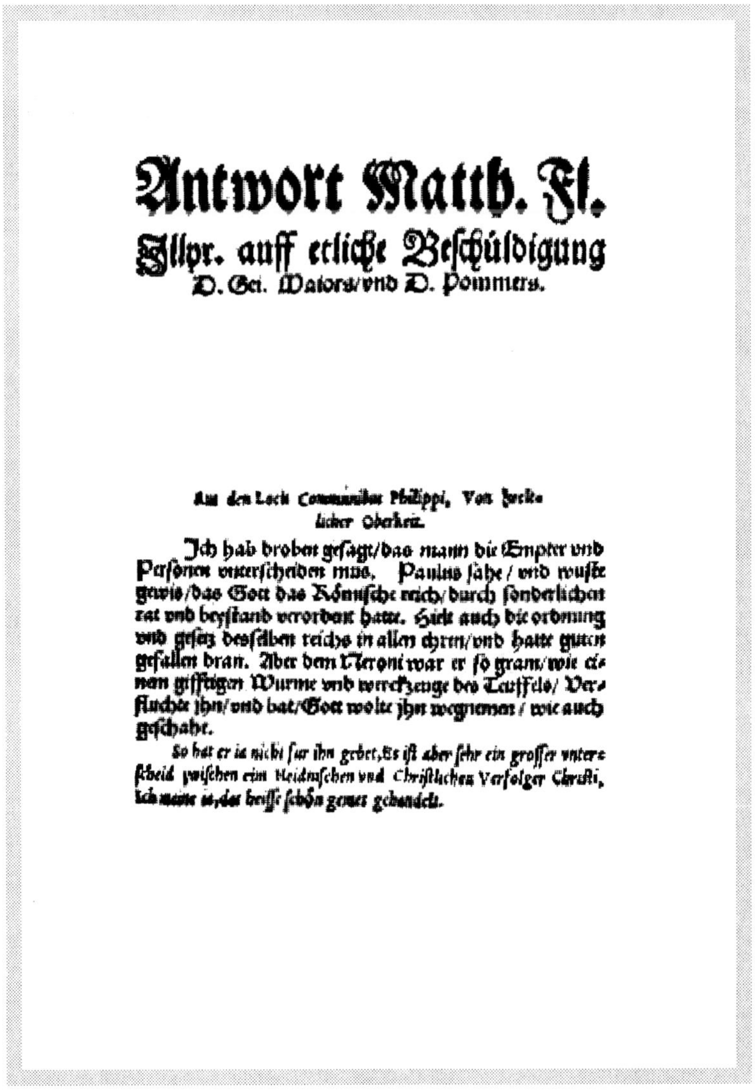

Antwort Matth. Fl. Illyr. auff etliche Beschüldigung D. Gei. Maiors, vnd D. Pommers.

[S.l. : s.n., 1550?]

[24] p. ; 20 cm. (4to) Signatures: A-C^4; [A] unsigned.

This volume was formerly in the W. H. Stifel Collection, #557. There is a bookplate on the inside, upper cover reading, "Gustav E. Stechert; 766 Broadway; New York."

BM STC German, p. 305; Preger, II, p. 549; VD 16, F 1259; OCLC: 18697478.

In the controversy over the Protestant response to the Interim, J. Bugenhagen and G. Major joined Melanchthon against Flacius. This is one of the latter's replies to some of their charges. Each side appealed to Luther's authority for their justification in the matter.

1550
Flac A

Antwort Matth. Fl.
Illyr. auff etliche Beschüldigung
D. Gei. Maiors/vnd D. Pommers.

Aus den Locis Communibus Philippi, Von weltlicher Oberkeit.

Ich hab droben gesagt/das mann die Empter vnd Personen vnterscheiden mus. Paulus sahe/vnd wuste gewis/das Gott das Römische reich/durch sonderlichen rat vnd beystand verordent hatte. Hielt auch die ordnung vnd gesetz desselben reichs in allen ehren/vnd hatte guten gefallen dran. Aber dem Neroni war er so gram/wie einem giefftigen Wurme vnd werckzeuge des Teuffels/ Verfluchte jhn/vnd bat/Gott wolte jhn wegnemen/ wie auch geschahe.

So hat er ia nicht fur ihn gebet, Es ist aber sehr ein grosser vnterscheid zwischen eim Heidnischen vnd Christlichen Verfolger Christi, Ich meine es, das heisse schön gemet gehandelt.

Flacius Illyricus, Matthias, 1520-1575.

CONTRA QVAEDAM INTERIMIstica & Adiaphoristica scripta, quae à multis Gasparo Huberino tribuuntur.

MAGDEBVRGI APVD CHRIstianum Rhodium [1550?]

[15] p. ; 15 cm. (8vo) Signatures: A^8; [A] unsigned, A8b blank.

Kuczynski, 841; Preger, II, p. 544; VD 16, F 1329; OCLC: 18730268.

Huberinus (Huber) was one of the Lutheran pastors who accepted the terms of the Interims. Flacius here presents a short refutation of his position.

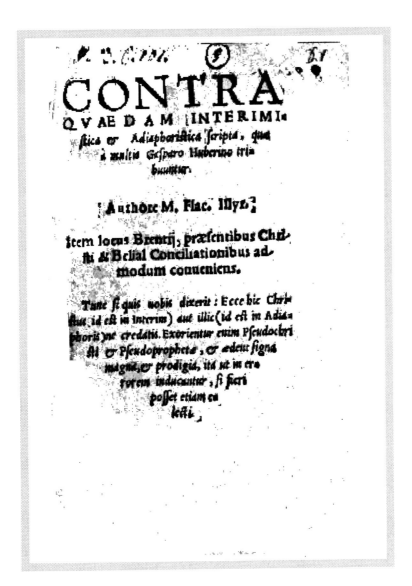

1550
Flac

Flacius Illyricus, Matthias, 1520-1575.

Ein Christliche vermanung M. Matthie Flacii Illyrici zur bestendigkeit, inn der waren reinen Religion Jhesu Christi, vnnd inn der Augspurgischen bekentnis, Geschrieben an die Meissnissche Kirche, vnnd andere, so das lauttere Euangelium Jhesu Christi erkant haben.

Gedrückt zu Magdeburgk durch Michael Lotther Anno 1550.

[60] p. ; 21 cm. (4to) Signatures: A-G^4 H^2; [A] unsigned; A1b blank.

There is a small bibliographical notation at the head of the title page. On the verso are two former ownership stamps, one reading, "Ad Bibl. Acad. Land.," and "U B M abgegeben."

BM STC German, p. 305; Kuczynski, 842; Pegg, Swiss, 1688; VD 16, F 1300; OCLC: 17540199.

This tract was written as a result of the adiaphoristic controversy in Lutheranism. Some Lutherans held that some things in the Church were adiaphora, that is, neither inherently good nor evil. They felt it was possible to compromise with Catholics and reach a mutually acceptable standard of religious practice. Flacius denied that there were adiaphora and rejected all compromise in matters of faith. The tract takes the form of an open letter to the Church of Meissen.

1550
Flac B

Flacius Illyricus, Matthias, 1520-1575.

Verlegung zweier schrifften, eines Augspurgischen Münchs, mit namen Joannes Fabri, von des Babsts Primat vnd von Beicht.

Gedruckt zu Magdeburgk bey Christian Rödinger [1550?]

[86] p. ; 21 cm. (4to) Signatures: A-I^4, K^3, L^4; [A], B3, C3 unsigned. Tentative date from p. [8].

This is the ninth item bound with Gallus' *Der Theologen bedencken ...* Gedruckt zu Magdeburgk durch Michel Lotther 1550.

There is a manuscript note on the title page, as well as manuscript marginalia in the text.

BM STC German, p. 307; Jackson, 1869; Pegg, Bibliotheca, 468; Pegg, Swiss, 1704; Preger, II, p. 548; VD 16, F 1519; OCLC: 18622876.

Flacius gathered all the material he could find against the Catholic Church and rushed it into print. This tract includes works by Flacius himself (against Johann Faber), eighteen reasons that St. Peter was never in Rome, a letter of consolation of Luther to the Church in Augsburg, and a treatise by Gregory of Heimburg against the usurpations of the papacy.

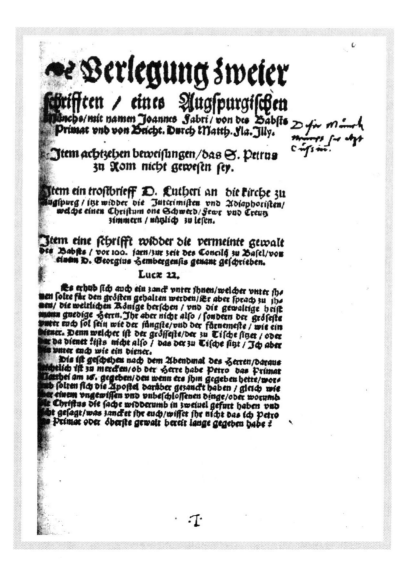

1550
Gall: 9

Flacius Illyricus, Matthias, 1520-1575.

Widder die newe Reformation D. Pfeffingers, des Meisnischen Thumbherrn.
Gedruckt zu Magdeburg, bey Christian Rödinger Anno D.M.L

[43] p. ; 21 cm. (4to) Signatures: A-E⁴, F²; [A], F2 unsigned, F2b blank.

This is the twenty-first item bound with Gallus' *Der Theologen bedencken* ... Gedruckt zu Magdeburgk durch Michel Lotther 1550.

BM STC German, p. 307; Hohenemser, 3594; Pegg, Bibliotheca, 469; Pegg, Swiss, 1707; Preger, II, p. 545; VD 16, F 1561; OCLC: 18618059.

Pfeffinger came into conflict with Flacius over the question of synergism. Pfeffinger believed that humanity cooperates with the Holy Spirit in effecting salvation, whereas Flacius believed that God acted alone and without human participation.

1550
Gall: 21

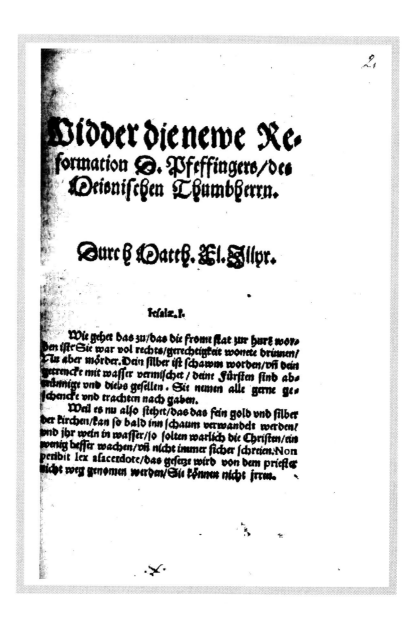

Flacius Illyricus, Matthias, 1520-1575.

Widder die vnchristliche Vermanungschrifft, des Bisthumbs zu Naumburg.
Gedruckt zu Magdeburg bey Christian Rödinger M.D.L.

[12] p ; 21 cm. (4to) Signatures: A⁴, B²; [A], B2 unsigned.

This is the twentieth item bound with Gallus' *Der Theologen bedencken ...* Gedruckt zu Magdeburgk durch Michel Lotther 1550.

BM STC German, p. 307;   Pegg, Bibliotheca, 470;   Pegg, Swiss, 1708;   Preger, II, p. 548;   VD 16, F 1565;   OCLC: 18586050.

Julius von Pflug, Bishop of Naumberg, published an admonition to the people of his diocese that they should return to Catholicism and give up the errors of Protestantism. Flacius here replies to von Pflug's order.

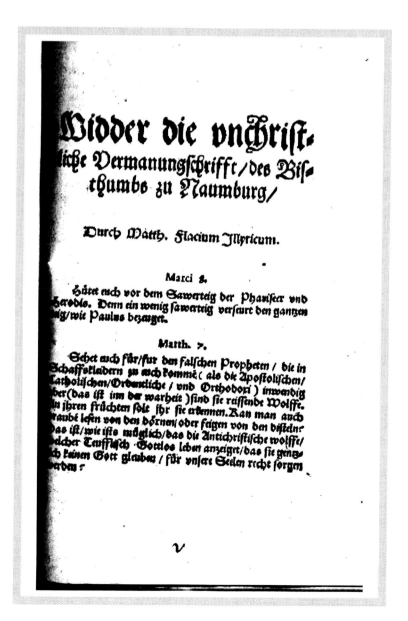

1550
Gall: 20

Flacius Illyricus, Matthias, 1520-1575.

Widderlegung der Predigten von der allerheiligsten Antichristische[n] MISSA des frembden Bischoffs von Sydon, Meintzischen Weihbischoff.

Gedruckt zu Magdeburg bey Christian Rödinger. Anno. M.D.L.

[91] p. ; 21 cm. (4to) Signatures: A·L^4, M^2; [A], M2 unsigned, M2b blank.

This is the eighth item bound with Gallus' *Der Theologen bedencken* ... Gedruckt zu Magdeburgk durch Michel Lotther 1550.

BM STC German, p. 308;   Pegg, Swiss, 1710;   Preger, II, p. 546;   VD 16, F 1567;   OCLC: 18580855.

At the Diet of Augsburg in 1548, M. Helding, Suffragan Bishop of Merseburg, preached ten sermons on the Mass. This tract is Flacius' reply to those sermons. Flacius' attacks are mostly ad hominem assaults on Helding's person and do not constitute a serious critique of his theology.

1550
Gall: 8

Flacius Illyricus, Matthias, 1520-1575.

Widderlegung des Catechismi des Laruen Bischoffes von Sidon.

Gedruckt zu Magdeburg [s.n.] 1550.

[43] p. ; 21 cm. (4to) Signatures: A-E^4,F^2; [A], F^2 unsigned; F2b blank.

This is the sixth item bound with Gallus' *Der Theologen bedencken ...* Gedruckt zu Magdeburgk durch Michel Lotther 1550.

Kuczynski, 844; Pegg, Swiss, 1711; Preger, II, p. 544; VD 16, F 1320; OCLC: 18580790.

This is a tract by Flacius Illyricus criticizing the catechism of M. Helding, Bishop of Merseburg. This work was first written in Latin in 1549.

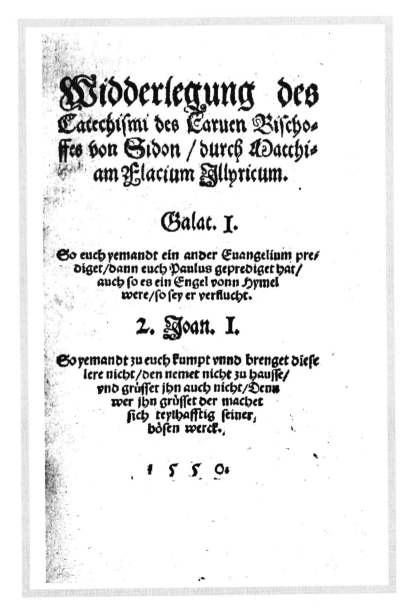

1550
Gall: 6

Flacius Illyricus, Matthias, 1520-1575.

Zwey Capitel Polydori Virgilij vom Name[n] vnd Stifftern der Mess, ausgangen zu eine[m] anfang widder des Sydonij predigten, Daraus erscheinet, wie er in seinen predigten öffentlich leugt, da er sagt, das die gantze Christenheit von 1500. Jaren her die Papistische Mess allezeit eintrechtiglich gehalten habe. Vnd das der Canon in allen seinen stücken von der Apostel zeit her im brauch gewesen sey.

Gedruckt zu Magegburg, bey Christian Rödinger. Anno M.D.L.

[44] p. ; 21 cm. (4to) Signatures: A-D^4, E^6.

This is the seventh item bound with Gallus' *Der Theologen bedencken* ... Gedruckt zu Magdeburgk durch Michel Lotther 1550.

BM STC German, p. 308; Pegg, Swiss, 1712; OCLC: 12852926.

P. Vergil was an English antiquary, whose book, "On the inventors of things," traced the discovery of all sorts of useful inventions and ideas. Chapters 9-10 of Book 5 deal with the early history of the Mass. Because Vergil argued that the Mass was a recent invention, Flacius reprinted the work with his own approving comments.

1550
Gall: 7

Gallus, Nicolaus, 1516-1570.

Der Theologen bedencken, odder (wie es durch die ihren inn offentlichem Drück genennet wirdt) Beschluss des Landtages zu Leiptzig, so im December des 48. Jars, von wegen des Auspurgischen Interims gehalten ist, Welchs bedenken odder beschluss wir, so da widder geschrieben, das Leiptzigsche Interim genennet haben.

Gedruckt zu Magdeburgk durch Michel Lotther 1550.

[118] p. ; 19 cm. (4to) Signatures: A-O^4, P^3 ; [A], P3 unsigned.

This volume is the first item in a bound collection, bound in blind-stamped, bleached pigskin over wooden boards, clasps intact.

There is, on the inside upper cover, a table of contents for works in the bound volume, as well as a hymn to the honor of Herzog Johann Friderich zuo Sachsen from 1555 on the upper flyleaves. On the lower flyleaves is a letter from Melanchthon to Carlwitz (?), 1548, on the Church, a song by Johann Gritel (?) of Eisleben, and a dedication on the inside lower cover. There are also manuscript notes on the title page in German.

BM, vol. 81, col. 568; BM STC German, p. 349; Jackson, 490; Kuczynski, 871; Pegg, Swiss, 1790; Preger, II, p. 544; OCLC: 12852911.

This is the first item in a large collection of Protestant polemical tracts dealing with the Interim. This tract attacks the Interim of Leipzig, a Protestant response to the Interim of Augsburg. The Magdeburg Lutherans proved utterly hostile towards any attempt at reconciliation with Catholicism. Included in this collected volume is a 4-page manuscript poem on the fidelity of Johann Frederich, Elector of Saxony.

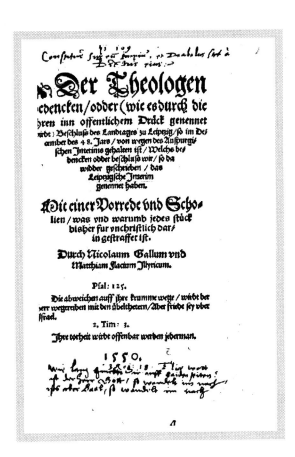

1550
Gall: 1

Gregory, of Nazianzus, Saint, 329?-389?

[Gregoriou tou Nazianzenou tou theologou hapanta ta mechri nun men heuriskomena hon echestin selis he deutera periechei. Tou hagiou bios, syngrapheis hypo Suida, Sophroniou kai Gregoriou tou Presbyterou (romanized form)]

En Basileia [i.e. Basel] J. Herwagen (romanized form), [1550].

[8], 140 [i.e. 340], 95 p. ; 35 cm. (fol. in 4s) Signatures: [alpha]4, a-z, A-P⁴, Q⁶, R-T⁴, ²[alpha]4, [beta]-[mu]4; [alpha] unsigned, [mu]4 blank.

This volume was from the Library of Samuel Stone, and donated to the Library of the Theological Institute of Connecticut. There is a bookplate on the inside upper cover reading, "J. Leslie, theological bookseller..." as well as a manuscript note reading, "Gregorii Nazian. opera Gr."

Adams, G-1133; BM STC German, p. 368; VD 16, G 3019; OCLC: 19464088.

Gregory of Nazianzus was a saint, the son of two saints and the brother of two more. He is counted as one of the fathers of the Eastern Church. He was by turns a rhetorician, a monk, a priest, and a bishop. He took a leading role in trying to counter the Arian heresy that denied the divinity of Christ.

1550
Greg
(OS)

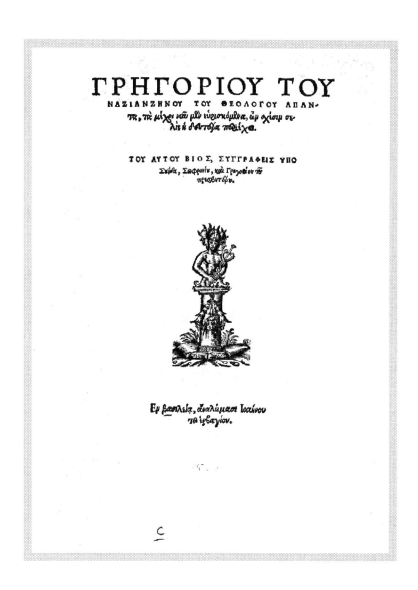

Hertzberger, Anton Otto.

Von dem frölichen Ablas auff das güldene Jar, des itzigen fünfftzigsten jars.

Gedrückt zu Magdeburg [Christian Rödinger] Anno 1550.

[31] p. ; 21 cm. (4to) Signatures: A-D⁴ ; D4b blank.

This is the twelfth item bound with Gallus' *Der Theologen bedencken ...* Gedruckt zu Magdeburgk durch Michel Lotther 1550.

Kuczynski, 3504; Hohenemser, 3596; Pegg, Bibliotheca, 566 (with printer as: "[M. Lotther?]"); Pegg, Swiss, 2197 (with printer as: "[M. Lotther]"); VD 16, O 1491 (under Otto, Anton; printer given as: "[Christain Rödinger d.Ä]"); OCLC: 10198623.

A. O. Hertzberger, who is also know as Anton Otto, was pastor in the Free Imperial City of Nordhausen. Besides this piece, he wrote another tract criticizing A. Osiander's doctrine of justification. This tract satirizes Paul III's declaration of a plenary indulgence for the Jubilee Year of 1550. Its tone is similar to that of other anti-Catholic propaganda emanating from the Gnesio-Lutheran camp at Magdeburg.

1150
Hert

HORTVLVS ANIMAE. *Lustgarten der Seelen: Mit schönen lieblichen Figuren.*
(Gedruckt zu Wittemberg durch Georgen Rhawen Erben), 1550.

[248] p. : ill., port., plates ; 21 cm. (4to) Signatures: A-Z^4, a-h^4; [A] unsigned.

This copy is bound in blind-stamped calfskin over paper board, with rolled panels of the Crucifixion and the Resurrection. The binding is dated, "1556," done for "IH," by binder, "FS." The clasps are missing.

This volume was a gift of Richard and Martha Kessler, 1987. There is a manuscript note on both sides of the lower flyleaf.

There are forty-three illustrations by L. Cranach, three by Hans Brosamer, and nine by Meister der Jacobsleiter in the text.

OCLC: *16949402.*

This is the first Protestant breviary of the Wittenberg Reformation. The readings are taken from Luther's catechetical writings and from Melanchthon's exposition of the Lord's Prayer. Luther's explanation of the Apostles' Creed is also included. Of special note is the well-preserved dated binding, 1556. The portrait of Luther by L. Cranach occurs only in the quarto editions of this work.

1550
Hort

Luther, Martin, 1483-1546.

Der ander Psalm Dauids, durch D. Martinum Luther heiliger gedechtnis ausgelegt, ...
Jtzt newlich Verdeudscht.

Gedruckt zu Magdeburg, bey Christian Rödinger. 1550.

[152] p. ; 19 cm. (4to) Signatures: A-T^4; [A] unsigned, A1b blank.

This volume was formerly in the Beck Lutherana collection, #348 and in the W. H. Stifel collection, #373/548.

VD 16, L 4541;   WA 40, 2, 192;   OCLC: 22167176.

Luther's lectures on Psalm 2 that form the basis for this commentary, were delivered in March-June 1532. The original Latin text was edited by Veit Dietrich based on transcripts by Rörer. It is not known who made the present German translation.

1550
Luth C

Luther, Martin, 1483-1546.

Des Ehrwirdigen vnd tewren Mans Doct. Marti. Luthers seliger gedechtnis meinung, von den Mitteldingen, durch M. Joachimu[m] Westphalum Pfarhern zu Hamburgk zusamen gelesen.

(Gedruckt zu Magdeburgk durch Michael Lotther) Anno 1550.

[68] p. ; 19 cm. (4to) Signatures: A-H^4, I^2; [A] unsigned, A1b blank.

This volume was formerly in the Beck Lutherana collection, #793.

BM STC German, p. 580;   VD 16, L 3471;   OCLC: 18216378.

In his theological battles with the Adiaphorists, Flacius Illyricus issued whatever writings by Luther and others that suited his purposes. This book is a collection of extracts from Luther's writings on Adiaphora. The collection was edited by J. Westphal.

1550
Luth B

Luther, Martin, 1483-1546.

PROPHETIAE ALIQVOT VERAE: ET SENTENTIAE INSIGNES REVERENDI PATRIS, Domini Doctoris Martini Lutheri, Tertij Heliae: De calamitatibus, defectione, & Tenebris, Germaniae obuenturis, eo in Domino mortuo, & perpetuo uiuente. Collectae per Iohannem Ammsterdamum Ecclesiae Dei ministrum in Brema. ET NVNC DENVO SVMMA CVra ac dilligentia castigatae. Accessit & altera pars, consolatoriarum sententiarum, eiusdem D. Lutheri.

[S.l. : s.n., 1550?]

[96] p. ; 16 cm. (8vo) Signatures: A-F^8; [A] unsigned, A1b blank.

This volume was formerly in the Stewart collection, #3951.

VD 16, L 3470; OCLC: 21494683.

The words of Luther were treasured by his followers, especially after his death. They collected his sayings on various topics and circulated them in collections such as this.

1550
Luth A

Melanchthon, Philipp, 1497-1560.

ENARRATIO BREVIS CONCIONVM LIBRI SALOmonis cui titulus est Ecclesiastes.

VITEBERGAE. Excudebat Ioseph Klug. ANNO. 1550.

[172] p. ; 15 cm. (8vo) Signatures: A-K^8, L^6; [A], E3, G3 unsigned, A7b, A8b blank.

Adams, M-1072; Hartfelder, 453; Kuczynski, 3446; VD 16, M 3158; OCLC: 28980458.

Melanchthon became quite a proficient trilingualist, working with Latin, Greek, and Hebrew. This commentary on the Book of Ecclesiastes is another example of his versatility. This is the first printing of the work.

1550
Mela A

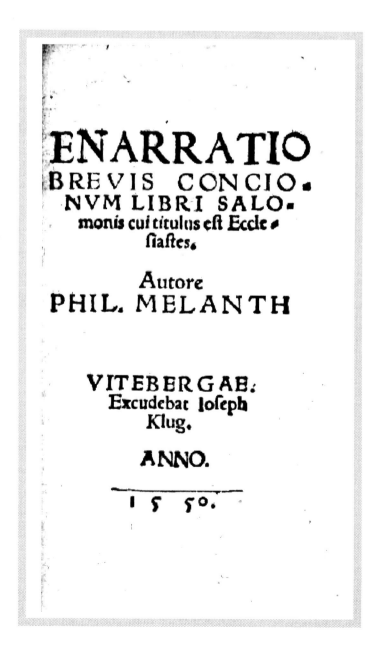

Melanchthon, Philipp, 1497-1560.

EROTEMATA DIALECTICES, *continentia fere integram artem: Ita scripta, ut Iuuen-tuti utiliter proponi possint.*

[Lyons : Antoine Vincent, ca. 1550.]

330, [33] p. ; 18 cm. (8vo) Signatures: a-z^8; [a] unsigned, z6b-8 blank.

This volume is bound in vellum binding.

There is a bookplate on the inside upper pastedown dated 1575 of Ludovicus Romanus, IVD, whose signature also appears on the title page with the date 1580.

BM, v. III, col. 838, Nr. 92 (with imprint "(S.l.n.d.)"); Pre '56 imprints, v. 374, p. 289, NM 0416787, (with date: "[15-?]"); OCLC: 12781317.

Melanchthon continued to write textbooks for his students and remained a popular teacher throughout his life. This textbook on rhetoric proceeds by question and answer, discussing the topics in a careful, thorough manner.

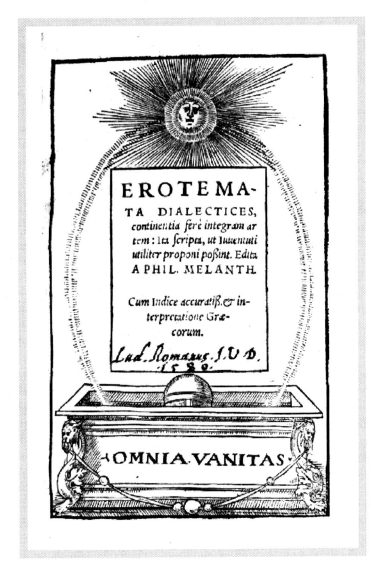

1550
Mela

Müntzer, M. R.

Zwey Schön new Geistlich lied, aus Göttlicher schrifft, von dem wüsten wesen der itzigen bösen Welt: zum schrecken den Gottlosen, vnd zu trost den Christen, Jm thon, Frisch auff ihr Lands [k]necht alle &c.

(Gedrückt zu Nürnberg durch Friedrich Christoff Gutknecht.) [ca. 1550.]

   [7] p. ; 14 cm. (8vo) Signature: unsigned.

   Wackernagel, 608;   OCLC: 26816806.

   Nothing is known about M. R. Müntzer, the author of these two hymns. The first is about the terrible condition of the present world, designed to terrify the godless and comfort the godly. The second is a prayer to God for forgiveness of sins, strengthening of faith, and a good death. The date of printing is conjectural.

1550
Munt

Naogeorg, Thomas, 1511-1563.

AGRICVLTVRAE SACRAE LIbri quinque.

BASILEAE [s.n.] (1550).

[8], 167, [37] p. ; 15 cm. (8vo) Signatures: [alpha]^4, A-K^8, L^4, m^8, n^{10}; [alpha]1b, [alpha]3b blank, n6, n7 signed.

This is the first item in a bound collection, bound in blind-stamped, bleached pigskin over paper boards, dated, "1592," with the quires bound upside down.

This volume was formerly in the Stewart collection, #4404. There is a manuscript note on the verso of the upper flyleaf.

Adams, N-30; BM STC German, p. 471; OCLC: 16113979.

T. Naogeorg was a playwright, who used his dramatic ability to foster the aims of the Reformation. He said that he owed the direction and insight that guided his life to the preaching of Luther. But he was no slavish Lutheran: he maintained his theological independence even when it cost him his position. In the years following the Interim of Leipzig (1548), he was frequently forced to change employment because of his religious views. This work is a long Latin poem, "Sacred Agriculture." The metaphor is the farm as a type of world and the pastor as the "cultivator" of the growth of souls. The other item with which this is bound is a long poem by Marco Probo (1455-1499) on the life of the Blessed Virgin Mary.

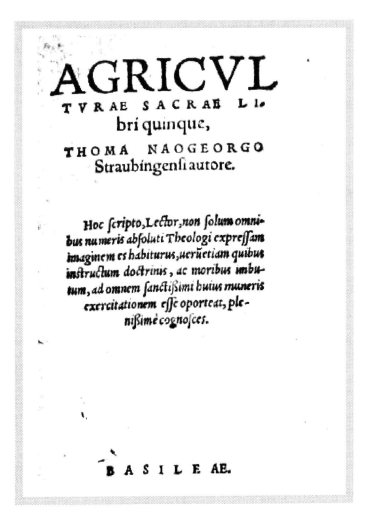

1550
Nang: 1

Ordenung vnd Mandat Keiser Caroli V. vernewert im April Anno 1550. Zu aussrotten vnd zu vertilgen, die Secten vnd spaltung, Welche entstanden sind, widder vnsern heiligen Christlichen glauben, Vnd wider die ordenung vnser Mutter der heiligen Christlichen Kirchen.

[S.l. : s.n., after April 1550.]

[76] p. ; 17 cm. (4to) Signatures: [leaf]^4, A-G^4, H^2; [leaf], H2 unsigned.

This is the twenty-fourth item bound with Gallus' *Der Theologen bedencken ...* Gedruckt zu Magdeburgk durch Michel Lotther 1550.

There are some manuscript marks in the text.

Pegg, *Bibliotheca*, 514; Pegg, *Swiss*, 1960 (with place and printer as "[Magdeburg: M. Lotter]"); VD 16, N 1581-1582; OCLC: 18634115.

This tract includes the second edition of the *Index of Prohibited Books* drawn up by theologians at the University of Louvain. This edition is edited by M. Flacius Illyricus and includes his commentary on the Interim and the Index.

1550
Gall: 24

Oresme, Nicole, 1330?-1382.

Lucifers Sendbrief, an die vermeinten Geistlichen, vor 140. Jaren geschrieben.
Gedruckt zu Magdeburg bey Christian Rödinger, M.D.L.

[36] p. ; 21 cm. (4to) Signatures: A-D^4, E^2; [A], E2 unsigned.

This is the eleventh item bound with Gallus' *Der Theologen bedencken ...* Gedruckt zu Magdeburgk durch Michel Lotther 1550.

BM STC German, p. 663;   VD 16, E 1702;   OCLC: 18633777.

This collection of "satanic" letters, written by Nicole Oresme in the fourteenth century, was translated and published by the Magdeburg Protestants in 1550.

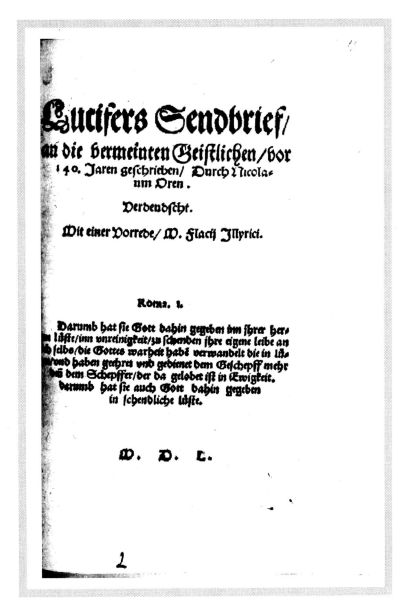

1550
Gall: 11

Paeonius, Martinus.

Von der krafft des Götlichen Worts, vnd des Glaubens. Drey schöne Trostbrieffe am Martin Arnoldt zu Bayreut in seiner Gefengknuss.

Gedruckt zu Nürnberg durch Johann Daubman, 1550.

[148] p. ; 19 cm. (4to) Signatures: A-S , T; [A], T2 unsigned.

This is the ninth item bound with Martin Luther's *Kurtz bekentnis*, Gedruckt zu Wittenberg, Durch Hans Lufft. M.D. XLIIII.

BM STC German, p. 670;   Hohenemser, 3601;   VD 16, P 75;   OCLC: 18653562.

M. Paeonius was a German Protestant theologian from Tirnava, Czechoslovakia, active in Nuremberg in the 1540s and 1550s. It is possible that among his works, he either wrote or translated a disputation on the layman's right to receive the cup in the Lord's Supper. However, it appears that he probably wrote only two other works, a sermon for Easter Sunday, printed in 1548, and a collection of three letters of consolation addressed to Martin Arnoldt. The letters stress the power of the Word of God and of faith. M. Arnoldt, a prisoner of conscience in Bayreuth, is reputed to have murdered his wife.

1544
Luth: 9

Paul III, 1468-1549.

BVLLA des Antichrists, dadurch er das volck Gottes widderumb inn den eisern ofen der Egiptischen gefengknis denckt zuziehen, gleichstimmig mit des Meintzischen Rabsakes briefe. Daraus wol zuuernemen, was der Teufel durch seine beide tugent, das ist, durch den Mörderische[n] krieg widder die Kirche Gottes, vnd durch sein lügen, als da sind, Concilium, Interim, Mittelding, Chorrock, denckt auszurichten.

Gedruckt zu Magdeburg durch Christian Rödinger. M.D.L.

[30] p.; 21 cm. (4to) Signatures: A-C , D ; [A] unsigned.

This is the fourth item bound with Gallus' *Der Theologen bedencken ...* Gedruckt zu Magdeburgk durch Michel Lotther 1550.

BM STC German, p. 755; Jackson, 480; Pegg, Swiss, 4654; VD 16, K 402-403 (further specification not possible); OCLC: 09462736.

This is a copy of the papal bull issued after the defeat of the Protestants at Muehlberg, issued with scurrilous notes by the Protestants of Magdeburg.

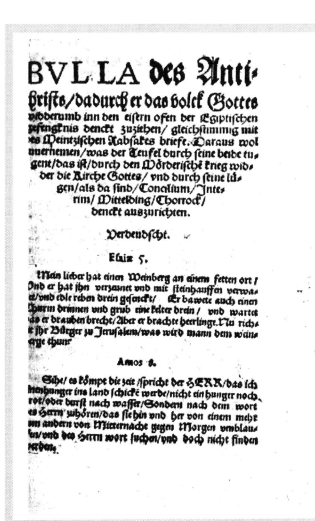

1550
Gall: 4

Pedioneus, Joannes.

IOANNIS PEDIONEI CONstantini Hymnorum Liber. EIVSDEM ODAE VII. ORA-TIO DE CICEROnis & eloquentiae laudibus.

INGOLSTADII excudebat Alexander Vueissenhorn. Anno L.

[117] p. ; 16 cm. (8vo) Signatures: A-H^8; I^3; [A], I2, 3 unsigned, A6b, I3b blank.

This is the first item in a bound collection.

There are manuscript marginalia in the text of this volume.

VD 16, P 1117; OCLC: 22837103.

J. Pedioneus was a Catholic priest from Constance, known for his fine Latin style. He was a teacher of the poet Peter Leichius, and became a professor of poetry and rhetoric in the University of Ingolstadt. He dedicated these "odes, hymns, and prose works" to some of the most notable cardinals of his day, men who were movers and shakers at the Council of Trent.

1550
Pedi: 1

IOANNIS
PEDIONEI CON.
  flantini Hymnorum Liber.

EIVSDEM ODAE VII.

ORATIO DE CICERO,
nis & eloquentiæ laudibus.

Cum gratia & priuilegio Imperatorio.

INGOLSTADII
excudebat Alexander
Vueissenborn.

ANNO L.

c̃

Pedioneus, Joannes.

IOANNIS PEDIONEI CONstantini, in D. Stephanum Hymnus, ad Vuolfgangum Episcopum Patauiensem. EIVSDEM ELEGIA, AD Georgium Loxanum.

INGOLSTADII excudebat Alexander Vueissenhorn. Anno M.D.L.

[31] p. ; 16 cm. (8vo) Signatures: A-B^8; [A] unsigned, A1b, B8b blank.

This is the second item bound with Joannes Pedioneus' *IOANNIS PEDIONEI CONstantini Hymnorum Liber....*, INGOLSTADII excudebat Alexander Vueissenhorn. Anno L.

VD 16, P 1118;   OCLC: 22837129.

J. Pedioneus dedicated this hymn to St. Stephen, to Wolfgang, Bishop of Padua, and the following elegy to Georgius Loxanus.

1550
Pedi: 2

IOANNIS
PEDIONEI CON-
lantini, in D. Stephanum Hymnus,
ad Vuolfgangum Episcopum
Patauiensem.

EIVSDEM ELEGIA, AD
Georgium Loxanum.

INGOLSTADII
excudebat Alexander
Vueissenhorn.

Anno M. D. L.

Rörer, Thomas.

Warer bericht vn[d] trost aus dem sechsten Capitel des Propheten Baruchs, allen betrübten gewissen, so in diesen kümmerlichen zeiten des Interims vnd Adiaphora halben, nicht wissen, wie sie sich halten sollen, Nützlich vnd tröstlich zu lesen.

Gedruckt zu Magdeburg bey Christian Rödinger, Anno M.D.L.

[62] p. ; 21 cm. (4to) Signatures: *·2*⁴, A-E⁴, F³; [*], B2 unsigned, *2 missigned "A2", A2 missigned "A3", B3-4 missigned "B2, 3" respectively.

This is the seventeenth item bound with Gallus' *Der Theologen bedencken* ... Gedruckt zu Magdeburgk durch Michel Lotther 1550.

There are some manuscript marginalia in the text.

There is a portrait of Luther on p. 2A3a.

BM STC German, p. 743; Pegg, Swiss, 4604; VD 16, R 3051; OCLC: 18586006.

T. Rörer was a Lutheran pastor in Cham, Bavaria. In this tract he comments on Baruch 6 from the Old Testament Apocrypha. Chapter 6 is also known as the Epistle of Jeremy and is a satire on idols.

1550
Gall: 17

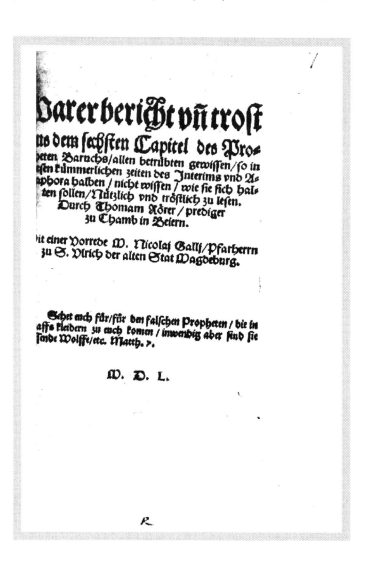

Sabinus, Georg, 1508-1560.

ELECTIO ET CORONATIO CAROLI .V. IMP. AVG.

COLONIAE Henricus Mameranus excudebat. [1550].

[208] p. ; 16 cm. (8vo) Signatures: A^8, ^{2}A^8, B-M^8; [A] unsigned, M8b blank, F5 missigned "v."

There is a manuscript inscription on the inside, upper pastedown. On the recto of the last leaf, at the foot of the page is a former ownership plate reading, "De Johnghe, Boulevard de l'Obervatione, 57."

VD 15, M 3090; OCLC: 10128346.

G. Sabinus was a son-in-law of P. Melanchthon. When Melanchthon wrote this history of the election and coronation of Charles V. as Holy Roman Emperor in 1544, he used his son-in-law's name as a pseudonym. The secret was apparently kept well enough that the printer, Henricus Mameranus, apparently a Catholic, sought and received a privilegium (a primitive form of copyright) to reprint the book for 10 years. This would not likely have been either applied for or granted if the true authorship had been known.

1550
Sabi

No. 1247 1550

Salvendensis, Basilius.

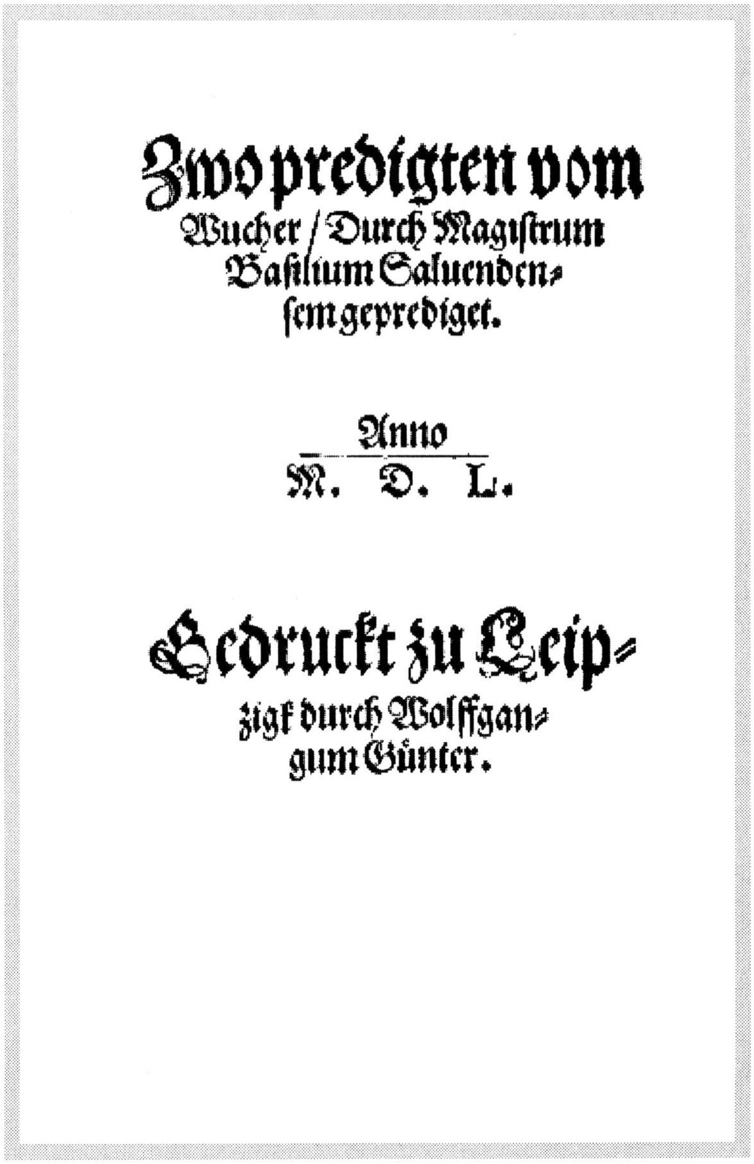

Zwo predigten vom Wucher.

Gedruckt zu Leipzigk durch Wolffgangum Günter. Anno M.D.L.

[37] p. ; 19 cm. Signatures: A-D , E ; [A] E3 unsigned E3b blank.

This is the fifth item bound with Martin Luther's *Kurtz bekentnis,* Gedruckt zu Wittenberg, Durch Hans Lufft. M.D. XLIIII.

VD 16, S 1339 (under S. Salfeld; VD transposes date "M.D.L." into imprint); OCLC: 18655086.

Neither Catholic nor Protestant divines sanctioned charging interest for loans. Both camps agreed that this practice violated standards of Christian conduct. B. Salvendensis here insists on this point in two sermons based on the book of Ezekiel.

1544
Luth: 5

Zwo predigten vom
Wucher / Durch Magiſtrum
Baſilium Saluenden-
ſem gepredigt.

Anno
M. D. L.

Gedruckt zu Leip-
zigk durch Wolffgan-
gum Günter.

Tes Kaines Diathekes hapanta evaggèlion = Nouum IESV Christi D.N. Testamentum.
EX BIBLIOTHECA REGIA.

LVTETIAE, Ex officina Roberti Stephani ..., [XVII Cal. Iul.] M.D.L.

[32], 272, 202, [2] p. ; 35 cm. (fol. in 8s).

Adams, B-1661;   *Mortimer*, 78;   *Renouard*, 75-76.1;   OCLC: 08103503.

Third edition of R. Stephanus' Greek N.T., called the "Editio Regia" or "Royal Edition." The "Textus Receptus" was substantially derived from this edition. This text has a critical apparatus that shows what other readings were to be found in manuscripts to which Stephanus had access. Stephanus' Greek text closely conformed to Erasmus' text.

1550
Bibl

Warhafftiger vnd gegrünter bericht, wider die vnerfindliche vnd ertichte antzeigung, So die verstockten der Röm. Key. Mai. Rebellen vnd Echtere, auch unser des Thumbcapittels vnnd Ertzstiffts Magdeburgk, vngehorsame, Ehren vnnd Eidtsvergessene Vnderthane, Burgermeistere, Rathmanne, vnd Innungsmeister, der Altenstadt Magdeburgk, neulicher zeit im druck vergesslich ausgegossen ...

[Magdeburg? : s.n.] Anno 1550.

[50] p. ; 19 cm. (4to) Signatures: A-F⁴, G¹; [A] unsigned, A1b blank.

BM STC German, p. 586; VD 16, M 153 (lists place and printer as: "[Leipzig : Valentin Bapst]"); OCLC: 23456967.

The Cathedral Chapter of Magdeburg here raises a protest against the dealings of the Protestants in the city during the Interim.

1550
Thum

[Zigerius, Emericus]

Ein schrifft, eines fromen Predigers aus der Türckey an Illyricum geschrieben, Darinnen angezeiget wird, wie es dort mit der Kirche vnd dem Euangelio zugehet.

(Gedruckt zu Magdeburg durch Michael Lotther), 1550.

[15] p. ; 21 cm. (4to) Signatures: A-B⁴; [A] unsigned, B4b blank.

This is the nineteenth item bound with Gallus' *Der Theologen bedencken ...* Gedruckt zu Magdeburgk durch Michel Lotther 1550.

There are manuscript marginalia in the text.

Hohenemser, 3586 (Latin ed.); OCLC: 14903121.

This is a letter to Flacius Illyricus from a former Schoolmaster in Illyria, describing the state of the church there under Turkish rule.

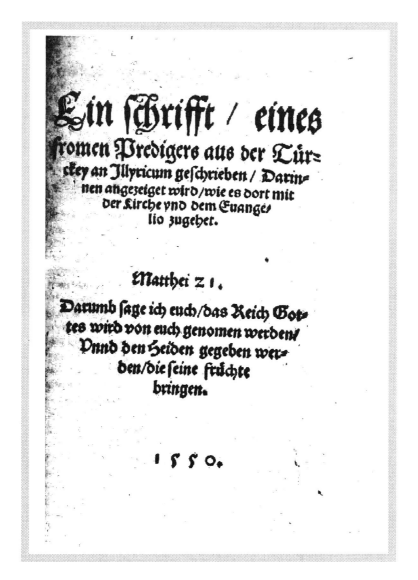

1550
Gall: 19

1551

Amsdorff, Nicolaus von, 1483-1565.

Vom Bapst vnd seiner Kirchen, das sie des Teufels, vnd nicht Christi vnsers lieben Herrn Kirche sey.

[Magdeburg : Michael Lotter] 1551.

> [12] p. ; 19 cm. (4to) Signatures: A^4, B^2; [A] unsigned.

> *BM STC German, p. 28;   Hohenemser, 3610;   Jackson, 1620;   Kolb, 53;   VD 16, A 2406;   OCLC: 17990349.*

> Following in Luther's footsteps, N. von Amsdorff makes a vitriolic attack on the Papacy.

1551
Amsd

Vom Bapst vnd seiner
Kirchen / das sie des Teufels / vnd
nicht Christi vnsers lieben Herrn
Kirche sey.

Nicolaus von Amsdorff.

EXVL.

1551.

Der Prediger zu Magdeburgk ware, gegründte Antwort, auff das rhümen ihrer Feinde, das sie auch GOTtes Wort reine, inhalts der Augspurgischen Confession, so wol als die zu Magdeburgk haben, Vnd was sie daraus mehr wider die Stadt einführen vnnd fürgehen dürffen.

(Gedruckt zu Magdeburgk durch Michael Lotther. 1551.)

[28] p. ; 19 cm. (4to) Signatures: A-C^4, D^2; [A] unsigned.

There is an old library label at the foot of the title page.

VD 16, P 4752-4753;   OCLC: 25489180.

In this pamphlet, the Magdeburgers reply to the assertion that the Catholics also had Scripture on their side. The city of Magdeburg capitulated to imperial forces on favorable terms shortly after this tract was printed. The tract is quite rare and does not appear in most Reformation bibliographies. The title page features the Magdeburg coat-of-arms.

1551
Pred

Deren zu Magdeburgk, so widder die Adiaphora geschrieben haben, jhres vorigen schreibens beschlus, auff der Adiaphoristen beschüldigung vnnd lesterung, die zeit jhrer belagerung, vnd jtzt zum teil neulich vnter diesen friedshandlungen wider sie ausgangen.

[Magdeburg : Michael Lotter] Anno 1551. am tag Simonis vnd Jude. 28. Octobris.

[23] p. ; 20 cm. (4to) Signatures: A-C^4; [A] unsigned, C4b blank.

There is a bookplate reading, "Bücherei von Otto Licht Magdeburg-Sudenburg," on the inside, upper cover.

BM STC German, p. 27; Jackson, 493; Pegg, Bibliotheca, 20; VD 16, A 2352-2353; OCLC: 13523166.

The Protestant pastors in Magdeburg continued their polemics against Melanchthon and the "Adiaphoristic Party." This pamphlet styles itself as a "Conclusion" to an earlier work, probably the "Confession and Defense" of the Magdeburg clergy. This is the sole edition of the work. It is bound in a piece from a eighteenth century music manuscript.

1551
Dere

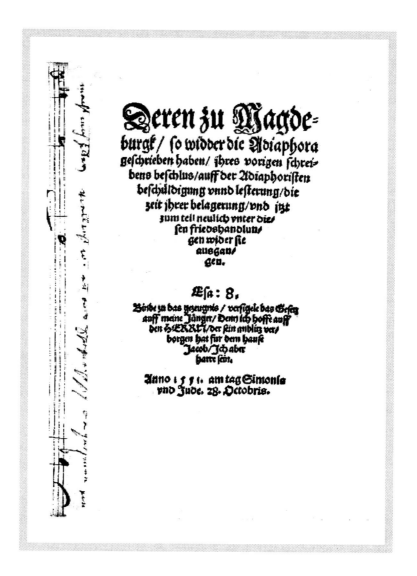

Flacius Illyricus, Matthias, 1520-1575.

Das alle verfolger der Kirchen Christi zu Magdeburgk, Christi des HERrn selbs verfolger sindt. Geschrieben zur warnung an alle Christen, vnd sonderlich an das Kriegesuolck der Feinde.

Gedruckt zu Magdeburgk, durch Michael Lotther, Anno 1551. April. 5.

[15] p. ; 20 cm. (4to) Signatures: A-B⁴; [A] unsigned, B4b blank.

BM STC German, p. 305;   Preger, II, 549;   VD 16, F 1426;   OCLC: 15151015.

Flacius kept up his attacks on the Interims and those who persecuted Magdeburg until the city capitulated to the besieging troops.

1551
Flac

Georg III, Fürst von Anhalt, 1507-1553.

Von dem hochwirdigen Sacrament des Leibs vnd Bluts vnsers HERREN Jhesu Christi, Drey Predigten.

Gedruckt zu Leipzig, durch Wolff Gunter. Anno M.D.LI.

[2] p. ; 19 cm. (4to) Signatures: 2A-2B , A-Z , a-e , f ; [2A] unsigned.

This is the second item bound with Martin Luther's *Kurtz bekentnis*, Gedruckt zu Wittenberg, Durch Hans Lufft. M.D. XLIIII. This copy is also imperfect: p. 145-146, leaf T, is wanting.

On the verso of the title page is an old ownership mark in ink: "Hanss Rubelt."

VD 16, G 1332;   OCLC: 18672657.

Prince Georg of Anhalt began his career as a Catholic prince and advisor to Archbishop Albert of Mainz. He became a Lutheran after reading the works of Luther and Melanchthon and was noted for his piety. These three sermons are on the Lutheran interpretation of the Lord's Supper.

1544
Luth: 2

Von dem hochwirdi-
gen Sacrament des Leibs vnd Bluts
vnsers HERREN Jhesu Christi/
Drey Predigten/
Durch
Fürst Georgen zu Anhalt/Thum-
probsten zu Magdeburg vnd Meissen/im
Dohen Stifft zu Mersburg
gethan/ Anno
1550.

Psalm. CXI.
Gros sind die werck des HERREN/wer jr ach
tet der hat eitel lust dran.
Was Er ordnet das ist löblich vnd herrlich/ vnd
seine gerechtigkeit bleibet ewiglich.
Er hat ein gedechtnis gestifftet seiner wunder/
der gnedige vnd barmhertzige HERR.
Er gibt speise/ denen so jn fürchten/ Er dencket
ewiglich an seinen Bund.
Er lest verkündigen seine gewaltigen thaten seinem Volck/das Er jnen gebe das Erbe der Heiden.

Hyalinus, Johannes.

Von den Versuchungen des Herrn Christi, beschrieben im Evangelio, Matth. 4. Ein Christliche auslegung.

Gedruckt zu Wittemberg, Durch Georgen Rhawen Erben. Anno 1551.

[123] p. ; 19 cm. (4to) Signatures: A-P , Q; [A], Q2 unsigned, Q2b blank.

This is the third item bound with Martin Luther's *Kurtz bekentnis*, Gedruckt zu Wittenberg, Durch Hans Lufft. M.D. XLIIII.

BM STC German, p. 427;   VD 16, G 2178 (under J. Glaser);   OCLC: 18692955.

This tract is a commentary on the temptation of Christ related in Matthew 4. Of Hyalinus little appears to be known. The preface is written by P. Melanchthon.

1544
Luth: 3

Jacobi, Leonardus, 1515?-1570?

Eine tröstliche Leichpredigt. Zur einweihung vnd bestetigung des newen Gottsackers zu Calbe gethan.

(Gedruckt zu Wittemberg, Durch Georg Rhawen Erben.) 1551.

[79] p. ; 15 cm. (8vo) Signatures: A-E^8; [A] unsigned, E8b blank.

There are some manuscript marginalia in the text of this volume.

VD 16, J 82; OCLC: 28942177.

L. Jacobi, was born in Nordhausen and educated in Erfurt. He is first mentioned in Calbe in 1548. This pamphlet includes the first funeral oration he preached at the new cemetary at Calbe opened after a three-year plague. This is the first, and probably only, edition of the work.

1551
Jaco A

Jacobi, Leonardus, 1515?-1570?

[Encheiridion (romanized form)] PRAECIPVORVM LOCORVM SACRAE SCRIP-
TVRAE, ORTHODOXO*rum patrum scriptis illustratum, & in gloriam Domini nostri
IESV CHRISTI, & Iuniorum Theologorum usum conscriptum.*

LIPSIAE EX OFFICINA VALENTINI PAPAE. M.D.LI.

[8], 133, [2] p. ; 16 cm. (8vo) Signatures: A-I^8; [A] unsigned, A1b, I8b blank.

There are former ownership marks on the title page as well as a stamp reading, "Bibliothek Zoffingen." There
are manuscript marginalia in the text.

BM STC, German, p. 434; VD 16, K 73; OCLC: 22618050.

L. Jacobi was a Lutheran preacher in Laucha and Magdeburg in the 1540's and thereafter in Calbe until his death around
1570. This work is his commentary on selected biblical texts.

1551
Jaco

Luther, Martin, 1483-1546.

Chronica des Ehrnwirdigen Herrn D. Mart. Luth. Deudsch.

Witeberg. Widerumb gedruckt durch Hans Lufft, 1551.

[246] p. : charts ; 16 cm. (8vo) Signatures: A^8, a^8, B-O^8, P^3; [A] unsigned, D7b, 8 blank.

This volume is bound in contemporary blind-stamped, polished calf over wooden boards, dated, "1553" and headed, "Chronic Martin." The clasps are missing.

This volume was formerly in the Beck Lutherana collection, #258 and the W. H. Stifel collection, #333. There is a former ownership mark dated, "1569," on the inside upper cover as well as the initials, "F.L.," and date, "1586," in red ink. On the title page is an ownership mark: "Carolus Gotthilff Oettrich (?) Dres: Nur:"

BM STC German, p.569;   VD 16, L 6720;   WA 53, 16ff;   OCLC: 21801493.

This is J. Aurifaber's German translation of Luther's "Chronological table of the years of the world." The Latin work was finished in manuscript in 1540 and first published in 1541. Luther's interest in writing this work was not primarily eschatalogical. This is the second printing of the German translation. Of special interest in this copy is the hand drawn bookplate on the inside front cover of Mathias Somm[er?], dated 1564. The binding is also dated (1553) and lettered, "Chronica Martin." The bookplate is important as an early dated example of this form of German folk art.

1551
Luth

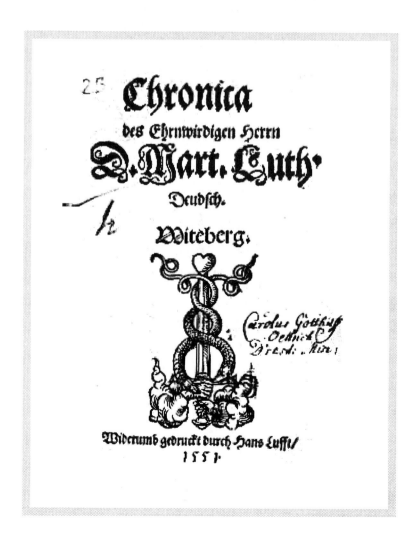

Major, Georg, 1502-1574.

ENARRATIO PSALMI SEXAGESIMI OCTAVI, EXVRGAT Deus & dissipentur inimici eius &c.

LIPSIAE EXCVDEBAT GEORGIVS HANTZSCH. ANNO M.D.LI.

[116] p. ; 15 cm. (8vo) Signatures: A-F^8, G^4, H^6; [A], A3 unsigned, A1b blank.

This volume was formerly in the Stewart collection, #3990.

VD 16, M 2029 *(under: "Meier, Georg, aus Nürnberg");*   OCLC: 28005294.

This is a commentary by G. Major on Psalm 68 (Arise, O Lord, and let your enemies be scattered). Major wrote this commentary in Wittenberg, shortly before becoming Superintendent in Eisleben. While at Wittenberg he took part in the adiaphoristic controversy.

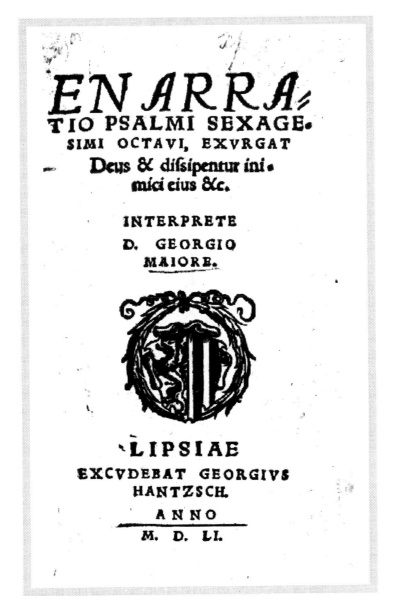

1551
Majo

Major, Georg, 1502-1574.

SENTENTIAE VETERVM POEtarum, per Georgium Maiorem in locos communes digestae, ac tandem post authoris supremam manum, multum auctae et locupletatae.

LVTETIAE Ex officina Roberti Stephani typographii Regij. M.D.LI.

240, [8] p. ; 18 cm. (8vo) Signatures: a-p^8, q^4; [a] unsigned, k printed as "lz".

This work is bound in polished calf with the gold-embossed coat-of-arms of the former owner, Herbert Norman Evans.

This volume was formerly in the Stewart collection, #3985. There is a bookplate on the inside, upper cover of "Herbert Norman Evans."

OCLC: 22832076.

Georg Major was a Lutheran theologian who spent most of his adult life at the University of Wittenberg. He became embroiled in the Adiaphoristic controversy and also in the "Majoristic Controversy" on the efficacy of good works. This volume is a collection of extracts from the major Latin poets of statements concordant with Christian virtue.

1551
Sent

SENTENTIAE VETERVM POE-
tarum, per Georgium Maiorem in locos communes
digestae, ac tandem post authoris supremam manum,
multum auctae ac locupletatae.

ANTONII MANCINELLI DE
Poetica virtute Libellus.

Index sententiarum & prouerbiorum.

LVTETIAE
Ex officina Roberti Stephani typographi Regij.
M. D. LI.

Melanchthon, Philipp, 1497-1560.

DE CONIVGIO PIAE COMMONEFACTIONES.

VVITEBERGAE EXCVDEBAT IOHANNES CRATO. ANNO MDLI.

[16], 32, [13] p. ; 16 cm. (8vo) Signatures: A-C^8, D^7; [A], A4, D4 unsigned, D7b blank.

Hartfelder, 470; Jackson, 2117; VD 16, M 2813; OCLC: 12781330.

One of the rifts between Protestants and Catholics concerned their views on marriage, especially clerical marriage. This little handbook, prepared by Melanchthon, offers advice and counsel to pastors on matters relating to marriage and divorce.

1551
Mela B

DE CONIV,
GIO PIAE COMMO,
NEFACTIONES COL=
LECTAE A PHI=
LIPPO MELAN
THONE.

VVITEBERGAE
EXCVDEBAT IO=
HANNES CRA=
TO.

ANNO

MDLI.

Melanchthon, Philipp, 1497-1560.

EXPLICATIO PROVERBIORVM SALOMONIS IN SCHOLA VVITEMBER-GENSI RECENS DICTATA.

FRANCOFORTI EX OFFICINA PEtri Brubachij, Anno Domini M.D.LI.

227, [5] p. ; 15 cm. (8vo) Signatures: A-Q^8; [A] unsigned.

This volume was formerly in the Stewart collection, #4057.

VD 16, M 3330; OCLC: 12652480.

Melanchthon published a Latin translation of the Book of Proverbs in 1524. The next year his version was issued with notes but without his permission or approval. A year later, the German translation by J. Menius appeared. In 1529, a new edition of the work was published, and later the same year, Melanchthon issued a new version of his, "Notes on Proverbs." In 1550, a new version of the commentary was published, which was re-edited in 1555. This version represents the next-to-last phase of his work on the book.

1551
Mela A

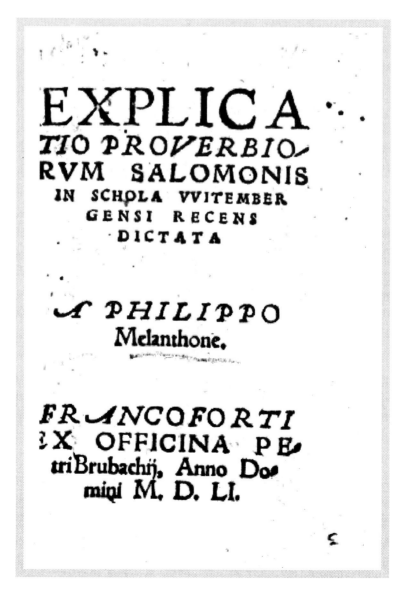

Menius, Justus, 1499-1558.

Vom EXORCISMO. *Das der, nicht als ein zeuberischer Grewel zuuerdamnen, sondern in der gewönlichen Action bey der Tauffe, mit Gott vnd gutem Gewissen, wol gehalten werden möge.*

(Gedruckt zu Wittemberg. Durch Veit Creutzer. Anno 1551.)

[91] p. ; 15 cm. (8vo) Signatures: A-E^8, F^6; [A] unsigned, A1b, F6b blank.

This volume was formerly in the Stewart collection, #7696.

VD 16, M 4586;   OCLC: 28005332.

The issue of exorcism in Baptism was a debated issue among Lutheran theologians. Luther accepted exorcism with some misgivings, primarily on account of tradition. J. Menius here writes a long essay demonstrating the efficacy of the exorcism. Menius sided mainly with the gnesio-Lutherans.

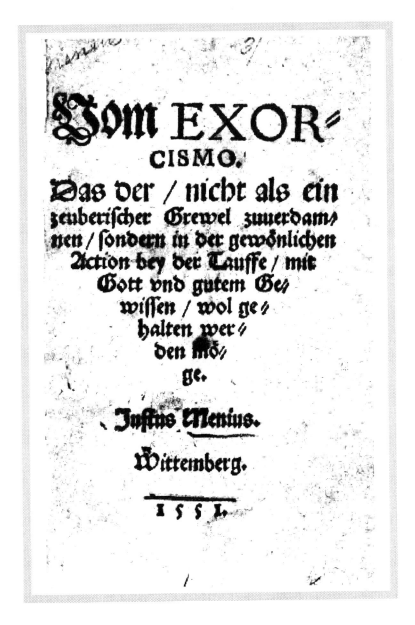

1551
Meni

Recusationschrifft der Christlichen Augspurgischen Confessions verwandten Stende, wider das vermeint, von Bapst Paulo dem dritten, weiland zu Trient indicirt vnd angefangen Concilium, sampt einer gebürlichen Prouocation vnnd erbietung, auff ein allgemein oder National, frey, Christlich vnnd vnparteisch Concilium inn Deudtschen Landen Mit einer Vorrede Matth.Fla. Illyr. vnd Nicolai Galli.

(itzt wider nachgedruckt, durch Michael Lotther, zu Magdeburg. Anno 1551.)

[44] p. ; 21 cm. (4to)

BM STC German, p. 363; *Hohenemser*, 3614; *Jackson*, 378; *Kuczynski*, 2217; *Preger*, II, p. 549-50; VD 16, E 4646; OCLC: 12034521.

This is a reprint of an earlier condemnation of the Council of Trent, prepared in Nüremberg in 1548. Flacius Illyricus and Nicolaus Gallus both wrote prefaces to this edition.

1551
Recu

Schwenckfeld, Caspar, 1489-1561.

Von der hailigen Schrifft, jrem Jnnhalt, Ampt, rechtem Nutz, Brauch vnd miszbrauch. Jtem, Vom vnderschaide der diener vnd prediger der hailigen Schrifft, vnd des worts Gottes. Was auch recht aigentlich Gottes wort sei.

[S.l. : s.n., 1551.]

[6], CXI, [1] leaves ; 20 cm. (4to) Signatures: [hand]^6, a-z^4, Aa-Ee^4; [hand], [hand]4 unsigned, d4 signed, y2 missigned "ijy", Ee4b blank.

BM STC German, p. 803; Corpus Schwenckfeldianorum, 12, Doc. 780; Pegg, Bibliotheca, 1945; VD 16, S 5052 (with imprint: "Ulm: Hans Varnier d.J.]"); OCLC: 22608590.

This is a treatise by Schwenckfeld on the distinction between inward spiritual life and external ceremonies. After 1553, Schwenckfeld came under attack from Flacius Illyricus for his definition of scripture as an external factor, distinct from the living presence of Christ as the only true "Word of God."

1551
Schwe

Westphal, Joachim, 1510?-1574.

PSALMVS QVADRAGESIMVS SExtus plenus mirificis consolationibus, quibus pij in summa rerum omnium perturbatione, & periculis confirmentur.

(Marpurgi excusum per Andream Colibium, expensis Petri Brubachij Anno MDLI.)

[56] p. ; 15 cm. (8vo) Signatures: A-C^8, D^4; [A] unsigned.

This is the fourth item bound with Martin Luther's *DE MISSA PRIVATA, ET VNCTIONE Sacer libellus,* Vitebergae (per Ioannem Lufft), M.D.XXXIIII.

Adams, W-83; Stickelberger-Folger, 148, VI; OCLC: 21721132.

J. Westphal was a Lutheran from Hamburg, who studied at Wittenberg under Luther and Melanchthon. He was pastor of St. Catherine's in Hamburg at the time he wrote this commentary (1551) on Psalm XLVI (God is our refuge and strength).

1534
Luth E: 4

1552

Besselmeyer, Sebastian.

*Warhafftige History, vnd beschreibung des Magdeburgischen Kriegs, vom anfang biss
zum ende, was sich die zeyt der Belegerung, innen vnd ausserhalb der Statt, zugetragen
vnd verlauffen hat, Auch von der Schlacht, vnd fürnemsten Scharmützeln....*
Gedruckt zu Magdeburg [s.n.], im Jar nach Christi geburt, tausent fünffhundert, zwey vnd fünfftzig.

[75] p. ; 19 cm. (4to) Signatures: A-I⁴, K²; [A], K2 unsigned, A1b blank, E2 missigned "F2."

This volume was formerly in the Stewart collection, #7933. On the verso of the title page is a sixteen-line
manuscript poem on the Magdeburg War, in three stanzas, as if by J. Sturmius, J. Sapidus, and R. Gwaltherius.

VD 16, B 2265;   OCLC: 23438327.

Sebastian Besselmeyer was a citizen of Magdeburg, who took part in the "Magdeburg War" of 1550-51, the Catholic
attempt to impose the Interim by force on Magdeburg. Ultimately the siege was successful, and Magdeburg was betrayed
into capitulation. The hard-won Catholic victory proved short-lived. Charles V's defeat by a coalition of Catholic and
Lutheran princes ultimately led to the Peace of Augsburg in 1555 in which Lutheranism was recognized by the Empire.
This work is an eyewitness account of the Magdeburg War as it progressed.

1552
Bess

Camerarius, Joachim, 1500-1574.

[Katechesis tou Christianismou, egoun, Kephalaia tes hygiousdidaches Christou te autou kai ton Apostolon (romanized form).]

[Leipzig : Valentin Bapst, 1552?]

[8], 499, [4] p. ; 16 cm. (8vo) Signatures: A-Z^8, a-i^8.

This volume is bound in blind-stamped pigskin over wooden boards, clasps intact.

There is a fore-edge shelf mark. A coat-of-arms is pasted on the inside, upper cover below a faded manuscript note, and a manuscript note on the upper flyleaf. There is an inscription on the title page reading, "Eximio theologo Al. Alesio v. cL. amico observa[n]do," that is said to be by P. Melanchthon, but it is more probably by J. Camerarius.

BM STC German, p. 177; VD 16, C 447; OCLC: 12575590.

Camerarius was an extraordinarily gifted Greek scholar, humanist-reformer, and one of Melanchthon's closest friends. In 1516, he received his B.A. from Leipzig, and in 1520, his M.A. from Erfurt. That same year he met Melanchthon who encouraged him in his Greek studies. This work is a Greek catechetical treatise on the major points of the Christian religion. It shows clearly Melanchthon's influence on Camerarius. The "Al. Alesio" on the title page of this copy is Alexander Alesius, a Scottish Lutheran theologian who translated the First Liturgy of Edward VI (1549) into Latin.

1552
Came

Confessio DoCTRINAE SAXONICARVM Ecclesiarum Synodo Tridentinae oblata, Anno Domini M.D.LI. in qua Christiane lector uidebis, qui nam e Catholicae Ecclesi[a]e gremio resilierint: & per quos stet, quo minus Ecclesiae pia concordia sarciatur.

BASILEAE, EX OFFICINA IOANnis Oporini, Anno salutis humanae M.D.LII, mense martio.

120 p. ; 15 cm. (8vo) Signatures: A-G^8, H^4; [A] unsigned, A1b blank.

There is a manuscript bibliographical note on the verso of the upper flyleaf.

BM STC German, p. 781; Kuczynski, 3057; VD 16, C 4803; OCLC: 17526775.

In 1551, at the request of Emperor Charles V, Melanchthon drew up a Protestant Confession of faith for presentation at the Council of Trent. This Confession is much less conciliatory than was the Augsburg Confession. This is the first printing of the work.

1552
Conf

Confelsio Do-

CTRINAE SAXONICARVM
Ecclefiarum Synodo Tridentinæ oblata, Anno Domini M. D. L I .in qua
Chriftiane lector uidebis, qui nam è
Catholicæ Ecclefiç gremio refilierint:
& per quos ftet, quo minus Ec-
clefiæ pia concordia
farciatur:

PSAL. CXIX.
Loquebar de teftimonijs tuis in confpectu
Regum, & non confundebar.

Anno Domini M. D. L I I.

Helding, Michael, 1506-1561.

BREVIS INSTITVTIO AD PIETATEM Christianam secundum Doctrinam Catholicam continens. EXPLICATIONEM Symboli Apostolici, Orationis Dominicae, Salutationis Angelicae, Decem Praeceptorum, Septem Sacramentorum. AD VSVM PVERORVM NObilium....

(MOGVNTIAE Excudebat Iuo Schoeffer, Anno M.D.LII.)

[150] p. : ill. ; 17 cm. (8vo) Signatures: A-S^8, T^3; [A], A3,4, B4, L2, M3,4, N3, T3 unsigned.

There are manuscript marginalia in the text.

BM STC German, p. 389; VD 16, H 1582; OCLC: 12706017.

M. Helding here writes a catechism for the instruction of the boys in the Mainz Cathedral School, where he first began teaching in 1531. The work takes up explanations of the Lord's Prayer, Apostles' Creed, etc. This work was prepared by Helding in response to M. Flacius Illyricus' attack on Helding's earlier catechetical writings.

1552
Held

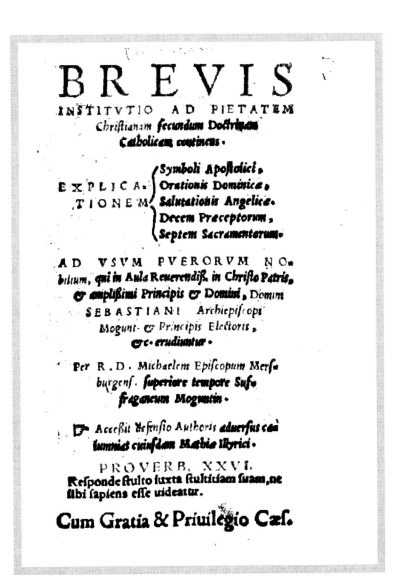

Innocent III, 1160?-1216.

OPERA.

Coloniae excudebat Ioannes Nouesianus. Anno M.D.LII.

[14], CCCL leaves ; 30 cm. (fol in 6s) Signatures: *6, 2*8, A-2L^6, 2M^4, 2N-3M^6, 3N^4; [*] unsigned, *6b, Q6b, 3N4b blank, L2 missigned "Lk2", 2I2 missigned "I2."

This volume is bound in limp vellum.

There are several old ownership marks in ink on the title page including one that reads, "Ex Libris ecclesiae Cathedralis Acetiensis." Below this are two illegible marks, and one reading, "Pr. Raymundi Forner Ord. Pred. Convtüs. Catherineae Pragae." To the right of this is "Ant. Augustini ep[iscop]i Herdensis (?)."

Adams, I-121;   VD 16, I 221;   OCLC: 19494881.

During Innocent III's reign the Fourth Lateran Council was convened, that approved the use of the word, "transubstantiation," to describe the action in the mass to make the bread and wine into Christ's body and blood. This volume includes all of Pope Innocent III's works.

1552
Inno

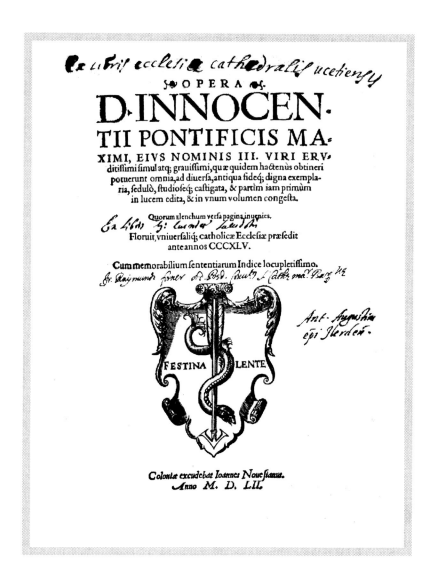

Jacobi, Leonardus, 1515?-1570?

Eine liebliche Trostschrifft, von der heiligen Christlichen Kirchen, Wie es damit in diesem zeitlichen leben eine gestalt hat, Vnd in dem zukuonfftigen, ewigen herrlichen vnd freudenreichen leben haben wird, Aus der andern vnd siebenden vision der Offenbarung Johannis gezogen, vnd mit besonderem fleis erkleret, Allen Christgleubigen itziger zeit zu trost.

Gedruckt zu Wittemberg Durch Veit Creutzer 1552.

[111] p. ; 15 cm. (8vo) Signatures: A-G^8; [A], A4, B4 unsigned, A1b G8b blank.

The title page has been re-backed but unfortunately without being able to preserve the complete title text.

VD 16, J 77;   OCLC: 28942039.

L. Jacobi, Lutheran pastor in Calbe, had this pamphlet printed in Wittenberg in 1552. This work is almost unknown in bibliographic literature. The only entry located has been in the sixteenth century German Union Catalog, VD 16.

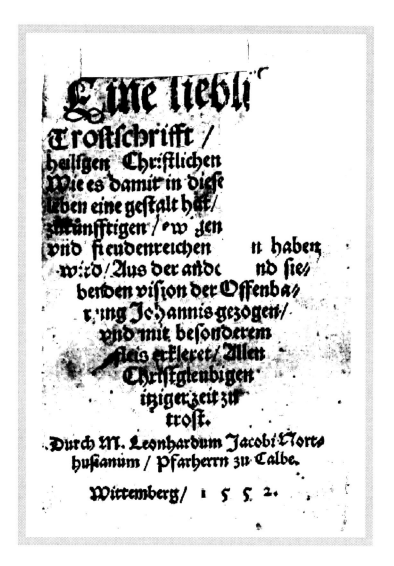

1552
Jaco

Kirchenordnung, wie es inn des durchleuchtigen hochgebornen Fursten vnnd Herrn,
Herrn Albrechts des Jungern Marggrauen zu Brandenburgs, zu Preussen, zu Stettin,
Pomern, der Cassuben vnd Wenden, auch in Schlesien zu Oppeln vnd Ratibarn etc.
Hertzogs, Burggrauens zu Nurmberg, vnnd Fürstens zu Rugen, Fürstenthumb, Landt,
Obrigkeit vnd gebiet, mit der lehr vnd Ceremonien bis auff vernere Christliche ver-
gleichung gehalten werden sol.

Gedruckt zu Leipzig durch Wolff Günter. M.D.LII.

[63], [94] leaves : music ; 31 cm. (fol in 6s and 4s) Signatures: A-G^6, H-I^4, K^6, L^4, a-b^6, c^4, d-e^6, f^4, g-h^6, i^4, k-l^6, m^4, n^6, o^4; [A], [a], c2 unsigned, L4. o4b blank.

This work is bound in blind-stamped, bleached skin over paper boards.

This volume was formerly in the Stewart collection, #3841. There is an old library bookplate dated 1746 pasted on the inside, upper cover and reads: "Ex Electorali Bibliotheca Sereniss Utriusque Bavariae Ducum." The title on the upper cover is defaced, with a loss of text.

BM STC German, p. 517; VD 16, B 6991; OCLC: 20023372.

The 1533 Brandenburg-Nuremberg church ordinance was perhaps the single most influential and widely copied work of its kind during the Reformation. Initially crafted through cooperation of theologians in Ansbach-Bayreuth and Nuremberg, it formed the basis for later ordinances throughout Germany, and influenced Brenz's work in Württemberg. This particular edition was printed after the failure of Margrave Albrecht Alcibiades to force the theologians in his territory to accept the Interim of Augsburg, and it is rarely referred to in the literature.

1552
Evan

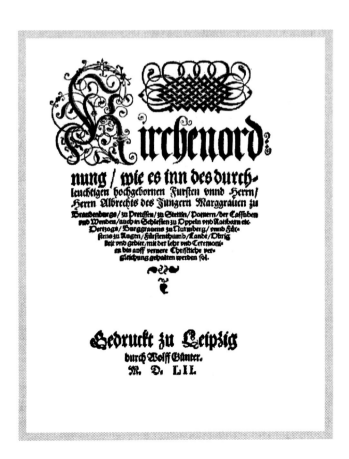

Luther, Martin, 1483-1546.

Etliche marhafftige weissagung, vnd fürneme spruche des Ehrwirdigen Vaters, Hern Doctor Martini Luthers, des dritten Helie, vom trübsal, abfal, finsternissen, oder aber verfelschungen reiner Lere, so Deudtschlandt künfftiglich nach seinem tode, widerfaren solle.

Gedruckt zu Magdeburgk, durch Michael Lotther. 1552.

[100] p. ; 20 cm. (4to) Signatures: A-M^4, N^2; [A] unsigned.

This volume was formerly in the Beck Lutherana collection, #11.

Hohenemser, 2717; VD 16, L 3474; OCLC: 21515823.

This is a collection of extracts from Luther's writings, considered to constitute predictions of future events. This edition was prepared by Johann Amsterdann and Albert Christian.

1552
Luth

Melanchthon, Philipp, 1497-1560.

Loci praecipui Theologici, NVNC POSTREMO' CVRA & diligentia summa recogniti, multisq[ue] in locis copiose illustrati, Cum appendice disputationis de Coniugio.

BASILEAE, PER IOANnem Oporinum, M.D.LII. Mense Nouembri.

702, [97] p. ; 18 cm. (8vo) Signatures: a-z^8, A-2D^8; [a], a5 unsigned, C3 missigned "C5", F2 missigned "G2", H4 missigned "F4", 2D8b blank.

This volume was bound in blind-stamped bleached pigskin over paper boards.

This volume was formerly in the Stewart collection, #4056. There is a former ownership mark on the title page reading, "Collegii Societatis Jesu Monachii."

Adams, M-1179;   VD 16, M 3652;   OCLC: 12701166.

After the colloquies of Worms and Regensburg, Melanchthon undertook a third major revision of the **Loci Communes**. This copy is a later printing of the third edition of the **Loci**, first published in 1543.

1552
Mela

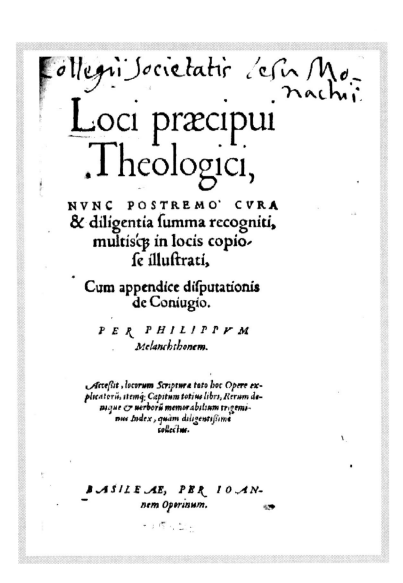

Schwenckfeld, Caspar, 1489-1561.

Ein Gebet zum Herrn Christo, in Kriegssnöten vnd geferlichen zeyten.
Gedruckt zuo Augspurg, Durch Hans Zimmerman. M.D.Lij.

[7] p. ; 21 cm. (4to) Signatures: A⁴; [A], A2 unsigned, A1b, A4b blank.

Corpus Schwenckfeldianorum, 10, Doc. 553C; Hohenemser, 3629; Kuczynski, 3587; OCLC: 22482571.

Schwenckfeld originally wrote this prayer in 1546 during the Schmalkaldic War. When hostilities renewed in 1552, he issued additional printings of the work, of which this is the first.

1552
Schwe

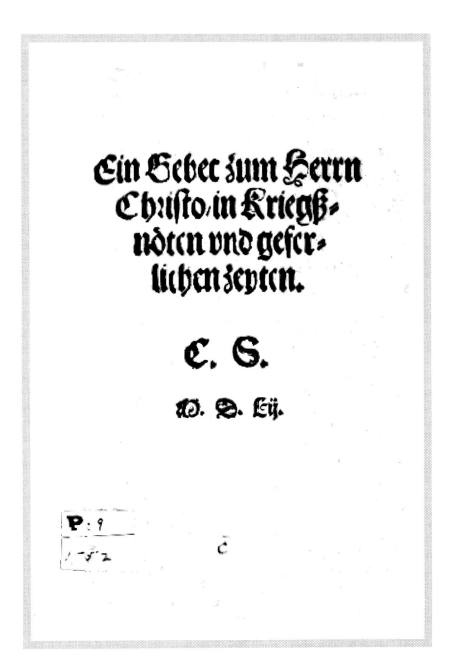

Schwenckfeld, Caspar, 1489-1561.

Vom[m] Euangelio Christi Vnd Vom Miszbrauch des Euangelij.

[S.l. : s.n., 1552.]

[11], CXLI, [2] leaves ; 20 cm. (4to) Signatures: A-Z, 2A-2P^4, 2Q^3; [A] unsigned, A1b blank.

BM STC German, p. 802; Corpus Schwenckfeldianorum, 12, Doc. 813A; Pegg, Bibliotheca, 1931; VD16, S 5013 (with imprint: "[Ulm : Hans Varnier, d.J., 1552]"); OCLC: 22465709.

As Schwenckfeld understood it, the Gospel was not the spoken word of the preachers, but the power of God penetrating the individual through Christ. Hence, the power of God is experienced directly, in an unworldly and spiritual manner.

1552
Schwe A

1553

Amsdorff, Nicolaus von, 1483-1565.

Vnterschreibung des Herrn Niclas Amsdorffs der Sechsischen kirchen Censurn vnd meinung, wider Doctor Georg Maiors Antichristische lere von guten wercken als zur seligkeit nötig.

Gedruckt zu Magdeburg, bey Christian Rödinger. Anno. 1553.

[12] p. ; 20 cm. (4to) Signatures: A^4, B^2; [A] unsigned, A3 missigned "B3", B2 unsigned.

There is a manuscript inscription on the title page, and on the verso of the title page.

Hohenemser, 3631; Jackson, 1623; Kolb, 61; VD 16, A 2397; OCLC: 17970377.

The role of works in the plan of salvation vexed Lutheran theologians from the beginning. Amsdorff here takes up the polemic against G. Major, who stressed the need of good works against Amsdorff, who stressed the efficacy of God's grace, freely given.

1553
Amsd

Flacius Illyricus, Matthias, 1520-1575.

Vom fürnemlichem stücke, punct, oder artickel der Schwenckfeldischen schwermerey.

[Magdeburg? : Michael Lotter?, 1553?]

[16] p. ; 20 cm. (4to) Signatures: A-B^4; [A] unsigned.

BM STC German, p. 307; Jackson, 2457; VD 16, F 1528; OCLC: 12720011.

Flacius' controversy with Schwenckfeld dragged on long after the issues had ceased to interest even the combatants. This tract is from near the beginning of their dispute. Flacius had not yet started calling Schwenckfeld, "Stenckfeld," (Stinkfeld) as he would do later on, but his condemnation of Schwenckfeld's "enthusiasm" is indicative of things to come.

1553
Flac

Juditium, eines Predigers inn der Schlesien: Uber Mathie Flacij Jllyrici büchlin, so er wider Chaspar Schwenckfelden im Truck hat lassen auszgehen.

[S.l. : s.n.] MDLIII.

> [39] p. ; 20 cm. (4to) Signatures: a-e^4; [a] unsigned, a1b, e4b blank.

> *Corpus Schwenckfeldianorum 13, Doc. 871;   VD 16, S 4922;   OCLC: 22690698.*

> A Silesian preacher, possibly S. Martini, here takes up the defense of Schwenckfeld against Flacius Illyricus. The book has been ascribed to A. Berner and to Schwenckfeld himself, but no proof of authorship is at hand. The book was printed in 1554, although dated 1553, the date of composition.

1553
Judi

Luther, Martin, 1483-1546.

Der Prophet Joel durch Doct. Mart. L. in Latinischer sprach gelesen vnd ausgelegt, Vnd newlich verdeudscht etc. Mit einer Vorrede herrn Niclas von Amsdorff.

(Gedruckt zu Jhena durch Christian Rödinger), 1553.

[319] p. ; 21 cm. (4to) Signatures: [clover]^4, 2[clover]^2, A-Z^4, Aa-PP^4,Qq^2; [clover] unsigned, [clover]1b blank, Qq2b blank.

This work is bound in red painted vellum.

This volume was formerly in the Beck Lutherana collection, #347 and in the W. H. Stifel collection, #334. There is a manuscript note on the inside, upper cover.

Pegg, Bibliotheca, 869;   *VD 16, B 3864;*   OCLC: 21429595.

In his continuing battle against the Interims and the Adiaphorists, N. von Amsdorff reprinted works by Luther to bolster his positions. This commentary on the Book of Joel is based on lectures Luther delivered in 1524/6 on the Minor Prophets.

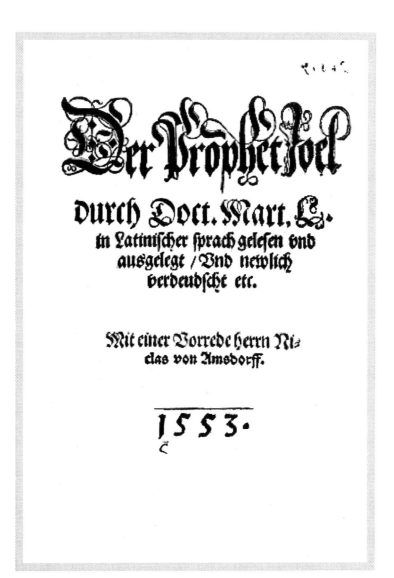

1553
Luth

Melanchthon, Philipp, 1497-1560.

LIBER DE ANIMA.

VVITEBERGAE EXCVDEBANT HAEREDES PETRI SEITZII. 1553.

[352] p. ; 17 cm. (8vo) Signatures: A-Y^8; [A] unsigned.

VD 16, M 2757; OCLC: 12996176.

Melanchthon studied the classical doctrine of the physical sciences for many years before producing his book on the soul in 1540. He lectured on this subject for several years before revising the work in 1552. This is the first printing of the revision. His doctrine of the soul was derived largely from Aristotle.

1553
Mela A

Melanchthon, Philipp, 1497-1560.

RESPONSIO DE CONTROVERSIIS STANCARI.

LIPSIAE IN OFFICINA VALENTINI PAPAE Anno M.D.LIII.

[39] p. ; 15 cm. (8vo) Signatures: A-B^8, C^4; [A] unsigned, C4b blank.

This volume was formerly in the Stewart collection, #4057. The manuscript marginalia in this volume, that has been somewhat shaved in rebinding, includes an old ownership mark in ink at the foot of the title page of "Johanni Dopporto" that has mostly been cut away.

Jackson, 2119;   VD 16, M 4100;   OCLC: 12701225.

Franciscus Stancarus was born in Mantua and forced to leave Italy because of his Protestant views. He became influential in the development of the Reformed Church in Poland, where he taught Hebrew and Old Testament. He held the opinion that Christ is a mediator by virtue of His humanity alone. This booklet by Melanchthon is a refutation of this and other errors of Stancarus.

1553
Mela

RESPONSIO
DE CONTROVER-
SIIS STANCARI.

SCRIPTA A
PHILIPPO MELAN.
ANNO M. D. LIII.

LIPSIAE
IN OFFICINA VALEN-
TINI PAPAE
Anno
M. D. LIII.

Spangenberg, Johann, 1484-1550.

Heubtartikel reiner Christlicher lere, Fragweise gestellt.
Wittemberg. Gedruckt durch Georgen Rhawen Erben, 1553.

[48] + p. ; 15 cm. (8vo) Signatures: A-C^8 + ; [A] unsigned.

This copy is incomplete, only the prefaces and Register are present. This is the second item bound with Martin Luther's *Die Heubtartikel des Christlichen Glaubens...*, Wittemberg. Gedruckt durch Peter Seitzen Erben. 1554.

BM STC German, p. 781;   VD 16, S 7867;   OCLC: 21709785.

J. Spangenberg was active as an educator and theologian in Nordhausen from 1524-1546. He issued a catechism based on Melanchthon's *Loci Communes* in the form of questions and answers. This is a fragment of that work.

1554
Luth B:2

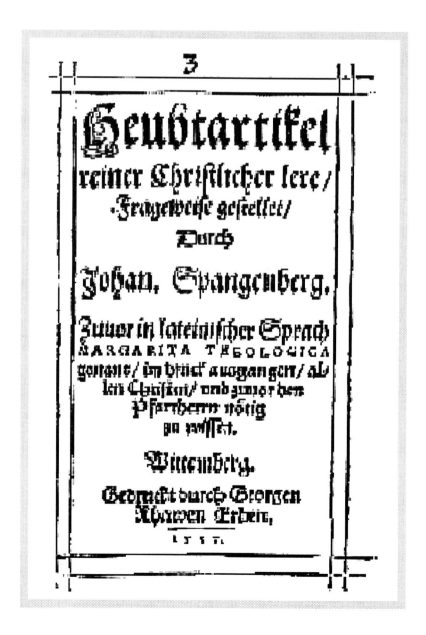

Vergerio, Pietro Paolo, 1498-1565.

CONCILIVM NON MODO TRIDENTINVM, SED OMNE PAPISTICVM PER-
petuo fugiendum esse omnibus pijs.
[S.l. : s.n.] Anno M.D.LIII.

[47] p. ; 20 cm. (4to) Signatures: A-F⁴; [A] unsigned, F4b blank.

This volume was formerly in the Stewart collection, #6636.

Kuczynski, 2698; OCLC: 22770718.

When P. Vergerio fled Italy in 1549, he went to Switzerland to preach to Italian Protestants living there. His preaching proved to be inflammatory, and his support for iconoclasm led to popular opposition to his ideas. In 1551, he compiled this collection of Catholic documents relating to the Council of Trent, showing how antithetical the conciliar decrees were to Protestant ideas. These documents are copiously annotated with Vergerio's caustic comments.

1553
Verg

D. XIV. D. 199.

꤮CONCILIVM
NON MODO TRIDENTINVM,
SED OMNE PAPISTICVM PER-
petuo fugiendum esse omnibus pijs.

AVTORE VERGERIO.

Anno M. D. LIII.

ĉ

1554

Amsdorff, Nicolaus von, 1483-1565.

Wie sichs mit des Durchleuchtigsten Hochgebornen Fürsten vnd Herrn, Herrn Johans Friederich, des Eldern, weiland Hertzogen zu Sachssen, vnd gebornem Churfürsten, Landgrauen in Düringen, vnd Marggrauen zu Meissen, meines gnedigsten Herrn, Christlichem abschied zugetragen hat. Sampt einer Leichpredigt, vber dem Begrebnis zu Weimar, Montag nach Letare gethan, Anno 1554.

Gedruckt zu Ihena, bey Christian Rödinger. Anno. 1554.

[37] p. ; 19 cm. (4to) Signatures: A-D^4, E^3; [A] unsigned, E3b blank.

This volume was formerly in the Beck Lutherana collection, #715. There is a manuscript note on the inside, upper cover.

BM STC German, p. 28;   Hohenemser, 3646;   Kolb, 64;   VD 16, A 2413;   OCLC: 18006182.

Johann Frederich the Magnanimous supported the publication of the Jena edition of Luther's works. This is a tribute to his life, death, and constancy under tribulation and imprisonment.

1554
Amsd

Camerarius, Joachim, 1500-1574.

Querela Martini Luteri, seu Somnium.

BASILEAE, EX OFficina Ioannis Oporini, Anno Salutis humanae M.D.LIIII. Mense Martio.

[63] p.; 17 cm. (8vo) Signatures: a-d^8; [a] unsigned, d8b blank.

Hohenemser, 3651 (under P. Melanchthon);   VD 16, C 522 (under J. Camerarius);   OCLC: 18978637.

This is a work written in support of Melanchthon's views on adiaphora. The attribution of this piece to Camerarius is conjectural.

1554
Came

Querela Mar-
tini Luteri, seu
Somnium.

CLEMENTIS AL

[Greek text]
[Greek text]

BASILEAE.
1554

Carranza, Bartolomé, 1503-1576.

Controuersia DE NECESSARIA RESIdentia personali Episcoporu[m] & aliorum inferiorum Ecclesiae Pastorum, Tridenti explicata.

ANTVERPIAE. Apud Ioan. Belleru[m] ad insigne Falconis. Anno, M.D.LIIII.

27, [1] p. ; 13 cm. (12mo) Signatures: A-I^{12}, K^6; [A] unsigned.

An old price notation on upper, right hand side of the title page is broken off with loss of text.

Klaiber, 591; OCLC: 16934317.

The Council of Trent undertook a serious reform of the Catholic Church. This work discusses the necessity for a bishop to reside in his own diocese. This requirement would avoid the amassing of benefices by a single person, a practice known in Germany as "Prebend eating" (Pfrundenfressen). At the time of this work, Carranza was working diligently to promote a Catholic restoration in England.

1554
Carr

CONFESSIO DOCTRINAE SAXONICARVM ECCLESIARVM, SCRIPTA ANNO DOMINI M.D.LI. VT SYNODO TRIDENTINAE EXHIBERETVR.

LIPSIAE IN OFFICINA VALENTINI PAPAE ANNO M.D.LIIII.

152, [22] p. ; 17 cm. (8vo) Signatures: A-K^8, L^7; [A] unsigned.

There are some manuscript marginalia in the text of this volume.

BM STC, German, p. 781; VD 16, C 4808; OCLC: 18854582.

The Saxon Confession was drawn up by Melanchthon in 1551 to be presented to the Council of Trent. It follows the outline of the Augsburg Confession, but it is much less conciliatory in tone. Special emphasis is laid upon the doctrine of the Church and the forgiveness of sins. This is the second Leipzig printing of the work.

1554
Saxo

CONFESSIO
DOCTRINAE
SAXONICARVM
ECCLESIARVM,

SCRIPTA ANNO
DOMINI M. D. LI. VT
SYNODO TRIDENTI-
NAE EXHIBE-
RETVR.

PSALM. CXIX.
Loquebar de testimonijs tuis in conspectu
Regum, & non confundebar.

LIPSIAE
IN OFFICINA VALEN-
TINI PAPAE
ANNO M. D. LIIII.

Kirchenordnung: Wie es mit Christlicher Lere, reichung der Sacrament, Ordination der Diener des Euangelij, ordenlichen Ceremonien, in den Kirchen, Visitation, Consistorio vnd Schulen, Im Hertzogthumb zu Meckelnburg etc. gehalten wird.

Witteberg. Gedruckt durch Hans Lufft. 1554.

144 leaves ; 20 cm. (4to) Signatures: A-Z, a-n^4; [A] unsigned, A1b blank.

There are manuscript notes on the title page. The manuscript marginalia in this volume include a manuscript note at the end, possibly in Swedish, and is only partly legible.

VD 16, M 1831;   OCLC: 22535438.

The first Lutheran church ordinance in Mecklenburg was published in 1540. Lutheranism was definitely established in 1549 at the Diet at Sternberg. A revised church ordinance was prescribed in 1552. Johann Aurifaber and David Chytrus, the authors of the church ordinance, were both prominent figures in the early history of the Lutheran church in Mecklenburg.

1554
Evan

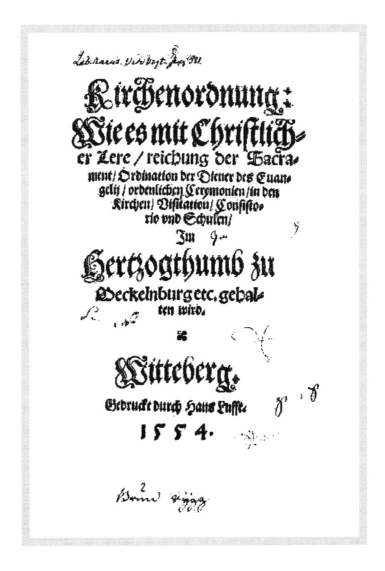

Luther, Martin, 1483-1546.

DE VSVRA TAXANDA AD PASTORES ECCLESIARVM commonefactio.

FRANCOFORTI apud Petrum Brub[achium], Anno Domini 1554.

182 p. ; 15 cm. (8vo) Signatures: A-L^8, M^3; [A] unsigned, A1b blank.

This is the second item bound with Martin Luther's *DE MISSA PRIVATA, ET VNCTIONE Sacer libellus*, Vitebergae (per Ioannem Lufft), M.D.XXXIIII.

Stickelberger-Folger, 148, V;   VD 16, L 3789;   WA 51, 328;   OCLC: 21721173.

This is a Latin translation of Luther's German work: *An Admoniton to Pastors to Preach against Usury*. The work is an exhortation to pastors to reprove both usury and usurers, for their practice is contrary to God's law. Civil authorities are also urged to protect their people in this matter.

1534
Luth E: 2

DE VSV=
RA TAXANDA AD
PASTORES ECCLESIARVM
commonefactio

In qua & Principes aliosq̃ Ma-
giſtratus atque etiam Iureconſultos
hortatur, ut officium ſuum in ea inhi-
benda diligenter faciant . Docet etiam , quomodo egentibus largien-
dum : quomodo item mutuandum:
& quæ ſancta ſit Vſura, alia-
que lectu digniſ-
ſima.

FRANCOFORTI
apud Petrum Brub.
Anno Domini
1 5 5 4 .

Luther, Martin, 1483-1546.

Die Heubtartikel des Christlichen Glaubens, Wider den Bapst, vnd der Hellen pforten zu erhalten. Sampt dem Bekentnis des Glaubens.

Wittemberg. Gedruckt durch Peter Seitzen Erben. 1554.

[223] p. ; 15 cm. (8vo) Signatures: A-O^8; [A], F4 unsigned, O8b blank.

This volume was formerly in the Beck Lutherana collection, #259 and in the W. H. Stifel collection, #335. There is a manuscript note on the title page reading, "Sumex libris Vlrici Holijj Ao 612 Vimariae Emi pro 15 gl[?]."

The title is printed in red and black within a double line border.

WA 50, 185; VD 16, L 4810; OCLC: 21709665.

The Schmalkald Articles of Luther were first called by that name in 1553. This edition of them also includes other Luther works and were first issued together in this form in 1543.

1554
Luth B: 1

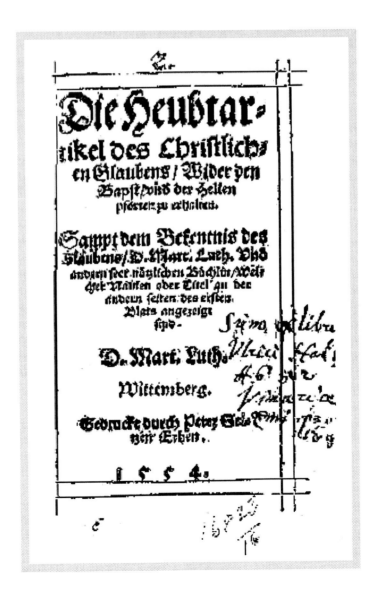

Luther, Martin, 1483-1546.

Fünff Predigten D. Martini Lutheri, von den fünff Heubtsünden, dauon Herr Niclas von Amsdorff, in der Leichpredigt vber dem Begrebnis des Durchleuchtigsten, Hochgebornen Fürsten vnd Herrn, Herrn Johans Fridrichen des Eltern etc. meldung thut, das vmb solcher Sünde willen Gott jtziger zeit Deudschland billich straffe.

(Gedruckt zu Jhena, bey Christian Rödinger Anno 1554.)

[82] p. ; 20 cm. (4to) Signatures: A-K^4, L^1; [A], K3 unsigned; A1b blank.

This volume was formerly in the Beck Lutherana collection, #586. There are manuscript marginalia in the text.

VD 16, L 3482;   OCLC: 21172503.

This collection of sermons on the "five chief sins," Amsdorff issued on the occasion of the death of Johann Frederich, Elector of Saxony.

1554
Luth

Luther, Martin, 1483-1546.

VERA ET PROPRIA ENARRATIO DICTI CHRISTI IOANNIS VI. Caro non prodest quicquam, &c. a Reuerendo uiro sanctae memoriae D. MARTINO Luthero scripta contra Sacramentarios, & in sermonem Latinum per IOACHIMVM Vuestphalum conuersa.

FRANCOFORTI apud Petrum Brub[achum] Anno Domini 1554.

[79] p. ; 15 cm. (8vo) Signatures: a-e^8; [a] unsigned, a1b, e8b blank.

This volume was formerly in the Beck Lutherana collection, #352.

VD 16, L 4279;   OCLC: 21266957.

This booklet includes a Latin translation of part of Luther's work, "That these words of Christ 'This is my body' will stand fast against the enthusiasts." The booklet does not appear in the bibliography of the Weimar edition of Luther's collected works; they list only a Latin translation of 1556.

1554
Luth A

Melanchthon, Philipp, 1497-1560.

Vnterricht der Visitation, an die Pfarhern im Kurfürstenthum zu Sachsen, Durch Doct. Mart. Luth. corrigirt. M.D.XXXVIII.

gedruckt zu Jhena, Durch Christian Rödinger. M.D.LIIII.

[95] p. ; 21 cm. Signatures: A-M^4; [A] unsigned, M4b blank; the 4th leaf is signed occasionally.

This volume was formerly in the Beck Lutherana collection, #419 and in the W.H. Stifel collection, #336. There is a manuscript bibliographical note on the title page.

BM STC German, p. 781; VD 16, M 2608; OCLC: 21169880.

Melanchthon wrote the Instruction for Church Visitations in 1527 in both German and Latin. He was himself one of the first visitors to put the work to use. As a result some changes were made to the manuscript, and the whole was sent to Luther for the purpose of securing a preface. Luther thought so highly of it that he "adopted" it, and revised it for publication in 1538. This fourth printing was occasioned by the visit of N. von Amsdorff.

1554
Mela

Vnterricht der Vi-
sitation / an die Pfar-
hern im Kurfürstenthum zu Sachsen / Durch Doct. Mart. Luth.
corrigirt. M. D. XXXVIII.

Itzt auffs newe wi-
der gedruckt zu Jhena / Durch
Christian Rödinger.

M. D. LIIII.

Mörlin, Joachim.

HISTORIA *Welcher gestalt sich die Osiandrische schwermerey im lande zu Preussen erhaben, vnd wie dieselbige verhandelt ist, mit allen actis, beschrieben.*

[Magdeburg : Michael Lotter, 1554?]

> [215] p. ; 21 cm. (4to) Signatures: A-Z, a-d⁴; [A] unsigned, A1b, d4b blank, F3 missigned "E3".

> This is the second item bound with Fridericus Staphylus' SYNODVS SANCTORVM..., NORIMBERGAE EXCVDEBAT Paulus Fabricius. Anno Salutis. M.D.LIIII. Mense Septembri.

> *BM STC German, p. 625;* VD 16, M 5879; OCLC: 23882568.

> J. Mörlin was a student of Luther, Melanchthon, and Bugenhagen in the years 1531-1536, while he was working on his M.A. In 1539, he became Luther's chaplain and a deacon in Wittenberg. In 1540, he received his Th.D. and became superintendent in Arnstadt. 1544-1550, he was pastor in Göttingen, but was forced out because of the Interim. About 1550, he became involved in the Osiander controversy over the doctrine of justification, at first siding with, then later against Osiander. In 1553, he had to leave Prussia because he refused to cease hostilities against Osiander and his partisans. This history of the Osiandrian controversy was written in 1554.

1554

Stap: 2

Peucer, Kaspar, 1525-1602.

DE DIMENSIONE TERRAE ET GEOMETRICE NVMERANdis locorum particularium interuallis ex Doctrina triangulorum Sphaerecorum & Canone subtensarum Liber, Denuo editus, sed auctius multo & correctius, quam antea.

(VVITTEBERGAE EXCVDEBAT IOHANNES CRATO M.D.LIIII.)

[16], 287 p., [3] leaves of plates: ill., plates; 16 cm. (8vo) Signatures: A-T^8, [chi]^3; [A], E5, N4 unsigned, A7-8, T8b blank.

There are manuscript marginalia in the text of this volume.

VD 16, P 1981; OCLC: 17743284.

K.Peucer, edited this volume containing material Melanchthon gathered for geographical, historical, and theological research.

1554
Peuc

DE DIMEN-
SIONE TERRÆ ET
GEOMETRICE NVMERAN
dis locorum particularium interuallis ex
Doctrina triangulorum Sphericorum & Canone subtensarum Liber, Denuo editus, sed auctius multo & correctius, quam antea.

AVTORE CASPARO
Peucero,

DESCRIPTIO LOCORVM TER-
ræ Sanctæ exactißimæ Autore quodam BRO-
CARDO MONACHO.

ALIQVOT INSIGNIVM LOCO-
rum Terræ Sanctæ explicatio & historiæ per
PHILIPPVM MELAN-
THONEM.

VVITTEBERGÆ
M. D. LIIII.

Sachs, Hans, 1494-1576.

Der Todt ein Endt, aller Yrdischen ding.

Gedruckt zu Nüremberg, durch Georg Merckel, [ca. 1554.]

[24] p. ; 19 cm. (4to) Signatures: A-C^4; [A] unsigned.

At the foot of the title page is an old library stamp reading, "Utile dulci."

BM STC German, p. 770 (with date as: "[1550?]");   Kuczynski, 2348 (no date);   Pegg, Bibliotheca, 1868 (with date as in BM STC German);   VD 16, S 561;   OCLC: 30339079.

In this "New Year's Wish," Hans Sachs considers the problem of a man facing death. He calls first upon his physical attributes--youth, beauty, strength, etc.--but finds they cannot help him. It is the spiritual factors of Sorrow, Confession, Repentance, Hope, Faith, and above all Love, that give him good counsel and rouse him from the dream of Death. This is the second printing of the revised version. The work was first written in 1542.

1554
Sach

Schwenckfeld, Caspar, 1489-1561.

Vom vnderschaide des worts Gottes vnd der Heyligen Schrifft. Auff Flacij Jllyrici ander Schmachbüchlin, Antwort.

[S.l. s.n., 1554?]

[30] p. ; 21 cm. (4to) Signatures: A-C^4, D^3; [A] unsigned, A1b blank.

BM STC German, p. 803; Corpus Schwenckfeldianorum, 13, Doc. 890B; Kuczynski, 2471; VD 16, S 5030 (with imprint: "[Ulm : Hans Varnier, d.J., 1554]"); OCLC: 22465518.

Schwenckfeld here replies to the second of Flacius Illyricus' booklets against him, "On the major parts, points, and articles of Schwenckfeldian heresy."

1554
Schwe A

Schwenckfeld, Caspar, 1489-1561.

Vom worte Gottes. Das khein ander wort Gottes sei, aigentlich zureden, denn der Suon Gottes Jesus Christus, Bewerung.

[Augsburg : Hans Wegler 1554.]

[4], CXLVII leaves ; 20 cm. (4to) Signatures: [pi]⁴, A-2N⁴, 2O³; [pi]b blank.

BM STC German, p. 803; Corpus Schwenckfeldianorum, 13, Doc. 889B; Pegg, Bibliotheca, 1939; VD 16, S 5034-5035; OCLC: 22478919.

Schwenckfeld maintained against Flacius Illyricus that the true Word of God is Christ himself.

1554
Schwe

Staphylus, Friedrich, 1512?-1564.

SYNODVS SANCTORVM PATRVM ANTIquorum contra noua dogmata Andreae Osiandri.

NORIMBERGAE EXCVDEBAT Paulus Fabricius. Anno Salutis. M.D.LIIII. Mensae Septembri.

[275] p. ; 21 cm. (4to) Signatures: a-b⁴, A-2I⁴, [chi]²; [a], 2C3 unsigned; a1b, b4b, [chi]4b blank, B3 missigned "A3", D2 missigned "D3".

This is the first item in a bound collection, half bound in blind-stamped calf over wooden boards. One clasp is missing.

At the head of the title page is an old ownership mark in ink and is only partly legible.

Klaiber, 2936; VD 16, S 8594; OCLC: 23882539.

When F. Staphylus returned to Königsberg in 1549, he became embroiled in a theological controversy with Osiander. The dispute drove Staphylus ever further into the Catholic camp. This work, stressing the authority of the Church Fathers against Osiander, was written in Danzig in 1552.

1554
Stap: 1

Vergerio, Pietro Paolo, 1498-1565.

DE IDOLO LAVRETANO. QVOD IVLIVM III. ROMA. *Episcopum non puduit in tanta luce Euangelij undiq[ue] erumpente, ueluti in contemptum Dei atq[ue] hominum, approbare.*

[Tübingen : U. Morhard] Anno M.D.LIIII.

[87] p.; 22 cm. (4to) Signatures: A-L⁴; [A] unsigned, A1b, L4b blank.

This is the third item bound with Johannes Brenz's APOLOGIAE *Confessionis Illustriss....*, FRANCOFORTI, EXcudebat Petrus Brubachius, Anno M.D.LVI.

There is a manuscript note on the title page, and manuscript marginalia in the text.

BM STC German, p. 888; OCLC: 25618333.

In the town of Loreto, Italy, there is a shrine of the Blessed Virgin Mary. According to legend, the shrine is the house where Mary grew up and nurtured Jesus. The house was brought to Loreto from Nazareth by angels. P. Vergerio scorns this legend in this book, which was translated by his nephew Ludovico Vergerio from Italian into Latin. The volume also includes a small picture of the Holy House.

1556
Bren: 3

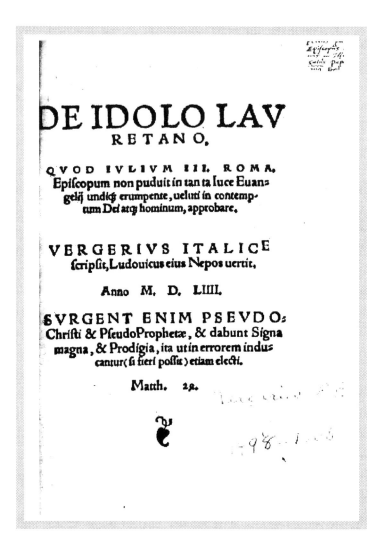

1555

Amsdorff, Nicolaus von, 1483-1565.

Das in der Schrifft ausdrücklich verkündigt ist, Das die Römische Kirche vom Christlichen glauben abfallen, Christum vnd sein Wort verleugnen vnd verdamnen sol.

Gedruckt zu Ihena durch Christian Rödinger. 1555.

[30] p. ; 20 cm. (4to) Signatures: A-C^4, D^3; [A] unsigned.

There is a former ownership stamp on the verso of the title page reading, "Suscipere et Finire; Ex Bibliotheca Fideicomm Ernesti ...(?)."

Kolb, 68;   *VD 16*, A 2341;   OCLC: 17965198.

Amsdorff here proves conclusively from Scripture itself that it is Roman Catholicism and not Protestantism that has fallen away from Christ and His teachings. The language and scurrilous form of argumentation closely follows Luther's polemical style.

1555
Amsd

Das in der Schrifft
ausdrücklich verkündigt ist / Das die
Römische Kirche vom Christlichen glauben abfallen / Christum vnd sein
Wort verleugnen vnd ver-
damnen sol.

Niclas von Amsdorff.

1. Timo. 4.
DER Geist aber saget deutlich/das in den letzten
zeiten/werden etliche von dem glauben abtretten/
vnd anhangen den verfürischen Geistern/vnd Leren
der Teufel / durch die/so in gleisnerey Lügenreder
sind/vnd Brandmal in jrem gewissen haben/vnd
verbieten Ehelich zu werden / vnd zu melden die
Speise etc.

2. Pet. 2.
DER HErr weis die Gottseligen aus der ver-
suchung zu erlösen/die Vngerechten aber behalten
zum tage des Gerichtes zu peinigen. Allermeist
aber die/so da wandeln nach dem Fleisch/in der
vnreinen Lust/vnd die Herrschafften verachten /
thürstig/eigensinnig/nicht erzittern die Majesteten
zu lestern etc.

1555.

Augustine, Saint, 354-430.

COLLECTANEA SENTENTIARVM.

RATISPONAE, EX OFFIcina Ioannis Carbonis. Anno. [MD]LV.

[127] p. ; 15 cm. (8vo) Signatures: A-H^8; [A] unsigned, H8b blank, H3 missigned "H5".

This volume was formerly in the Stewart collection, #6794. There is a manuscript biographical note on "Joachim Westphalus" in English on the second upper flyleaf.

BM STC German, p. 55;   VD 16, A 4170;   OCLC: 24031568.

Everyone in the Reformation era quoted St. Augustine to prove his own orthodoxy. And nearly everyone else disparaged his neighbor's Augustine quotations as out of context, irrelevant, or incorrect. Joachim Westphal, a Hamburg Gnesio-Lutheran preacher, here presents his collection of Augustine's sayings in an attempt to prove that the "Sacramentarians," who opposed Luther's view of the Lord's Supper, were misusing the Bishop of Hippo's words.

1555
Augu

Barnes, Robert, 1495-1540.

VITAE ROMANORVM PONTIficum, quos Papas uocamus.

BASILEAE [s.n., 1555?]

[24], 406, [26] p. ; 17 cm. (8vo) Signatures: [alpha]^8, [beta]^4, a-z^8, A-B^8, C^4, D^8, E^4; [alpha], h5, C4 unsigned, C4 blank.

There is a fore-edge shelf mark. On the upper flyleaf is a former ownership mark, "(?) Glen. Lucas. 1658," and at head of title page in ink is the name of a former owner, "C. Browne."

Adams, B-226;   BM STC German, p. 66;   VD 16, B 410;   OCLC: 25489135.

Robert Barnes was an Englishman who was converted to Luther's thought around the year 1523. He went to Europe for Henry VIII to negotiate the King's marriage with Anne of Cleves. While in Germany he tried to convince Melanchthon to come to England, but Elector Johann Frederich would not give his permission. Barnes was executed for heresy in 1540 at Smithfield. This printing of his *Lives of Roman Popes,* has a preface by Luther.

1555
Barn

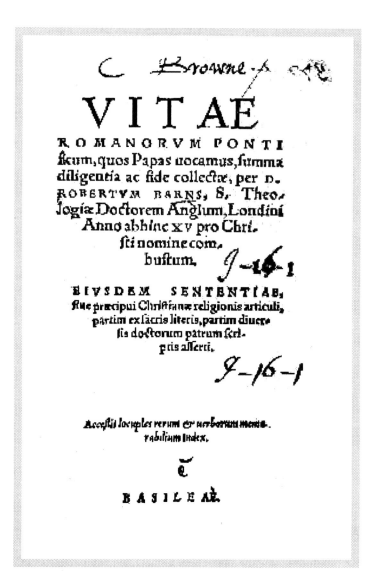

Brenz, Johannes, 1499-1570.

IN APOLOGIAM *Confessionis Illustrissimi Principis ac Domini, D. Christophori, ducis Vuirtenbergensis &c. [prolegomena].*

Francoforti apud Petrum Brubachium, Anno 1555.

191 p. ; 22 cm. (4to in 8s and 4s) Signatures: A^8, B-Z^4; [A] unsigned, Z4b blank.

This is the second item bound with Johannes Brenz's APOLOGIAE *Confessionis Illustriss...,* FRANCO-FORTI, EXcudebat Petrus Brubachius, Anno M.D.LVI.

There are scattered marginalia in the text.

VD 16, B 7702;   OCLC: 25618067.

Johannes Brenz's prolegomena to his Apology for the *Confessio Wirtembergica,* include historical and theological documents important for an understanding of that text. This volume has the prolegomena bound after Part I, possibly because the binder could not read the Greek words on the title page.

1556
Bren: 2

IN APOLOGIAM
Confessionis Illustrissimi
Principis ac Domini, D.
Christophori, ducis
Vuirtenbergen=
sis &c.

ΠΡΟΛΕΓΟΜΕΝΑ,

AVTORE IOANNE
BRENTIO,

Francoforti apud
Petrum Brubachium, Anno
1555.

Chytraeus, David, 1531-1600.

REGVLAE VITAE. VIRTVTVM OMNIVM METHODICAE DESCRIptiones in Academia Rostochiana propositae.

VVITTEBERGAE EXCVDEBAT IOHANNES CRATO. ANNO M.D.LV.

[128] p. ; 17 cm. (8vo) Signatures: A-H^8; [A] unsigned.

Adams, C-1604; VD 16, C 2732; OCLC: 15871755.

D. Chytraeus was born the son of a pastor in Ingelfingen near Schwäbisch-Hall. He studied in Wittenberg under Melanchthon. In 1550 Melanchthon recommended him to Rostock University where he worked for fifty years. This is the first printing of this work on Protestant educational reform. It formed the basis for the organization of schools in several Lutheran territories.

1555
Chyt

EPISTOLAE DVAE, DVORVM AMICORVM, EX QVIBVS uana, flagitiosaq[ue] Pontificum, Pauli tertij, & Iulij tertij, & Cardinalis Poli, & Stephani Gardineri pseudoepiscopi Vuintoniensis Angli, eorumq[ue] adulatorum sectatorumq[ue] ratio, magna ex parte potest intelligi.

[S.l. : s.n., 1555?]

[24] p. ; 15 cm. (8vo) Signatures: A^8, B^4; [A] unsigned, A1b blank.

This volume was formerly in the Stewart collection, #6509.

VD 16, E 1718 (which gives imprint: "[n.p. : 1555?]");   OCLC: 23743314.

A small anonymous tract on the English Reformation directed against Cardinal Pole and Stephan Gardiner, spearheads of the Counter-Reformation in England under Mary Tudor.

1555
Epis

EPISTO-

LÆ DVÆ, DVORVM

AMICORVM, EX QVIBVS
uana, flagitiosaḉ Pontificum, Pauli tertij, & Iulij tertij, & Cardinalis Poli, & Stephani Gardineri pseudoepiscopi Vuintoniensis
Angli, eorumḉ adulatorum sectatorumḉ
ratio, magna ex parte potest
intelligi.

✻   ✺   ✻

Apocalypsis Cap. 18.

Vobis quod suppleut dedit, illi reddite duplum,
Luctus si tantus, gloria quanta fuit?

CVM PAPAE PRIVILEGIO
ad momentum horæ.

Flacius Illyricus, Matthias, 1520-1575.

DE VOCE ET RE Fidei, contra PHARISAICVM HYPOcritarum fermentum: autore MATTHIA FLAcio Illyrico. Cum praefatione PHILIPPI Melanchthonis.

BASILEAE, PER IOannem Oporinum. [1555.]

[30], 161, [10] p. ; 17 cm. (8vo) Signatures: [alpha]-[beta]^8, a-k^8, l^6; [alpha] unsigned; [alpha]b blank, l6a colophon, l6b blank.

This is the third item bound with Martin Luther's PROPOSITIONES.., EXCVSVM VVITENBERgae, typis Ioannis Lufft. Anno M.d.XXXVIII. V. idus Septembris.

BM STC German, p. 306; Jackson, 1880; Pegg, Bibliotheca, 460; VD 16, F 1526; OCLC: 11932675.

Flacius was one of the first theologians to recognize the importance of the study of the meaning and origins of words for a thorough understanding of the Scriptures. This is his first work and was first printed in 1549. The present copy appears to be the second printing of the work.

1538
Luth A: 3

Luther, Martin, 1483-1546.

IN PRIMVM LIBRVM MOSE ENARRATIONES.

Impressum Noribergae in officina Iohannis Montani; & Vlrici Neuberi, Anno Domini M.D.LV. [1555-1560.]

4 v. bd. as 2 ; 33 cm. (fol. in 6s).

Both volumes are bound in blind-stamped pigskin over wooden boards. Volume 3-4 has one clasp missing.

These volumes were formerly in the Beck Lutherana collection, #351. Both volumes have fore-edge shelf marks. Volume 1-2 has a manuscript inscription on the upper flyleaf, as well as two former ownership marks on the title page and manuscript marginalia on the text.

VD 16, B 2999 (T.1-1555);   VD 16, B 2998 (T.4-1554);   OCLC: 05131050.

Luther began his lectures on Genesis on June 1, 1535, and concluded them on November 17, 1545. The editors of these notes were students of Melanchthon, hence some "Philippist" tendencies may be noticed from time to time. On the whole, however, the thought and most of the words are Luther's.

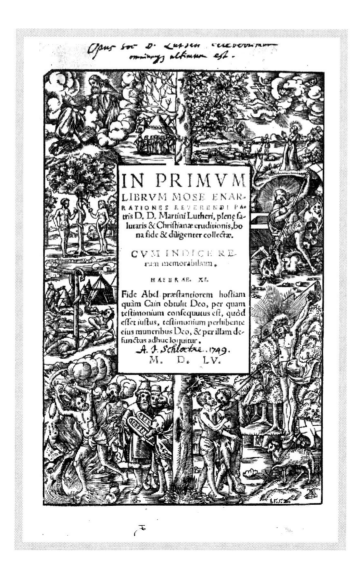

1555
Luth
(OS)

Melanchthon, Philipp, 1497-1560.

Vita Lutheri. Vonn dem Leben vnd Sterben, des Ehrwirdigen herrn D. Martini Lutheri trewlich vnd warhafftiglich geschrieben.

[S.l. : s.n.] Anno 1555.

[304] p. ; 16 cm. (8vo) Signatures: A-T^8; [A] unsigned, T8b blank.

This volume was formerly in the Beck Lutherana collection, #869. There are scattered manuscript marginalia in the text.

BM STC German, p. 612?;   VD 16, M 3427 (which lists place and publisher as: "[Frankfurt/Main: David Zöpfel]"); OCLC: 12661428.

After Melanchthon had preached the funeral sermon for Luther he felt a more permanent memorial was in order. Melanchthon then wrote this biography of Luther, first published in Latin in Wittenberg in 1548. It was subsequently translated by M. Ritter into German and printed in 1554.

1555
Mela

Nausea, Friedrich, 1480/1496-1552.

REVERENdiss. in Christo patris & Domini, Domini Frederici Nauseae Blancicampiani, Episcopi Viennensis, de Consummatione seculi, Libri IIII. De nouissimo Iesu Christi Aduentu & Iudicio, Libri III. Nunquam hactenus typis excusi.

COLONIAE, Excudebat Iaspar Genuep[a]eus. Cum Priuilegio C[a]esare[a]e Maiestatis. Anno M.D.LV.

[16], 303 p. ; 17 cm. (8vo) Signatures: a^8, A-T^8; [A] unsigned, A1b, T8b blank, G5 unsigned.

This volume was formerly in the Stewart collection, #4409. The manuscript marks on the title page have been inked out.

Adams, N-83; VD 16, N 222;   OCLC: 28004484.

F. Nausea was Bishop of Vienna in 1555 when he published these two works. Roman Catholics of the sixteenth century were not especially interested in eschatological speculation, hence Nausea's interest in this subject makes this work noteworthy.

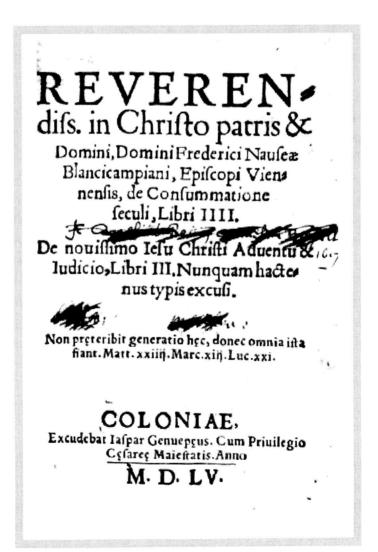

1555
Naus

Sachs, Hans, 1494-1576.

Ein ernstliche ermanung an die Weltkinder, so in leybs wollust ersuffen sindt, wieder zukeren.

(Gedruckt zu Nürmberg, durch Georg Merckel, auffm newen baw bey der Kalckhütten. 1555.)

[8] p. ; 19 cm (4to) Signatures: i-ij4; [i] unsigned.

Hohenemser, 4714; not in VD 16 as a separate work, but cf. VD 16, S 259 for this edition in a collection of works of H. Sachs; OCLC: 20379117.

H. Sachs was an early supporter of Luther. He was especially influential because of the popularity of his poetry and verse-plays.

1555
Sach

Schwenckfeld, Caspar, 1489-1561.

Ableinung D. Luthers Malediction, so erst durch Flacium Illyricum wider mich im[m] truck ist publicirt worden.

[S.l. : s.n.] MDLV.

[85] p. ; 19 cm. (4to) Signatures: A-K^4, L^3; [A] unsigned, L3b blank.

There is a former ownership mark on the inside, upper cover reading, "A.F. Schneider Berlin 1836. Aus einer Auktion in Berlin."

BM STC German, p. 800;   Corpus Schwenckfeldianorum, 14, Doc. 942;   Kuczynski, 2453;   Stickelberger-Folger, 693; VD 16, S 4835 (with imprint "[Ulm: Hans Varnier d.J.]");   OCLC: 05509147.

In 1555, Flacius Illyricus published a false text of the curse Luther had laid on Schwenckfeld. Schwenckfeld decided to publish "the true" text in order to vindicate himself. This booklet is the result.

1555
Schwe

Ableinung D. Luthers
Malediction/ so erst durch Flacium
Illyricum wider mich im truck
ist publicirt worden.

Caspar Schwenckfelde.

ITEM

Vom rechten grund vnd verstande des
H. Sacraments des HER-
REN Nachemals.

M D LV.

Schwenckfeld, Caspar, 1489-1561.

Von der Götliechn kindtschaft, vnd herrlichait des ganntzen Sones Gottes Jesu Christi.
[S.l. : s.n.] 1555.

> [47] p. ; 16 cm. (8vo) Signatures: A-C^8; [A] unsigned, A1b, C8b blank.
>
> C. Schwenckfeld's name crossed out in ink on title page of this copy, and replaced in margin in ink.
>
> *Corpus Schwenckfeldianorum, 14, Doc. 941; VD 16, S 4971 (with imprint: "[Ulm: Hans Variner d.J.]");* OCLC: *22535412.*
>
> It was one of Schwenckfeld's theological tenets that the flesh of Christ did not originate in the first or Adamic creation, but represented the first fruits of God's new creation. This view was opposed by Lutherans who stressed Christ's ubiquity consequential to his presence in the Lord's Supper. Schwenckfeld rewrote this tract several times trying to produce a brief exposition of his doctrine for interested inquirers.

1555
Schwe A

Sleidanus, Johannes, 1506-1556.

IOAN. SLEIDANI, DE STATV RELIGIONIS ET REIPVBLICAE, CAROLO QVINTO, CAESARE, Commentarij.

ARGENTORATI Excudebat Vuendelinus Rihelius. Anno M.D.LV.

[4], 470 leaves ; 33 cm. (fol. in 4s) Signatures: a^4, A-Z^4, Aa-Zz^4, 2a-2z^4, 2A-3Z^4,3a^4, 3b^6; a-2z^4; [a] unsigned, 3b6b blank. Errors in foliation: leaves 230 and 358 are misnumbered 229 and 357 respectively.

This volume is bound in blind-stamped, bleached pigskin over wooden boards.

There are manuscript marginalia in the text.

Adams, S-1285; VD 16, S 6669; OCLC: 16850163.

J. Sleidanus was born in Aachen and studied to be a diplomat. He wrote this history on the basis of extensive use of archival sources, some of which were not to be used again until the nineteenth century. Thus this work is important to Reformation historiography as presenting the only access to original sources available to sixteen-nineteenth century historians.

Soto, Pedro de, 1495/1500-1563.

ASSERTIO CATHOLICAE FIDEI CIRCA ARTICVLOS CONFESSIONIS NOM-INE ILLVSTRISSIMI DVCIS Wirtenbergensis oblatae per Legatos eius Concilio Tridentino, XXIIII. Ianuarij Anni M.D.LII.

COLONIAE, Ioannes Nouesianus excudebat, Anno M.D.LV.

[307] p. ; 20 cm. (4to) Signatures: A-Z, a-z, 2a-2e^4; [A] unsigned, 2e4b blank.

This volume is bound in a leaf of medieval manuscript, possibly from a missal.

This volume was formerly in the Stewart collection, #6170. There is an old ownership mark on the inside front flyleaf: "Duplum Bibliothecae regiae Monacensis."

Adams, S-1505; BM STC German, p. 929; Klaiber, 2924; VD 16, S 7072; OCLC: 23887967.

Christoph, Duke of Württemberg was a Lutheran who took a great deal of interest in religious affairs in his territory. This volume includes a text of the Württemberg Confession with Pedro de Soto's notes as a running commentary in the margins. P. de Soto was a Spanish Catholic theologian who was confessor to Emperor Charles V from 1542-1548. The Interim of Augsburg was drafted in part by de Soto. He went on to become a professor of theology at Dillingen and Procurator of the German Province of Dominicans, which order he had professed in 1519. He died as Paul IV's theologian at the Council of Trent.

1555
Soto

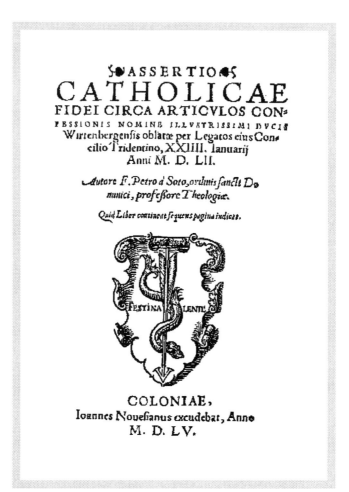

1556

Artopoeus, Petrus, 1491-1563.

VATICINIVM SACRVM, DE Ecclesia, totoq[ue] ministerio Euangelij, sub Antichris-
tianismo, usq[ue] ad finem mundi. Ex Apocalypsi capite XI.

[S.l. : s.n.] 1556.

23 p. ; 16 cm. (8vo) Signatures: a^8, b^4; [a] unsigned, b4b blank.

This is the sixth item bound with Philipp Melanchthon's *IVDICIVM D. Philippi MeLANCHTHONIS DE controuersia Coenae Domini.* BASILEAE, [s.n.] 1560.

VD 16, B 5263; OCLC: 12691419.

P. Artopoeus (Greek for "Becker") was born in Cosslin. He studied in Wittenberg, and returned to Cosslin to teach. He later became a pastor in Stettin, but was deposed for breaking with Lutheran orthodoxy on the issue of justification. This tract is a commentary on Revelation 11.

1560
Mela A:7

Brenz, Johannes, 1499-1570.

APOLOGIAE Confessionis Illustriss. Principis ac Domini, d. Christophori Ducis Vuirtenbergensis &c. [perikope prote].

FRANCOFORTI, EXcudebat Petrus Brubachius, Anno M.D.LVI.

407 [i.e. 411] p. ; 22 cm. (4to in 4s and 8s) Signatures: a^4, b-z, A-B^8, C^4, D^6; [a] unsigned, g2 missigned "g4", D6b blank.

This is the first item in a bound collection covered in bleached, panel-stamped pigskin over wooden boards, one clasp intact.

This volume was formerly in the Stewart collection, #6633. There are scattered marginalia in the text.

VD 16, B 7486 (Pt. I only); OCLC: 25617991.

Johannes Brenz wrote the *Confessio Wirtembergica* in 1552. In response to an attack by Pedro de Soto, he began a defense of the Confessio Wirtembergica in 1554. The Prolegomena were finished in 1555, and Part I, this document, was printed in 1556. Parts II-III were printed in 1557 and 1559.

1556
Bren: 1

Brottuff, Ernst, 1497?-1565.

GENEALOGIA Vnd Chronica, des Durchlauchten Hochgebornen, Königlichen vnd Fürstlichen Hauses, der Fürsten zu Anhalt, Graffen zu Ballenstedt vnd Ascanie, Herrn zu Bernburgk vnd Zerbst, auff 1055. Jar....

Gedruckt zu Leipzigk, durch Jacobum Berwaldt, wohnhafftig in der Nickels Strassen. 1556.

[10], 105 [i.e. 108], [26] leaves : geneal. tables, coats-of-arms ; 30 cm. (fol. in 6s) Signatures: [section mark]10, A-T⁶, V², 2[section mark]4, 2A⁶, 2B⁸; [section mark] unsigned, E3 unsigned, 2B8b blank.

This volume was a gift of Richard and Martha Kessler, 1987. There is a former ownership stamp on the upper flyleaf, "Thorvald Rützou Kjobenhavn."

BM STC German, p. 155; *VD 16, B 8434;* OCLC: *16991138.*

Richly illustrated genealogical work on the House of Anhalt, important to this collection because of Melanchthon's preface tying the family into the contemporary scholarly community.

1556
Brot

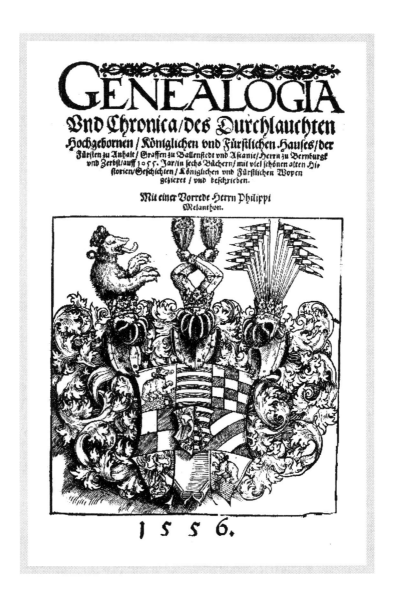

Eck, Johann, 1486-1543.

ENCHIRIDION LOcorum communium aduersus Lutherum & alios hostes ecclesiae.
INGOLSTADII IN OFficina Alexandri et Samuelis Vueissenhornio. M.D.LVI.

[8], 253, [4] leaves ; 14 cm. (12mo in 8s and 4s) Signatures: A^8, B^4, C^8, D^4 ... Z^8, a^4,b^8 ... x^4; [A] unsigned, g3 missigned "g5", s3 missigned "s5".

This volume is bound in a vellum leaf of a medieval music manuscript.

This volume was formerly in the Beck Lutherana collection, #736. There is a manuscript note on inside, lower cover about the controversy between Eck and Luther and may be from the sixteenth century. It is signed by Polycarpus Scheiblinus Nordlingensis.

Metzler, 51 (63); OCLC: 19088530.

This is a later edition of Eck's *Handbook of theological topics against Luther,* written as an extension of his refutation of the Augsburg Confession.

1556
Eck

Eitzen, Paulus de.

PROPOSITIONES DE QVIBVS disputabit.

VVITEBERGAE. [s.n.] Anno 1556. Die Maij 18.

[32] p. ; 17 cm. (8vo) Signatures: A-B^8; [A] unsigned.

This is the second item bound with Melanchthon's *EPISTOLAE PAVLI SCRIPTAE ad Romanos, Enarratio,* VVITEBERGAE [Veit Kreuzer] 1556.

Hartfelder, 595;   VD 16, E 925 (under P. Eitzen, without mention of P. Melanchthon's role);   OCLC: 25572519.

Bound with Melanchthon's commentary on St. Paul's Epistle to the Romans, this is a rare doctoral dissertation. These theses were written by Melanchthon and defended by Paul von Eitzen. The work is about how one might recognize the true Church and distinguish it from false (heretical) churches. The contemporary pigskin over wooden boards binding is a good example of the kind of work that the bookbinders were doing in the latter half of the sixteenth century.

1556
Mela C: 2

Flacius Illyricus, Matthias, 1520-1575.

Catalogus testiVM VERITATIS, QVI ante nostram aetatem reclamarunt Papae.
BASILEAE, PER IOANnem Oporinum, Anno Christi M.D.LVI. Mense Martio.

[32], 1095 p. ; 18 cm. Signatures: [alpha]8, a^8, A-3A^8, 3b^4; [alpha], m4 unsigned; 2D4 missigned "Dc4".

This volume is bound in blind-stamped pigskin over wooden boards.

There are manuscript notes on the inside upper cover and both sides of the upper flyleaf, and manuscript marginalia in the text.

BM STC German, p. 305; Jackson, 1883; Pegg, Bibliotheca, 458; Preger, II, p. 555; VD 16, F 1293; OCLC: 07346793.

One of the results of Flacius' investigations into church history was the discovery that there had been a large number of men who had protested the usurpation of power by the Bishop of Rome. Flacius here gathers these testimonies together in a catalog, designed to show how widespread and pervasive this testimony had been in the past.

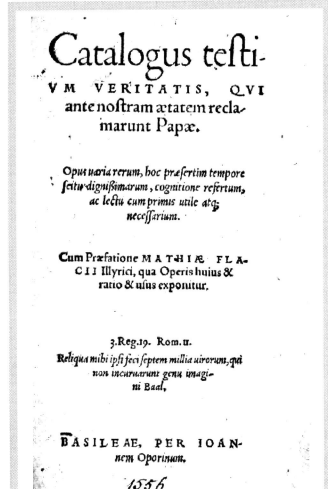

1556
Flac

Luther, Martin, 1483-1546.

EPISTOLARVM REVERENDI PATRIS Domini D. Martini Lutheri, Tomus primus, [-secundus], continens scripta viri Dei, ab anno millesimo quingentesimo septimo, usque ad annum vicesimum secundum A IOHANNE AVRIfabro, aulae Vinariensis concionatore collectus.

[Jena/Eisleben : Christianus Rhodius/Andreas Petri, 1556-1565.]

2 v. ; 21 cm. (4to).

These volumes are a created set, and not bound uniformly. Volume one is bound in blind-stamped, bleached pigskin over wooden boards and is dated "1576" with a former owner's initials: "I.R.I." Volume two is bound in polished pigskin over wooden boards stamped with a portrait of Luther.

These volumes were both in the Stewart collection, #3819. Volume one has manuscript notes relating to Luther's life on the title page, an inscription in Greek on the verso, and references to various figures in the correspondence with page numbers on the last blank page. Volume two has manuscript marginalia in the text.

Adams, L-1805, 1806; BM STC German, p. 535; VD 16, L 4649; WA 14, 577-578, 372ff (includes historical, bibliographical, and biographical information); OCLC: 05205945.

J. Aurifaber edited these two volumes of Luther's letters. A projected third volume was never printed. Vol. 1: IHENAE Excudebat Christianus Rhodius [1556], Vol. 2: Eislebii Excudebat Andreas Petri [1565].

1556
Luth

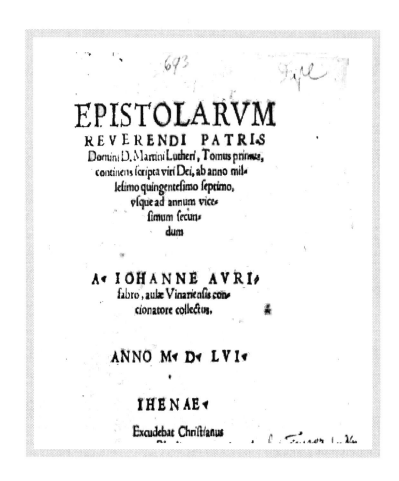

Luther, Martin, 1483-1546.

TOMVS PRIMVS [-quartus et idem ultimus] OMNIVM OPERVM.
IENAE EXCVDEBAT Christianus Rhodius. 1556-1558.

4 v. ; 33 cm. (folio in 6s).

These volumes are all bound in blind-stamped pigskin over wooden boards in 1556 for "M.R." Only volume 3 has a clasp intact.

This work was presented to Hartford Seminary by "Dea Sam[uel] Stone." Each volume has a fore-edge shelf mark, and manuscript marginalia in the text. There is a manuscript note on the inside lower, cover of volume one.

Aland, p. 584;   OCLC: 15490931.

This is the first printing of the four-volume Jena edition of the Latin works of Luther. N. von Amsdorff was editor: he was also one of the leading gnesio-Lutherans.

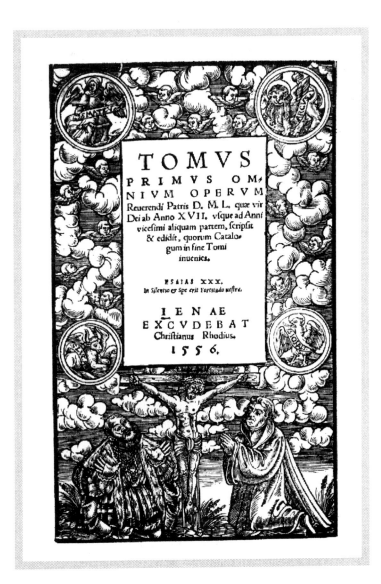

1556
Luth
(OS)

Melanchthon, Philipp, 1497-1560.

DEFINITIONES MVLTARVM APPELLATIONVM, QVARVM IN ECCLESIA VSVS EST, TRADITAE A PHILIPPO MELANTH. TORGAE ET VVITEBERgae, Anno 1552. & 1553.

VVITTEBERGAE [Peter Seitz' Erben] 1556.

[80] p. ; 16 cm. (8vo) Signatures: a-d^8, E^8; [a] unsigned, E8 blank.

There are two old ownership marks in ink on the title page that are only partly legible, dated 1556 and 1613 respectively.

BM STC German, p. 611; Hartfelder, 515; Jackson, 2124; VD 16, M 2933-34 *(printer and date from VD 16)*; OCLC: 12781434.

This little dictionary of theological terms first appeared in 1554 in an edition of the *Loci communes.* It received widespread circulation by being included in Melanchthon's handbook for the examination of candidates for ordination as well as in subsequent printings of the *Loci.* This is the second printing of the work.

1556
Mela A

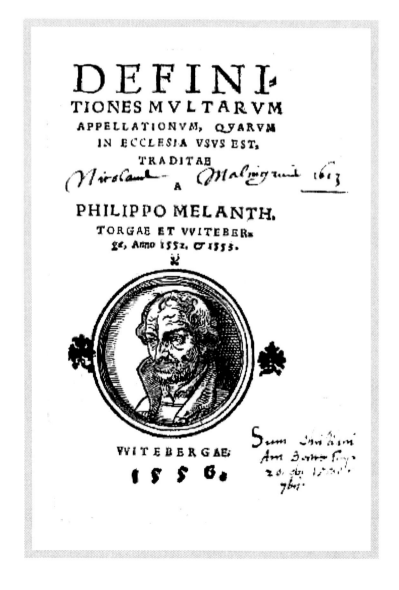

Melanchthon, Philipp, 1497-1560.

EPISTOLAE PAVLI SCRIPTAE ad Romanos, Enarratio.

VVITEBERGAE [Veit Kreuzer] 1556.

[8], 89 [i.e. 86], 160 leaves ; 17 cm. (8vo) Signatures: A-M, a-u^8; [A], G3, p4, u3 unsigned, g5 missigned, "5g".

This is the first title in a bound collection, bound in blind-stamped, bleached pigskin over wooden boards, clasps missing.

On the title page are a handwritten inscription by Melanchthon to Christopher Piscator (Fischer) and on old ownership entry in ink reading, "Andreas Virgander Lüneb."

BM STC German, p. 611; Hartfelder, 592; VD 16, M 3216 (with pagination error "88" for "86"); OCLC: 25572216.

Melanchthon's work as a humanist Christian scholar necessitated close study of the text of the Bible. He spent a lifetime studying the Epistle of Paul to the Romans. At least three of his commentaries are in the Kessler Reformation Collection (1523, 1532, and 1556-this present work). Melanchthon continued to grow and deepen his thought throughout his life, and this commentary grew in size and depth over the years. This is the first printing of this version or stage of the work. The text is in Latin and Greek, including a Latin translation of selections from Paul's Epistle to the Romans.

1556
Mela C: 1

Melanchthon, Philipp, 1467-1560.

EXAMEN EORVM QVI AVDIVNTVR ANTE RITVM PVBLICAE ORDINA-
TIONIS, QVA commendatur eis ministerium EVANGELII. Traditum Vuitebergae
Anno 1554.

VVITEBERGAE EXCVDEBANT HAEREDES PETRI SEITZII. ANNO 1556.

[376] p. ; 17 cm. (8vo) Signatures: A-Z^8; [A] unsigned; Z8b blank.

This volume was formerly in the Stewart collection, #4057.

BM STC German, p. 611;   Kuczynski, 3448;   VD 16, M 3928;   OCLC: 12324692.

Melanchthon's examination for candidates for ordination first appeared in German as part of the Mecklenberg Church
Ordinance of 1553. Melanchthon translated his examination into Latin in 1554 and it was printed as a separate work
that same year.

1556
Mela B

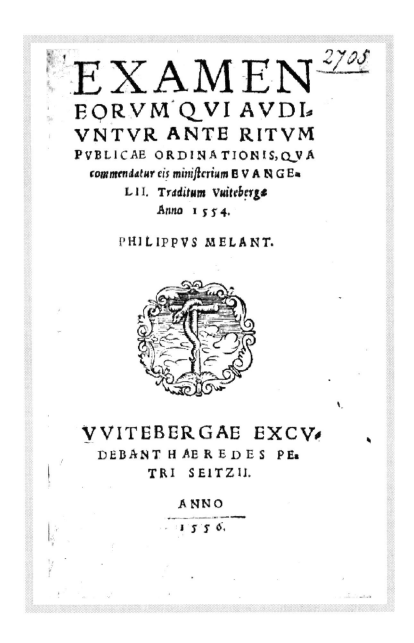

Melanchthon, Philipp, 1497-1560.

LOCI PRAECIPVI THEOLOGICI. NVNC DENVO CVRA ET DILIGENtia summa recogniti, multisq[ue] in locis copiose illustrati, Cum appendice disputationis de Coniugio.

LIPSIAE OMNIA IN OFFICINA VALENTINI PAPAE ELABORATA ATQUE EDITA, ANNO M.D. LVI.

[16], 888, [78] p. ; 21 cm. (8vo) Signatures: A-Z^8, a-z^8, 2A-2Q^8; [A], o5, t3 unsigned, c3 missigned "c2", 2Q7b, 8 blank.

This volume is bound in blind-stamped, bleached pigskin over wooden boards, both clasps intact.

This copy includes an eight line inscription in Greek by Philipp Melanchthon. Below this, in a different hand, is "7. octob. Anno 1558." On the title page in the same hand is the name "Christophoro." The family name has been cut away.

VD 16, M 3658; OCLC: 18736257.

This is a printing of the third Latin version, of Melanchthon's *Loci Communes* published in 1556. This copy is historically significant because it includes an eight-line inscription in Greek in Melanchthon's own hand. The surname of the person to whom the book was given has been cut away, but scholars believe it was Christoph Pezel (1539-1604), who later became a Lutheran pastor and editor of Melanchthon's letters.

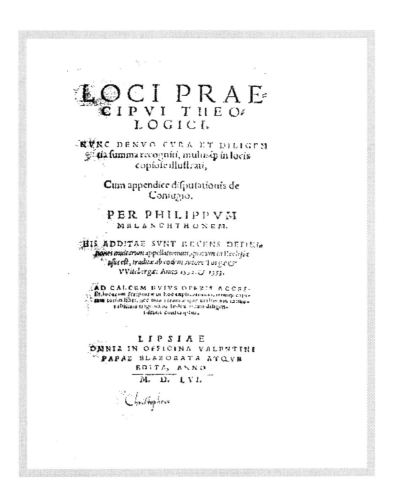

1556
Mela

Moronessa, Jacobus.

IL MODELLO DI MARTINO LVTERO.

IN VINEGIA APPRESSO GABRIEL GIOLITO DE FERRARI ET FRATELLI. MDLVI.

[26], 432, [56] p.; 17 cm. (8vo) Signatures: $*^8$, A-2G^8, 2H^4; [*] unsigned.

This volume is bound in limp vellum.

There is a former ownership mark on the title page and the following page as well.

Adams, M-1822; Klaiber, 2140; Lauchert, p. 633-639; OCLC: 17970334.

This is a standard Catholic critique of Lutheran theology, printed in Venice. It is noteworthy for its description of disturbances in Naples in 1547. Also included is the recantation of John Dudley, Earl of Warwick and Duke of Northumberland, given before his execution for heresy and rebellion in 1553.

1556
Moro

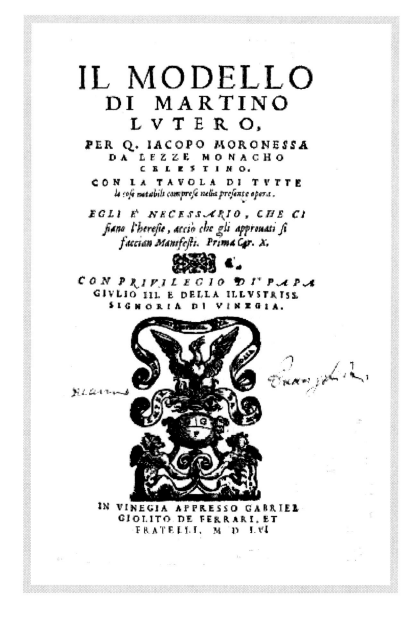

Savonarola, Girolamo, 1452-1498.

HOMILIAE.

SALMANTICAE, Excudebat Ioannes a Canoua. M.D.LVI.

[4], 288, [7] leaves ; 21 cm. (4to in 8s) Signatures: [*]^4, A-Z^8, 2A-2N^8, 2O^7; [*] unsigned, H5, M5, O5, Q5, 2C5, 2E5, 2F5 unsigned; F5 missigned "E5", G4 missigned "C4", 2H2 missigned "H".

This volume is bound in vellum. Three of the four vellum straps to tie the book closed are intact.

This volume was formerly in the Stewart collection, #5760. There are censorship notices in manuscript on the title page of this copy. Leaves 76-87 have been removed and Leaf 88a has been inked out.

OCLC: 28005436.

This volume contains sermons by Savonarola printed in Spain. The work is dedicated to Joanna, daughter of Charles V.

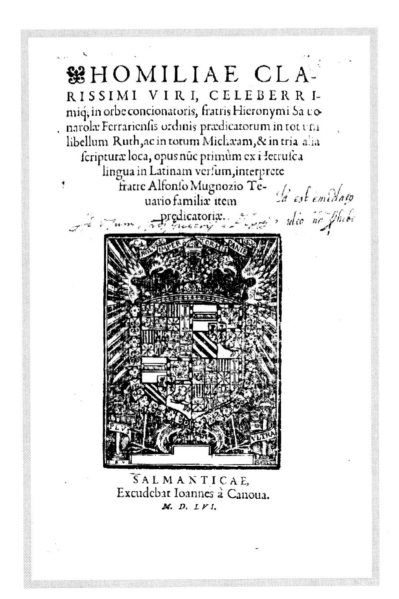

1556
Savo

Sleidanus, Johannes, 1506-1556.

IOANNIS SLEIDANI DE STATV RELIGIONIS ET REIPVBLICAE, CAROLO QVINTO, CAESARE COMmentarij.

BASILEAE, [s.n.] M.D.LVI.

[8], 342, [12] p. ; 33 cm. (fol. in 6s) Signatures: a^4, A-2E^6, 2F^4, [*]^6; [a] unsigned, [*]6b blank, 2F4b blank. Signature "I" is bound out of sequence in this copy, though all pages are present.

This copy is bound in blind-stamped, bleached pigskin over boards.

There is an old bibliographical note in manuscript on the verso of the upper flyleaf.

Adams, S-1288; VD 16, S 6676; OCLC: 19878117.

This is a later edition of Sleidan's history of the Protestant Reformation, based on archival sources.

1556
Slei

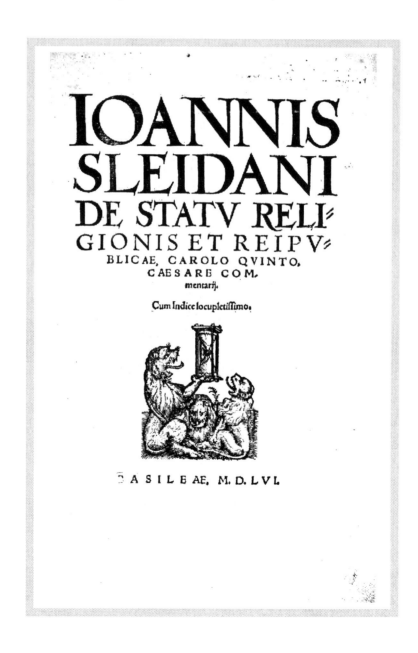

Vergerio, Pietro Paolo, 1498-1565.

RETRATTATIONE.

[S.l. : s.n.] Nell' Anno [MD]LVI.

[55] p. ; 16 cm. (8vo) Signatures: A-C^8, D^4; [A] unsigned, A1b, D4b blank.

This volume was formerly in the Stewart collection, #6507. At the foot of the title page are catalog numbers from two former libraries.

BM STC German, p. 888 (that lists place and printer as: "[U. Morhard's Widow, Tübingen]"); OCLC: 23826289.

In 1556, P. Vergerio was again in Tübingen working on plans for a diplomatic alliance between Duke Christoph of Württemberg, the Polish King, the French King, Elizabeth of England, and others. Nothing came of all these negotiations, but not for want of effort on Vergerio's part. Vergerio was also an active Protestant polemicist. He wrote in Italian, as here, because he hoped to win Italy for Protestantism. The retraction, or review of writings, is a defense of himself and his works.

1556
Verg

RETRAT-
TATIONE DEL
VERGERIO.

Misericordiam sum consecutus quod
ignorans fecerim per in-
credulitatem.

Pr. ad Timoth. p5.

Bb 6321

Nell' Anno LVI.

1557

Agricola, Theophilus, pseudonym.

Widerlegung der Lutherischen eingefürter Sophistischen lehre von Mitteln, in der gerecht vn[d] seligmachung des menschen. Vnd was erstlich D. Luther selbst vnd andere Theologi, wie auch weyland die allten Christlichen Lehrer der Kirchen darwider haben geschribe[n].

[S.l. : s.n.] Anno 1557.

[77] p. ; 19 cm. (4to) Signatures: A-I^4, K^3; [A] unsigned, K3b blank.

This volume was formerly in the Beck Lutherana collection, #710 and in the W. H. Stifel collection, #377/625.

Corpus Schwenckfeldianorum 15, Doc. 1000, p. 152; *Stickelberger-Folger, 700, 2; VD 16, M 1704; OCLC:* 22690520.

Georg Mayer (d. after 1572) of Leeder, Germany, was an associate and defender of Schwenckfeld. He wrote, and had this work printed under the pseudonym, "T. Agricola." It includes quotations from Luther and other Lutherans intended to prove that the doctrine of grace, as articulated in Article V of the Augsburg Confession, is inconsistent with earlier positions taken by Luther and his co-workers.

1557
Agri

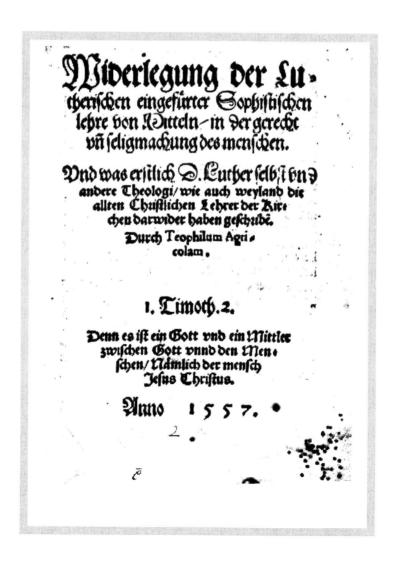

Brenz, Johannes, 1499-1570.

IN EVANGELION, *quod inscribitur, secundum Lucam, duodecim priora capita, Homiliae centum & decem.*

Francoforti : Ex Officina Petri Brubachij, Anno Domini M.D.LVII.

2 pts bd. as 1 v. (1404 [i.e. 1350], [43] p.) ; 33 cm. (fol. in 6s) Signatures: A-Z, a-z, 2A-2Q^6, 2R^4, 2S-2Z, Aa-Zz, 3a-3z, 3&, 3[recipe]^{6,} $^{3[que]4,}$ $^{2a-2c6}$; A1b, 2R4, 2S1b, [que]4b, 2c6b blank; S4, c4 unsigned, Nn2 missigned "N2", Xx2 missigned "X2", 3u4 missinged "3u3."

This volume is bound in bleached, panel-stamped pigskin over wooden boards. The title page of Part II includes the printer's statement and is dated M.D.LVI. The pagination and signatures of Part II are continuous with Part I.

There are fore-edge and top-edge shelf marks on this volume. There are former ownership marks on the pastedown end papers of Nicolaus Fry, the Jacobi Minoris Bibliotheca, and Concordia Seminary, St. Louis, Missouri. There are scattered manuscript marginalia in the text.

Adams, B-2792 (title page dated 1563, but internally appears identical to this ed.); Jackson, 1673; *VD 16, B 7738-7739;* OCLC: 23896319.

When Johannes Brenz first published these sermons in 1540-1543, he was pastor in Schwäbisch-Hall. He had been active in introducing the Protestant Reformation in Hall since 1522, where he remained until 1548 when the Interim forced him into exile. These two volumes, here bound together, include sermons on the Gospel of Luke, and sermons on the Passion of Christ. Brenz was, after Luther himself, one of the most important Lutheran biblical interpreters of the Reformation period. After Luther's death Brenz became one of the chief spokesmen for Lutheranism and played a key role in the formation of several territorial churches in Southern Germany.

IN EVANGELION,
quod inscribitur, secundum Lu=
cam, duodecim priora capita,
Homiliæ centum & decem,

AVTORE IOANNE
BRENTIO.

Eiusdem Homiliç octoginta in
duodecim posteriora capita, ac
in historiam Passionis & Resur
rectionis Christi.

CVM INDICE COPIOSO
AC VTILI.

EVANGELION CHRISTI POTENTIA
Deiest, adsalutem omnicredenti. Rom. 1.

Francoforti Anno Domini
M. D. LVII.

1557
Bren

Helding, Michael, 1506-1561.

CATECHISMVS, *Das ist, Christliche Vnderweisung vnd gegründter Bericht, nach warer Euangelischer vnd Catholischer lehr, vber die Fürnembste stücke vnsers hailigen allgemeinen Christen glaubens.*

Maintz Druckts Frantz Behem, Im Jar M.D.LVII.

[4], CCLXXIX [i.e. 284] leaves : 30 cm. (fol. in 6s) Signatures: A⁴, ²A⁶, B-Z, Aa-Yy⁶, Zz⁴, Aaa⁵; [A], V4 unsigned, R2 missigned "R3", A1b blank.

Pasted onto the upper pastedown is an old library bookplate: "Bibliotheca P.P. Capucinorum Surlaci." On the title page is an old ownership mark in ink: "Ad Prum. F. Frid. Capucinorum Surlaci."

Klaiber, 1476 (but not this ed.);   VD 16, H 1595;   OCLC: 29768717.

Helding preached the eighty-four sermons that underlie this catechism in the Cathedral of Mainz between 1542 and 1544. They were first published in 1551 at the request of the Archbishop of Mainz, Sebastian von Heusenstamm.

1557
Held

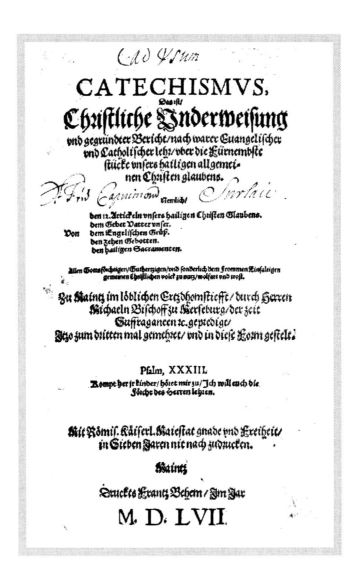

Kirchen Ordnung Wie es mit der Reynen Lehr des Euangelij, Administration der heyligen Sacrament, Annehmung, verhörung, vnd bestetigung der Priester, Ordentlichen Ceremonien in den Kirchen, Visitation vnd Synodis, in der Herrschafft Waldeck gehalten werden soll. Anno Domini 1556. Mense Martio auffgericht.

Getruckt zuo Marpurg bei Andres Colben 21. Augusti. Anno D[omi]ni. M.D.LVII.

[138] p. : music ; 19 cm. (4to) Signatures: A-Q^4, R^5; [A] unsigned, A1b blank.

This volume is bound in blind-stamped, bleached pigskin over paper boards, clasps missing. The front cover has vignette titled, "Iustitia," and the back cover has a vignette titled, "Lucretia."

This volume was formerly in the Stewart collection, #3722. There is a former ownership mark on the title page, and a fore-edge shelf mark.

OCLC: 22603794.

This is the Church ordinance issued by the Counts of Waldeck. Although the county was a fief of Hesse-Kassel, this ordinance differs considerably from the Hessian Church Ordinance of 1539.

1557
Evan

Luther, Martin, 1483-1546.

Hundert vnd zwanzig Propheceyunge, oder Weissagung, des Ehrwirdigen Vaters Herrn Doctoris Martini Luthers, von allerley straffen, so nach seinem tod vber Deutschland von wegen desselbigen grossen, vnd vielfaltigen Sünden kommen solten.

Gedruckt zu Eisleben durch Vrbanum Kaubisch Jm Jahr 1557.

[182] p. ; 20 cm. (4to) Signatures: A-Y⁴, Z¹ + ; [A] unsigned, D2 missigned "C2"; all after "Z¹" wanting from this copy.

This volume was formerly in the Beck Lutherana collection, #12.

VD 16, L 3484;   OCLC: 21580406.

This is a further example of apocalyptic writing from the mid-sixteenth century. Such collections of Luther's "prophecies" were especially useful for preserving his memory after his death.

1557
Luth

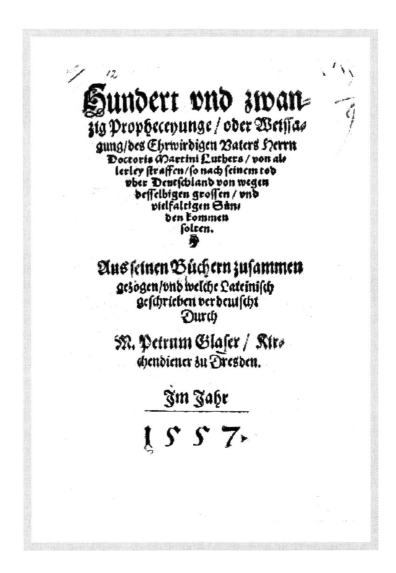

Luther, Martin, 1483-1546.

Warnunge Doctor Martini Luther, ann seine liebe Deutschen, vor etlichen jarren geschriben auff disen fall, so die feinde Christlicher warheyt, dise Kirchen vnnd Land, darinne reyne lehr des Euangelij gepredigt wirdt, mit Krieg vberziehen, vnnd zerstören wolten. Mit einer Vorrede Philippi Melanthon.

Gedruckt zu Nuornberg durch Christoff Heussler. M.D.LVII.

[80] p. ; 20 cm. (4to) Signatures: A-K^4, L^3; [A] unsigned, A1b blank.

This volume was formerly in the Beck Lutherana collection, #209.

VD 16, L 7356;   OCLC: 21709595.

This is the twelfth printing after Luther's death of his *Caution to his beloved Germans*. There is some confusion as to the date of issue. While the title page gives 1557, the colophon reads 1556. The later date appears to be correct.

1557
Luth A

Melanchthon, Philipp, 1497-1560.

ENARRATIO BREVIS CONCIONVM LIBRI SALOMONIS, CVIVS TITVLVS EST ECCLESIASTES.

VVitebergae. (Excudebant Haeredes Petri Seitzij), 1557.

[127] p. ; 17 cm. (8vo) Signatures: A-H^8; [A], A4 unsigned, A1b, H8b blank.

This is the second item bound with P. Melanchthon's *IN DANIELEM PROPHETAM Commentarius*, [Vitebergae (Per Iohannem Lufft), Anno 1543.

Hartfelder, Cf. 457; OCLC: 28905608.

Melanchthon wrote the first version of this Ecclesiastes Commentary in 1550. This "SECVNDA EDITIO" from 1557 is not in VD 16, so it is not possible to judge how much, if any, revision has taken place.

1543
Mela B: 2

Melanchthon, Philipp, 1497-1560.

EPISTOLAE PAVLI SCRIPTAE AD ROMANOS.

VVITEBERGAE. EX OFFICINA TYPOgraphica Viti Creutzer, sumptibus Conradi Rhüel. Anno 1556.

[8], 247 [i.e. 248] leaves ; 17 cm. (8vo) Signatures: A-Z^8, a-i^8; [A] unsigned, i8 blank.

This volume is bound in blind-stamped calf, clasps intact.

Not cited in the bibliographies we consulted; OCLC: 12815338.

This is the second printing of Melanchthon's third commentary on St. Paul's Epistle to the Romans. The coat-of-arms on the title page is that chosen by Melanchthon.

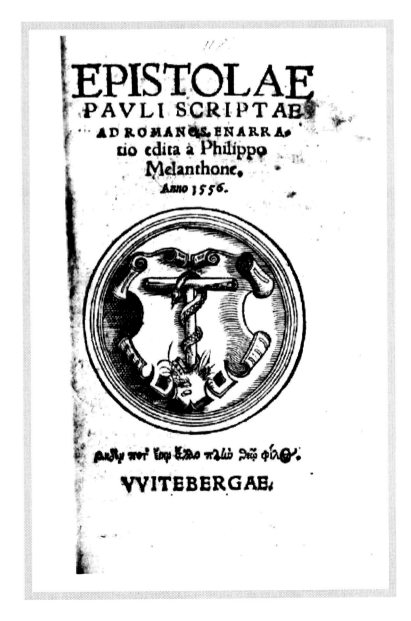

1557
Mela

Sleidanus, Johannes, 1506-1556.

Warhafftige Beschreibung Geystlicher vnd Weltlicher historien, vnder dem gross-
mechtigen Keyser Carolo dem fünfften verloffen.

Gedruckt zuo Basel [s.n.] im iar M.D.LVII.

[16], DCCCCXCVI, [12] p. ; 23 cm. (4to) Signatures: a-b⁴, A-Z⁴, ²a-²b⁴, Aa-Zz⁴, 2A-2Z⁴, 2a-2z⁴, Aaa-Lll⁴; [a],
l2 unsigned, A3 missigned "B3", 2F3 missigned "2E3", Bbb3 missigned "Aaa3", a1b blank.

This volume is bound in blind-stamped, bleached pigskin over wooden boards, clasps intact.

This volume was formerly in the Beck Lutherana collection, #1220. There is a manuscript note on the inside
upper flyleaf, as well as a doodle and a former ownership mark on the title page. On the inside lower pastedown
are contemporary manuscript notes referring to pages in the text.

VD 16, S 6693 (with printer: "[Nikolaus Brylinger]");   OCLC: 23438379.

This is a German translation of Sleidan's Reformation history, prepared in 1557 by Heinrich Pantaleon, a Basel theologian
and medical doctor.

1557
Slei

Soto, Pedro de, 1495/1500-1563.

ASSERTIO *Catholicae fidei cir*CA ARTICVLOS CONFESSIONIS NOMINE ILLVSTRISSIMI DVCIS VVIRtenbergensis oblatae per Legatos eius Concilio Tridentino, XXIIII. *Ianuarij Anni M.D.LII. Accessit his defensio aduersus Prolegomena Brentij.*

ANTVERPIAE. Apud Martinum Nutium sub Ciconijs. Anno Salutis. M.D.LVII.

2 v. bound as 1 ; 21 cm. (8vo) Signatures: Part I: A^4, B-T^8; Q5 missigned "P5". Part II: A- 2K^8, 2L^6; G missigned "H", G3-5 missigned "H3-5" respectively, H2 missigned "I2", I4 missigned "K4".

At the head of the title page is an almost illegible manuscript motto, under which is an former ownership mark, written in a different hand, reading, "Sum Guil. Charci(?)."

Adams, S-1506; Klaiber, 2924; OCLC: 12226805.

This is a later printing of Soto's response to Brenz's Württenberg confession.

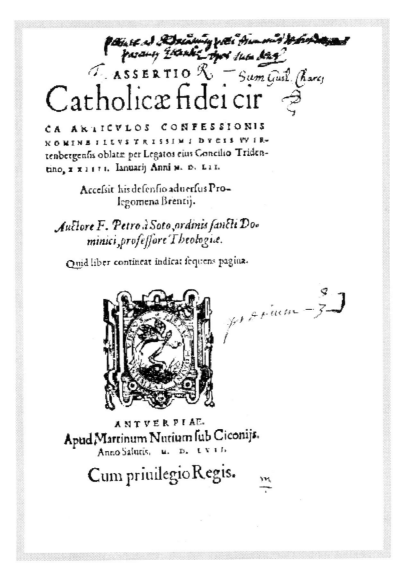

1557
Soto

Tauler, Johannes, 1300?-1361.

HOMILIAE SEV SERMONES IN EVANGELIA, TAM de Tempore quam de Sanctis, cumque pluribus aliis in calce additis.

LVGDVNI. Apud Sebastianum de Honoratis. 1557.

[4], 81, [3], 777, [12] p. ; 18 cm. (8vo) Signatures: a^8, e^8, i^8, o^8, u^8, $\&^4$, a-z^8, A-Z^8, Aa-Cc^8, Dd^4; G4 missigned C4; Dd4 blank; p. 80 misnumbered 773.

On the title page is an old library stamp reading, "Cartusia Repausatorii."

Adams, T-277; OCLC: 08923410.

The sermons of J. Tauler are apparently the only authentic works of his that we now possess. This Latin translation was prepared by Surius in 1548. J. Eck had a low opinion of Tauler's sermons, an opinion that the Abbot of Liesse, L. Blasius, attempted to refute in the introduction he wrote for this collection. The "Life" of Tauler included in this volume is a sixteenth century forgery.

1557
Taul

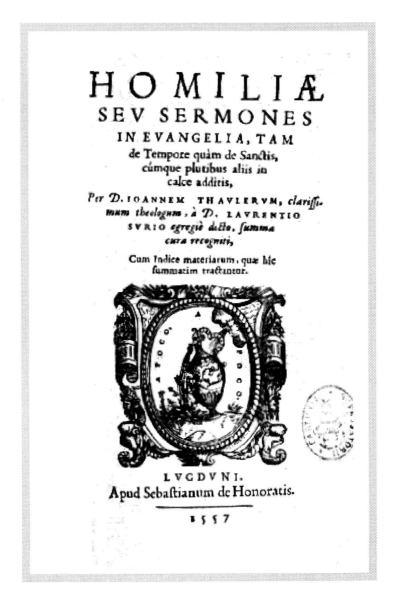

1558

AD TOTIES CVM FASTIDIO ET NAVSEA REPETITAS VIRVLENTISSIMAS ET FALSISSIMAS CRIMINATIOnes Flacij uera responsio, decerpta summatim ex tota rerum gestarum Historia.

VVITEBERGAE [s.n.] ANNO M.D.LVIII.

[71] p. ; 20 cm. (4to) Signatures: A-I^4; [A], E3 unsigned, I4b blank.

Preger, I, 425-426; VD 16, M 2421; OCLC: 17738292.

Flacius was a staunch defender of Luther despite his constant disagreements with the University of Wittenberg on questions of doctrine. This is a reply by members of the theological faculty at Wittenberg to Flacius' views on original sin.

1558
Schol

Camerarius, Joachim, 1500-1574.

CAPITA PIETATIS ET RELIGIONIS CHRISTIANAE, VERSIBVS GRAECIS COMPREHENSA AD INSTITVTIONEM PVERILEM, CVM INTERPRETATIONE LATINA.

LIPSIAE IN OFFICINA HAEREDVM VALENTINI PAPAE. ANNO M.D.LVIII.

[79] p. ; 16 cm. (8vo) Signatures: A-E^8; [A] unsigned, A1b, E8b blank.

There is a bookseller's label on the inside upper cover of "Gustav E. Stechert."

VD 16, C 359; OCLC: 23712436.

At the time of the publication of this work, J. Camerarius was Classics Professor at the University of Leipzig, where he had gone in 1541 on Melanchthon's recommendation. This book was designed for students studying fairly advanced Latin and Greek. It includes poetic translations and excerpts in those languages from the Bible and from approved classical authors.

1558
Came

CLARORVM VIRORVM EPISTOLAE LATINAE, GRAECAE, & *Hebraicae, uarijs temporibus missae ad Ioannem Reuchlin Phorcensem, LL. Doctorem.*

TIGVRI APVD CHRISTOPHOrum Froschouerum. M.D.LVIII.

78 leaves ; 15 cm. (8vo) Signatures: A-I^8, K^6; [A] unsigned, A1b, K6b blank.

This copy was formerly in the "Bibl. ad. aed. Mar. Magdeb.," or the City Library of Magdeburg and "Stadt- und Bezirksbibliothek 'Wilhelm Weiting.'"

Adams, E-276; BM STC German, p. 733; VD 16, R 1243; OCLC: 23437903.

In the battle with Johann Pfefferkorn over Jewish books, Reuchlin received testimonial letters from humanist supporters and well-wishers. These "Letters of famous men addressed to Johann Reuchlin" were repeatedly reprinted after his death.

1558
Clar

Cogelerus, Johannes, fl. 1558-1588.

IMAGINES ELEGANTISSIMAE QVAE MVLTVM LVCIS AD intelligendos doctrinae Christianae locos adferre possunt, Collectae, partim ex praelectionibus Domini Philippi Melanthonis, partim ex scriptis Patrum.

VITEBERGAE. EXCVDEBAT IOHANNES CRATO. ANNO M.D.LVIII.

[109] p. : ill. ; 16 cm. (8vo) Signatures: A-F^8, G^7; [A] unsigned, G7b blank.

There is a former ownership bookplate on the inside upper cover reading, "Pro Viribus Summus Contendo; Ex Libris," and a former ownership mark on the upper flyleaf.

Some of the woodcuts in this volume are by Hans Brosamer.

BM STC German, p. 215;   VD 16, K 1693 or K 1694;   OCLC: 23261007.

J. Cogelerus was a student of Melanchthon in Wittenberg. He mentions Melanchthon on the title page of this work as inspiring some of this volume's contents. This volume includes twenty-four mostly quarter-page woodcuts of biblical and theological subjects. Some of the woodcuts are by Hans Brosamer. The work is a precursor to the "emblem books" that united theology and pictures and were quite popular later in the sixteenth century. The preface is by G. Major, and the dedication is to King Christian of Denmark. The copy is from the Broxbourn Library and is bound in a leaf of fifteenth century manuscript.

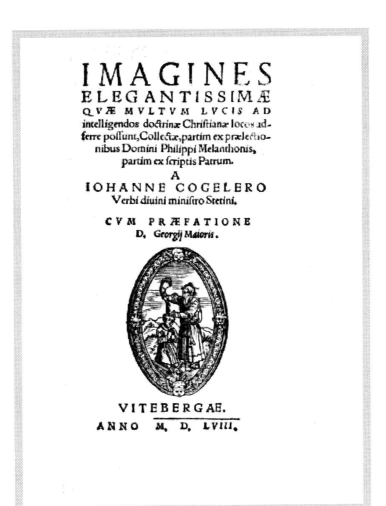

1558
Coge

DE ECCLESIASTICA HISTORIA: QVAE MAGDEBVRGI CONTEXITVR, NAR-RATIO, CONTRA MENIVM, ET SCHOLASTICORVM VVITTEBERGENSIVM EPISTOLAS.

EDITA VVITEBERGAE [s.n.] Anno M.D.LVIII.

[52] p. ; 21 cm. (4to) Signatures: A-F⁴ G²; [A] unsigned.

VD 16, E 242; OCLC: 12443076.

M. Flacius Illyricus formed the committee that wrote the "Magdeburg Centuries," the first large-scale Protestant church history. This pamphlet includes both an attack on that history and a defense of it by students from the University of Wittenberg.

1558
De

Erasmus, Desiderius, 1466?-1536.

ADAGIORVM CHIliades quatuor cum sesquicenturia.

[Geneva] Oliua Roberti Stephani. M.D.LVIII.

[64] p., 1126 columns; 35 cm. (fol. in 8s.) Signatures: ^{3}8, ^{8}8, 8, 38, a-z^8, A-L^8, M^{10}; [3] unsigned.

Haeghen, I, p. 5; OCLC: 08094099.

This is a later printing of Erasmus' proverb collection. Erasmus frequently appended the work in an effort to provide students with a clearer understanding of the significance of the proverbs.

1558
Eras A

Erasmus, Desiderius, 1466?-1536.

DE RECTA LATINI GRAECIQVE SERmonis pronunciatione.

BASILEAE, Froben, MDLVIII.

287, [1] p. ; 18 cm. (8vo) Signatures: a-s[8]; [a] unsigned, a1b blank.

This is the first item in a bound collection, and the only Kessler item. The volume is bound in vellum.

There is a table of contents for this volume on the verso of the upper flyleaf.

BM STC German, p. 281;   VD 16, E 3612;   OCLC: 28005519.

This is Erasmus' guide to the pronunciation of Greek and Latin.

1558
Eras: 1

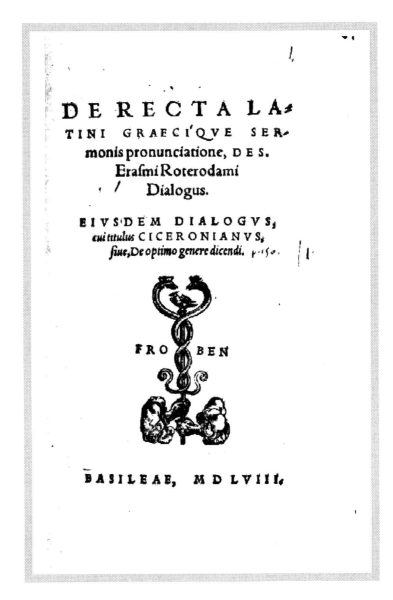

DE RECTA LA-
TINI GRAECI'QVE SER-
monis pronunciatione, D E S.
Erasmi Roterodami
Dialogus.

EIVSDEM DIALOGVS,
cui titulus CICERONIANVS,
siue, De optimo genere dicendi.

FRO BEN

BASILEAE, MDLVIII.

Fröschel, Sebastian.

CONCIONES EXPLICANTES INTEGRVM EVANGELIVM S. MATTHÆI.
[Wittenberg] EXCVSÆ AB HÆREDIBVS GEORGII RHAVV. M.D.LVIII.

[888] p. : ill. ; 17 cm. (8vo) Signatures: [flower]⁸,)(⁸, A-3G⁸, 3H⁴; [flower] unsigned, 213, 204 unsigned, 3H4b blank.

This volume is bound in blind-stamped pigskin over wooden boards, clasps intact.

There is a sixteenth century Latin inscription referring to Melanchthon's postil on the inside upper pastedown.

Hartfelder, 636;   VD 16, M 2811 (under P. Melanchthon);   OCLC: 12682338.

Sebastian Fröschel was a student at Leipzig at the time of the famous disputation. He followed Luther back to Wittenberg and continued his studies there. Fröschel was ordained in Magdeburg, but was arrested and exiled on account of his Protestant preaching. He returned to Wittenberg and became Bugenhagen's assistant in the *Stadtkirche*. This explication of the Gospel according to Matthew is the first in a series of sermons, presented with additional commentary.

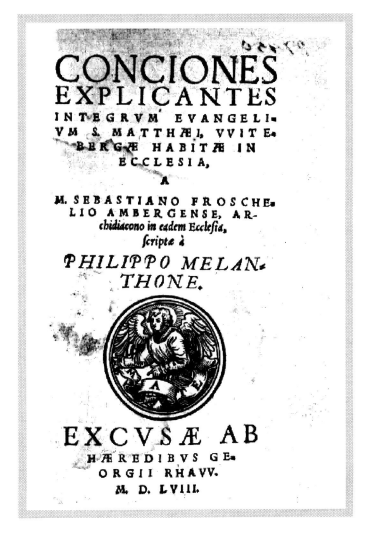

1558
Fros

Hus, Jan, 1369?-1415.

IOANNIS Hus, et HieRONYMI PRAGENSIS CONFESSORVM CHRISTI HISTORIA ET MONVMENTA.

Impressa Noribergae, in Officina Ioannis Montani, & Vlrici Neuberi. Anno Domini M.D.LVIII.

2 pts. bd. as 1 v. : ill. ; 33 cm. (fol. in 6s) Signatures: (Pt. 1): a^8, A-Z^6, a-z^6, 2A-3O^6, 3P^4; H4 unsigned, G4, N4, V4, 2R, 2Y missigned "H4," "O4," "T4," "rr," "yy" respectively. (Pt. 2): A^8, B-2N^6, 2O-2P^8, 2Q-3)6, 3P^8; 2H4 unsigned, Z3, 2G4, 2Y2 missigned "X3," "G4," Yz2" respectively.

This volume is bound in blind-stamped, bleached pigskin over wooden boards, clasps missing. The binding dated, "1591," and lettered on front, "Iohannis Hus Opera."

This volume was presented to the Library of the Theological Institute of Connecticut by Dea[con] Samuel Stone.

Adams, H-1207 and H-1208 (for both parts);   BM STC German, p. 438;   VD 16, H 6154;   OCLC: 16159824.

J. Hus and Jerome of Prague were the chief leaders of the Bohemian theological school in the late fourteenth and early fifteenth centuries. The prefaces in this volume are by Luther, taken from an earlier edition of Hus' letters.

1558
Hus

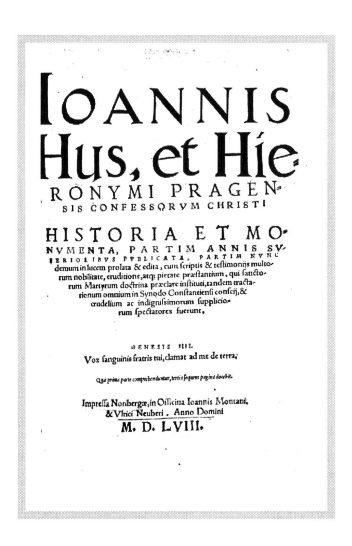

Ignatius Loyola, Saint, 1491/1495-1556.

CONSTITVTIONES SOCIETATIS Iesv. Anno 1558.

Romae, in aedibus Societatis IESV. 1558.

159, [8] p. ; 18 cm. (8vo) Signatures: A-K^8, ^{2}A^4; [A], 2A2-3 unsigned, K8b, 2A4b blank.

This is the fourth item bound with Ignatius Loyola's *CONSTITVTIONES SOCIETATIS IESV*, Romae in aedibus Societatis IESV, Anno 1559.

Page 159 of this title has been cut away after the text.

Backer-Sommervogel VI, col. 75, no. 2, item 3 (p. 159 of this copy is not like either of the two transcribed, though shares features of each);   OCLC: 23826422.

This is a 1558 extended edition of the constitution of the Society of Jesus.

1559
Cons: 4

Luther, Martin, 1483-1546.

*PROPOSITIONES THEOLOGICAE REVERENDORVM VIrorum D. Mart. Luth.
Et D. Philippi Melanth. Continentes summam doctrinae Christianae, scriptae &
disputatae VVitebergae, inde usq[ue] ab anno 1516. De quo tempore uaticinatus est
Iohannes Hilten, initium fore reformationis Ecclesiae anno 1516. Cum praefatione D.
PHILIP. MELANTH.*

VVITEBERGAE. [s.n.] 1558.

[670] p.; 16 cm. (8vo) Signatures: A-Z^8, a-s^8, t^7; [A], E4, X5, a4, d4 unsigned, Z5 missigned "Z3", K3 missigned "K2".

This volume is bound in vellum.

This volume was formerly in the Stewart collection, #3481. Below the medallions on the title page is the former ownership mark of "Johannes Henric[us] Schmidi[us] a[nn]o 1666."

VD 16, L 5748; OCLC: 12648000.

This is a collection of academic dissertations from 1516 onward. Of note are the title page portraits of Melanchthon and Luther. Joannes Hilten was an Augustinian monk (d. 1502) incarcerated for predicting a general reformation of the church.

1558
Luth

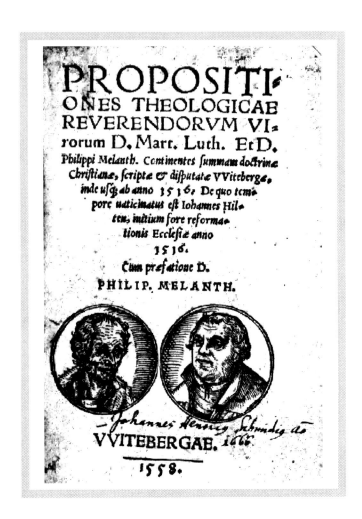

Melanchthon, Philipp, 1497-1560.

CHRONICON CARIONIS LATINE EXPOSITVM ET AVCTVM MVLTIS ET VETERIBVS ET RECENTIBVS Historijs, in narrationibus rerum Graecarum, Germanicarum & Ecclesiasticarum.

VVITEBERGAE EXCVSVM IN OFFICINA HAEREDVM GEORGII RHAVV. ANNO M.D.LVIII.

[416] p. ; 16 cm. (8vo) Signatures: [Double dagger]⁸, A-Z, Aa-Bb⁸; [double dagger]1 unsigned, M3 unsigned.

This copy bound in blind-stamped, bleached pigskin over paper boards. The binding was done in "1558" for "I.D.D."

This copy includes a three page Latin manuscript commentary on the inside upper cover and flyleaf on Daniel 2:31-44, entitled "De Monarchijs" by P. Melanchthon--in his own handwriting--and signed at end, "Scriptu[m] manu Philippi."

Hartfelder, 628; VD 16, M 2698; OCLC: 30340026.

Johannes Carion was a slightly younger contemporary of Melanchthon. His *Chronica* was "adopted" by Melanchthon, who produced his own augmented edition of the work. This is the first printing of the second, revised edition.

1558
Mela A

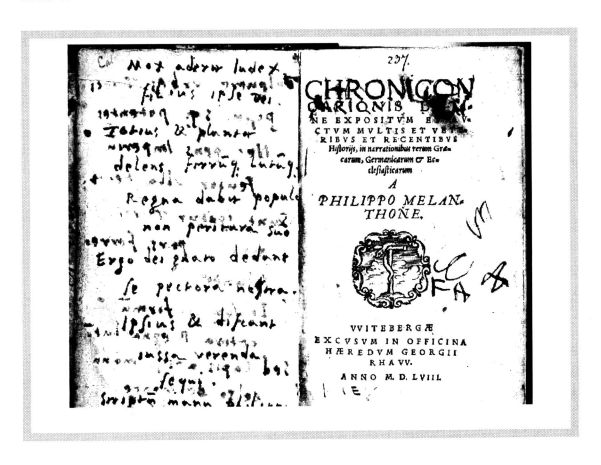

Melanchthon, Philipp, 1497-1560.

RESPONSIO AD CRIMINATIONES STAPHYLI ET AVII.

VVITEBERGAE. [Peter Seitz' Erben] 1558.

[32] p. ; 21 cm. (4to) Signatures: A-C^4, D^3; [A], C3 unsigned.

Not in the Corpus Reformatorum ed. of Melanchthon's works; BM STC German, p. 614; VD 16, M 4126-27, that lists printer as: "[Veit Kreutzer]"; OCLC: 12796319.

Johannes a Via (ca. 1520-1582) and Friedrich Staphylus (1512 or 1513-1564) were two Catholic opponents of Melanchthon in his last years. Staphylus had studied with Melanchthon at Wittenberg but had returned to Catholicism by 1552. Via was a Catholic priest who became cathedral preacher in Worms in 1556. This work, a reply to libels made against Melanchthon by these two men, is so rare that it was missed by both Hartfelder and the Corpus Reformatorum edition of Melanchthon's works. The coat-of-arms on the title page is that of Melanchthon.

1558
Mela

Pfeffinger, Johann, 1493-1573.

In hoc Libello CONTINENTVR VTILES DISPVtationes de praecipuis capitibus doctrinae Christianae, quae propositae fuerunt in academia Lipsica.
(FRANCOFORTI EX OFFIcina Petri Brubachij. Anno 1558. Mense Iunio.)

103 leaves ; 17 cm. (8vo) Signatures: A-M^8, N^7.

This is the fourth item bound with Martin Luther's PROPOSITIONES, (EXCVSVM VVITENBERgae, typis Ioannis Lufft. Anno M.D.XXXVIII. V. idus Septembris.)

VD 16, P 2356; OCLC: 11932706.

J. Pfeffinger began his public career as Foundation-Preacher in Passau in 1521 but then fled to Wittenberg, and later moved to Sonnenwalde to became a preacher in 1527. Pfeffinger married in Sonnenwalde, and the Bishop of Meissen drove him out of office. Later he obtained a position as preacher in Electoral Saxony and became Superintendent of Leipzig. He became the first Protestant Doctor of Theology after the reformation of the University at Leipzig. In 1550, his dissertation on the cooperation of man in his salvation occasioned the Synergistic Controversy, over whether man can do anything in his own salvation. This volume includes a series of theses, or disputations, presented in the University of Leipzig.

1538
Luth A: 4

Pighius, Albertus, 1490-1542.

HIERARCHIAE ECCLESIASTICEA ASSERTIO PER ALBERTVM PIGHIVM CAMPENSEM.

COLONIAE AGRIPPINAE Apud Iohannem Birckmannum, Anno 1558.

[8], 344 leaves ; 30 cm. (fol. in 4s) Signatures: *·2*⁴, A⁴, B-3K⁶, 3L⁸; [*] unsigned, 3L8b blank.

This volume was formerly in the Stewart collection, #5098. At the head of the title page is a former ownership mark in ink of "Monasterij S[anc]ti Clementis MerT (?) O.S.B. 1764," and at the foot a mark reading, "Ludolphus Omesius (?) possedeio Anno 62."

Adams, P-1194; Klaiber, 2515; VD 16, P 2756 (under Pigghe, Albert); OCLC: 20023491.

This assertion of the ecclesiastical hierarchy by A. Pighius is probably his most important work. It was first published in 1538.

1558
Pigh

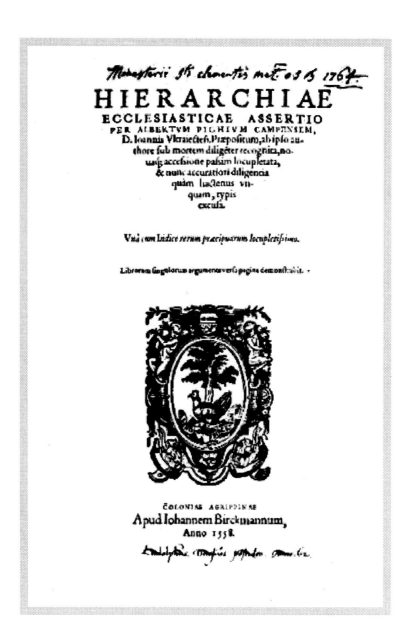

PRIMVM AC GENERALE EXAMEN IIS OMNIBVS, QVI IN Societatem IESV admitti petent, proponendum.

Romae in aedibus Societatis IESV, 1558.

51, [1] p. ; 18 cm. (8vo) Signatures: A-C^8, ^{2}A^4; [A] unsigned, C7-8 blank, 2A2 unsigned.

This is the third item bound with Ignatius Loyola's *CONSTITVTIONES SOCIETATIS IESV*, Romae in aedibus Societatis IESV, Anno 1559.

Backer-Sommervogel VI, Col. 75, no. 2, item 2; BM, v. 116, col. 142; OCLC: 23826360.

The Jesuits have always paid careful attention to candidates' qualifications and vocation. This, in part, underlay Jesuit reforms in education and pedagogy.

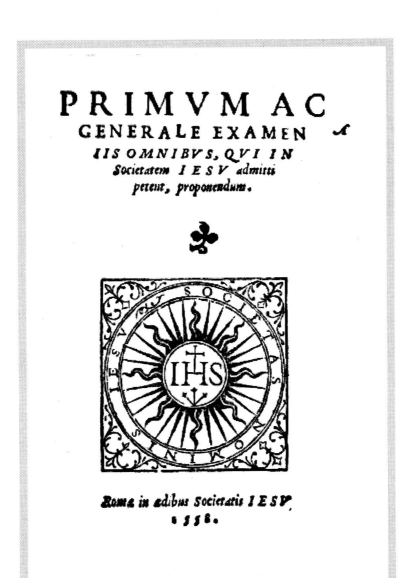

1559
Cons: 3

SCHOLASTICORVM ACADEMIAE VVITEBERGENSIS AD OMNES PIOS CIVES ECCLESIARVM. *quae unam & eandem communi consensu cum ipsis amplectuntur ac profitentur doctrinam, ex scriptis Propheticis & Apostolicis repetitam in libro Confessionis Augustanae & reliquis publice approbatis, EPISTOLAE DVAE, TERTIA ET QVARTA.*

VVITEBERGAE [s.n.] M.D.LVIII.

[117] p. ; 21 cm. (4to) Signatures: A-P^4; [A] unsigned, P3b, 4 blank.

BM STC German, p. 921; VD 16, S 3805-1806; OCLC: 17975938.

The quarrel between Flacius and Melanchthon regarding the Interim of Augsburg in 1548 here branches out into other areas of theology. The students who supported Melanchthon take Flacius to task for his failure to properly understand the theology of the Augsburg Confession. Also included is Melanchthon's reply to a delegation of Catholic theologians from Saxony.

1558
Schol A

Schwenckfeld, Caspar, 1489-1561.

Avff das Wirtte[m]bergische, jüngst im[m] 1558. Jare durch den Truck aussgangne Mandat, in der Religion, Caspar Schwenckfeldts entschuldigung, so vil jhne darinnen belanget. Mit bekan[n]tnus seiner Lehre vnnd glaubens, das jn auch die jrrigen verdampten Puncten, oder Item, im[m] Mandat begriffen, gar nichts angehn, vnnd sein Nam[m]en derhalb vnbillich mit eingemengt, diffamiert vnd beschwärdt werde.

[Augsburg : Hans Gegler] M.D.LVIII.

[58] p. ; 21 cm. (4to) Signatures: A-F⁴, G⁵; [A] unsigned, A1b blank.

BM STC German, p. 800; Corpus Schwenckfeldianorum, 16, Doc. 1053; Kuczynski, 2455; VD 16, S 4844; OCLC: 22608722.

When Duke Christoph of Württemberg renewed his edict of June 14, 1554, against Schwenckfeld on June 25, 1558, Schwenckfeld felt compelled to issue a reply. The mandate against Schwenckfeld was renewed again in 1564, three years after his death.

1558
Schwe

Schwenckfeld, Caspar, 1489-1561.

Bericht, Warinn der yetzigen Theologen vnd Predicanten spahn mit C. Schwenckfelden stande, im[m] Artickel von der Glorien vnd Herrligkeit Christi.

[Augsburg : Hans Gegler] 1558.

[26] p. ; 20 cm. (4to) Signatures: A-B⁴, C⁵; [A] unsigned, A1b blank.

Corpus Schwenckfeldianorum, 16, Doc. 1034;   VD 16, S 4887;   OCLC: 22669642.

The Württemberg theologian Jakob Andreae claimed to have found two hundred errors in Schwenckfeld's books. Yet he also pretended not to know or understand Schwenckfeld's theology of the Lord's Supper and of the two natures of Christ. To explain his position more fully Schwenckfeld re-edited a letter written in 1542 to Wolfgang Neidthardt, bailiff of Erbach and a Catholic sympathetic to Schwenckfeld's position.

1558
Schwe A

Sleidanus, Johannes, 1506-1556.

IOAN. SLEIDANI, DE statu Religionis & Reipublicae, Carolo Quinto, Caesare, Commentariorum libri xxvj.

ARGENTORATI (per Haeredes Vuendelini Rihelij), Anno M.D.LVIII.

[38], 469 leaves; 33 cm. (fol. in 4s) Signatures: a^6, A-H^4, ^{2}A-^{2}H^4, I-2Z^4, 2a-2z^4, ^{2}2A-^{2}2Z^4, 3A-3Z^4, 3a^4, ^{2}3a, ^{2}3a^2, 3b^3, 3b^4, 3b^5, 3b^6; [a], 3a3 unsigned.

This copy is bound in blind-stamped pigskin over wooden boards, clasps intact.

This volume was formerly in the Stewart collection, #5922. There is a fore-edge shelf mark and manuscript marginalia throughout the text.

OCLC: 19882908.

This is a later edition of Sleidan's history of the Reformation, based on archival sources. As is often the case, the colophon date for this edition (1555) is incorrect.

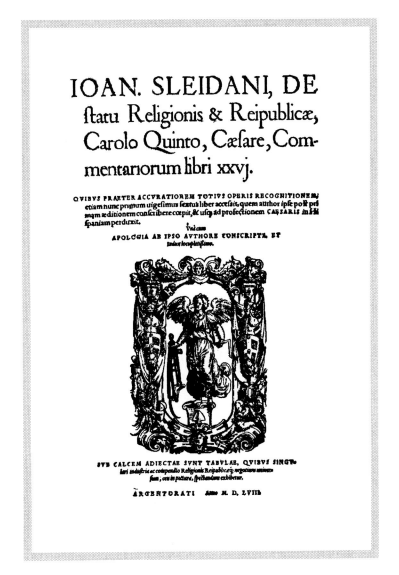

1558
Slei

Soto, Pedro de, 1495/1500-1563.

TRACTATUS DE INSTITUTIONE SACERDOTUM, QUI SUB EPISCOPIS ANI-MARUM CURAM GERUNT.

DILINGAE PER SEBALDUM MAYER. Anno D[omi]ni M.D.LVIII.

[36], 524, [8] p. ; 22 cm. (4to) Signatures: a-d^4, e^2, A-3T^4, 3V^2, 3X^4; [a], 2E3, 2S2, 2X2 unsigned, 2M3 missigned "2M4", 3T2 missigned "3T3".

This volume was formerly in the Stewart collection, #6171. There is an armorial bookplate pasted to inside upper cover, of William Dansey, and a former ownership mark on the verso of the upper flyleaf.

Adams, S-1513; VD 16, S 7091; OCLC: 05157410.

This is a study on the administration of the sacraments, written by de Soto and dedicated to the Bishop of Augsburg.

1558
Soto

TRACTATUS

D E

INSTITUTIONE

SACERDOTUM,

QUI SUB EPISCOPIS

ANIMARUM CURAM GERUNT.

AVTHORE

R·P·F· PETRO DE SOTO

ORDINIS SANCTI DOMINICI

PROFESSORE THEOLOGIÆ.

JUSSU ET AUTHORITATE REVEREND.

AC ILLUST·D·OTHONIS

Cardinalis & Episcopi Augustani editus.

Salvo in his omnibus judicio & Censura S. R. Ecclesiæ.

Attendite vobis & universo gregi, in quo vos Spiritus Sanctus posuit
Episcopos regere Ecclesiam Dei, quam acquisivit sanguine suo. Ad. 10.

Cum Gratia & Privilegio Cæf. atque Catholicæ Majeß.

DILINGÆ PER SEBALDUM MAYER,

Anno Dñi M. D. LVIII.

Werner, Johann Sigismund, 1491-1554.

Postill. Kurtze Ausslegung vber die Euangelienn so man pflegt zuoläsen an den fürnemsten Festen durchs gantze Jar, sampt den Sum[m]arien darüber: Christlich vnd einfaltig gepredigt vnd beschriben.

[Pfortzheim : Georg Rab] M.D.LVIII.

3 pts bd. as 1 v. (lxxxv, cxiii, lxxviii leaves) ; 30 cm. (fol. in 6s).

This is the first item in a bound collection, bound in blind-stamped calf over wooden boards, clasps missing.

This copy is incomplete. The missing pages, except for the "Vorwort" that is bound after the title page, are bound in at the end as 42 leaves in seventeenth-eighteenth century manuscript.

Corpus Schwenckfeldianorum 15, Doc. 1026A;   OCLC: 30338599.

Johann Sigismund Werner was a Protestant preacher in Silesia. He preached in Liignitz from 1523 to 1539, and in Regensdorf (Glatz) from 1540 until his death in 1554. He wrote down all his sermons in the form of a Postil, that was sent to Schwenckfeld by several Silesian noblemen after Werner's death. Schwenckfeld arranged for their publication after satisfying himself that the sermons were doctrinally sound and free from scurrilous language. This particular copy was badly damaged and incomplete. Missing portions of the printed text appear in manuscript form, written in a seventeenth or perhaps an eighteenth century hand. Many works in the Schwenckfeldian tradition only survived in manuscript form, even if printed editions had once appeared.

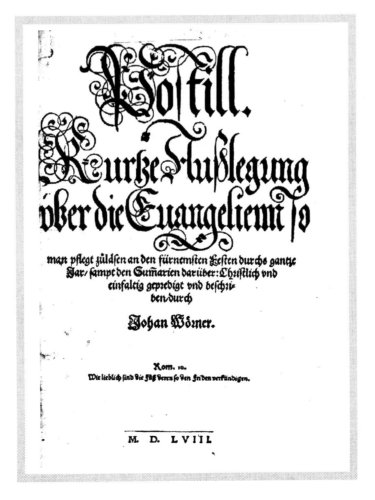

1558
Wern: 1

1559

DEPVLSIO CALVMNIARVM, QVIBVS ATHANASIVS QVIDAM in Epistola, &
alij nonnulli, CARDINALEM insectantur: cum explicatione duarum sententiarum de
Eucharistia.

[Dillingen : S. Mayer] Anno d[omi]ni M.D.LIX.

[51] p. ; 16 cm. (8vo) Signatures: A-C^8, D^2; [A] unsigned, A1b, D2b blank.

This is the second item bound with Conradus Brunus' *ADVERSVS NOVAM HISTORIAM ECCLESIAS-*
TICAM..., DILINGAE APVD SEBALDVM MAYER. M.D.LXV.

VD 16, D 585;   OCLC: 21794342.

This is an anonymous tract attacking Pietro Paolo Vergerio and defending an unnamed cardinal. Vergerio had discussed
religious issues with Luther in 1535, and attempted to institute extensive reforms after becoming Bishop of Capodistria
in 1536. Vergerio was accused of heresy and fled to Switzerland and ultimately Poland after being summoned to Rome
to face charges.

1565
Brun: 2

DEPVLSIO
CALVMNIARVM,
QVIBVS ATHANASIVS QVIDAM
in Epiſtola, & alij nonnulli,
CARDINALEM inſectantur:
cum explicatione dua-
rum ſententiarum de
Euchariſtia.

PSALM. 118.
Feci iudicium & inſtitiam, non tradas me calum-
niantibus me.

IVDAS APOSTOLVS.
In nouiſsimis temporibus venient illuſores, ſe-
cundum deſideria ſua ambulantes in impietati-
bus : hi ſunt qui ſegregant ſemetipſos.

Anno dñi M. D.LIX.

Erasmus, Desiderius, 1466?-1536.

DES. ERASMI ROT. ADAGIORVM CHILIADES QVATVOR, ET SESQVICEN-TVRIA.

LVGDVNI APVD HAERED. SEBAST. GRYPHII. M.D.LIX.

[80] p., 1316 columns, [1] p. ; 34 cm. (fol. in 8s) Signatures: 2a-2e^8, a-z^8, A-O^8, P-T^6, V^4; [2a] unsigned; V4b blank, I2 missigned "2."

Haeghen, I, p. 5; OCLC: *04571696.*

This is another printing of Erasmus' proverb collection. The number of editions of the *Adagia* suggest the extent of its popularity.

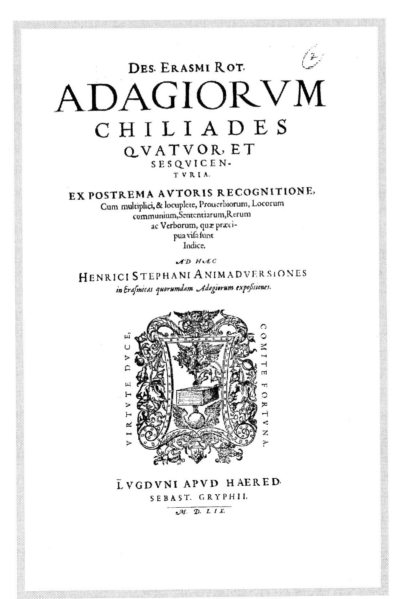

1559
Eras

Flacius Illyricus, Matthias, 1520-1575.

ECCLESIASTICA HISTORIA.

BASILEAE, PER IOANnem Oporinum, [1559-1574; see below for details.]

13 v. bd. as 8 ; 34 cm.

Each century after the third has a special title page. This history was written by Matthias Flacius Illyricus, Johann Wigand, Matthaus Judex, Basilius Faber, Andreas Corvinus, and Thomas Holzhuter.

All the volumes are bound in blind-stamped pigskin over wooden boards. All the clasps are intact, except for volume two, that has only one.

These volumes were donated to the Theological Institute of Connecticut in 1831 by "Dea[con]. Sam[ue]l Stone." On the inside upper cover of each volume is a large armorial bookplate in red, green, and white.

Jackson, 1786; Preger, II, p. 559, says v. 1 appeared in 1559; OCLC: 01905013.

In about 1553, Flacius conceived the plan of writing a Protestant church history. Over the next several years he gathered a committee of scholars and church historians at Magdeburg. These were charged with collecting the material for this monumental undertaking. The work is divided into "centuries" whence the popular name of the work, "Magdeburg Centuries." The first volume was undated (a second edition appeared in 1562). Later volumes appeared between 1559-1574. Flacius himself was dropped from the committee as a result of his stand on original sin. The printing information for the volumes is as follows: Vol. I: BASILEAE, PER IOANnem Oporinum. [1559] Vol. II: BASILEAE, PER IOANNEM OPORINVM, ANNO SALVTIS HVmanae M.D.LX.Vol. III: BASILEAE, EX OFFICINA IOANNIS OPORINI, ANNO SALVTIS HVMAnae M.D.LXII. Mense Martio.Vol. IV: BASILEAE, EX OFFICINA IOANNIS OPORINI, ANNO M.D.LXVII. mense Martio.Vol. V: BASILEAE, EX OFFICINA IOANNIS OPORINI, ANNO SALVTIS humanae M.D.LXV. Mense Septembri.Vol. VI: BASILEAE, EX OFFICINA PAVLI QVECI, SVMTIBVS IOANNIS OPORINI, ANno Salutis humanae per CHRISTVM partae, M.D.LXVII. Mense Septembri.Vol. VII: BASILEAE, EX OFFICINA OPORINIANA. 1569. Vol. VIII: BASILEAE, EX OFFICINA OPORINIANA, Anno Salutis humanae M.D.LXXIIII. Mense Ianvario.

1559
Flac

ECCLESIASTICA

HISTORIA, INTEGRAM ECCLESIAE

CHRISTI IDEAM, QVANTVM AD LOCVM,
Propagationem, Perfecutionem, Tranquillitatem, Doctrinam, Hærefes, Ceremonias, Gubernationem, Schifmata,
Synodos, Perfonas, Miracula, Martyria, Religiones extra
Ecclefiam, & ftatum Imperij politicum attinet, fecundum
fingulas Centurias, perfpicuo ordine complectens: fingu-
lari diligentia & fide ex uetuftifsimis & optimis
hiftoricis, patribus, & alijs fcripto-
ribus congefta:

Per aliquot ftudiofos & pios uiros in urbe
Magdeburgica.

TYPOGRAPHVS LECTORI.

Hoc opere nullum aliud ab Orbe condito, eiufdem quidem argumēti, Rei-
pub. Chriftianæ & utilius & magis neceffariū, in lucem effe editum, æquus
atq̃ finceri iudicij Lector, uel ex Præfatione, qua etiam contexendi huius
caufa exponuntur, adiectaq̃ in primis hiftorici operis Metho-
do ac fingulorum capitum metis generalibus,
facile deprehendet.

Accefsit etiam cùm Rerum uerborumq̃; in fingulis Centurijs præcipuè
memorabilium, tum Locorum Scripturæ explicato-
rum copiofus ac geminus INDEX.

BASILEAE, PER IOAN-
nem Oporinum.

Fröschel, Sebastian.

Kurtze Auslegung etlicher Capitel des Euangelisten Matthei, als des V. VI. VII. und VIII.

Witteberg. [Lorentz Schwenk] M.D.LIX.

[14], [652], [4] p. ; 17 cm. (8vo) Signatures:)(^{8}, A-Z^8, a-s^8; [)(] unsigned, r4 missigned "4", s8b blank.

This copy was bound in blind-stamped, polished calf over wooden boards, clasps missing.

There is a former ownership mark on the inside, upper cover.

VD 16, F 3092; OCLC: 12231098.

This volume includes the original German version of part of S. Fröschel's "Sermon-Commentary on the Gospel of Matthew." Fröschel relied so heavily on Melanchthon that some authorities have attributed the Latin edition of these Sermons to Melanchthon himself.

1559
Fros

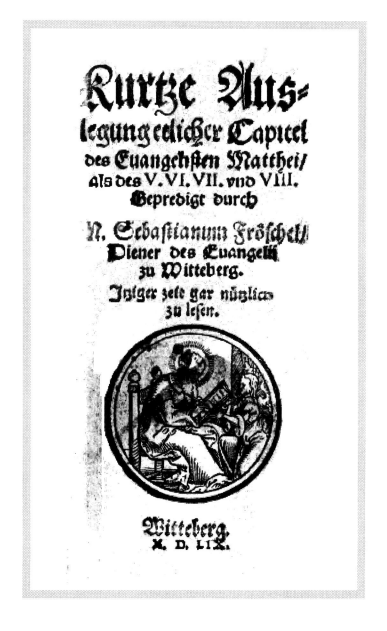

Ignatius Loyola, Saint, 1491/1495-1556.

CONSTITVTIONES SOCIETATIS IESV.

Romae in aedibus Societatis IESV, Anno 1559.

[10] p. ; 18 cm. (8vo) Signatures: Unsigned.

This is the first item in a bound collection, bound in vellum. The titles in this volume are bound out of sequence according to Backer-Sommervogel.

This volume was formerly in the Stewart collection, #3247. At the head of the title page is a former owner's signature.

Backer-Sommervogel VI, col. 75, no. 2, item 1; OCLC: 23854481.

The Society of Jesus established by St. Ignatius Loyola, was given papal approbation on September 27, 1540, in the bull *Regimini militantis Ecclesiae of Pope Paul III.* Initially the Society's membership was strictly limited, but this restriction was removed after a few years. The chief aim of the Society was the restoration of the Catholic Church through their unswerving obedience to the Pope. This volume gathers five items relating to the Society's organization and polity. These are all first printings of the respective works.

1559
Cons: 1

Johann Frederich II, Duke of Saxony, 1529-1595.

Des Durchleuchtigen hochgebornen Fürsten vnd Herren, Herrn Johans Friderichen des Mittlern, Hertzogen zu Sachssen, ... in Gottes wort Prophetischer vnd Apostolischer Schrifft gegründete Confutationes, Widerlegungen vnd verdammung etlicher ein zeit her zu wider demselben Gottes wort, vnd heiliger Schrifft, auch der Augspurgischen Confession Apologien, vnd den Schmalkaldischen Artickeln.

Gedruckt zu Jhena durch Christian Rödingers Erben. 1559.

[6], 84 leaves : coat-of-arms ; 19 cm. (4to) Signatures: ()^6, A-X^4; [()] unsigned, X4b blank, A, A3 missigned "B", "B3" respectively.

OCLC: 22832332.

This is a refutation of various heresies, issued in Ernestine Saxony. Among the "heresies" condemned are those of Servetus, Schwenckfeld, Zwingli, and the Anabaptists.

1559
Joha

Kurtzer bericht, was sich für ein kleglich Schawspiel, verflossens ein vnd zweintzigsten tags May, dieses Lix. Jarss, mit etlichen frommen Christen inn Hispanien zu Valladolid zugetragen.

[Nuremberg : Georg Kreidlein, 1559?]

[16] p. ; 20 cm. (4to) Signatures: [A]4, B^4; [A], A2 unsigned.

There is a collector's stamp on inside front pastedown.

VD 16, K 2746, *or* K 2748;   OCLC: 15600439.

In 1559, Charles V's Court Preacher, Augustin de Cazalla, was executed along with some other court officials for being Lutherans. This is one of three contemporary printings of the announcement of his death and is extremely rare.

1559
Kurt

LITTERAE APOSTOLICAE, QVIBVS INSTITVTIO, confirmatio, & varia priuilegia, & indulta Societati IESV a Sede Apostolica concessa continentur.

Romae, in aedibus Societatis IESV 1559.

[67] p. ; 18 cm. (8vo) Signatures: A-D^8, E^2; [A], E2 unsigned, A1b, E2b blank.

This is the second item bound with Ignatius Loyola's *CONSTITVTIONES SOCIETATIS IESV*, Romae in aedibus Societatis IESV, Anno 1559.

There is a signature at the end of this work of an Apostolic Notary. Unfortunately the signature is illegible.

Backer-Sommervogel VI, col. 75, no. 2, item 5;   BM, v. 116, col. 144;   OCLC: 23854361.

This volume includes all the Papal documents relating to the first 19 years of the Society of Jesus.

1559
Cons: 2

Melanchthon, Philipp, 1497-1560.

RESPONSIONES SCRIPTAE A PHILIPPO MELANTHONE AD IMPIOS ARTIculos Bauaricae Inquisitionis.

VVITEBERGAE EXCVDEBANT HAEREdes Georgij Rhaw. ANNO M.D.LIX.

[77] p. ; 16 cm. (8vo) Signatures: A-I^8, K^7; [A] unsigned, K7b blank.

This copy is bound in vellum.

Beuttenmüller, 2196; Hartfelder, 649; Jackson, 2127; VD 16, M 4169-71; OCLC: 12756864.

When the Jesuits set up the Holy Office in Bavaria, they issued a questionnaire of thirty-one items to persuade Protestants to forsake their errors. Melanchthon published this document, together with an introduction and his own comments. He also refutes other heresies of the day. This is the first printing of the work.

1559
Mela

Naogeorg, Thomas, 1511-1563.

Regnum Papisticum: Nunc postremò recognitum & auctum.

(BASILEAE EX OFFICINA IOannis Oporini), 1559. Mense Septembri.

243 [i.e. 343], [31] p. ; 17 cm. (8vo) Signatures: a-y^8, z^4, A-B^8; [a] unsigned, A1b, 24b, B8b blank, Y3 unsigned.

This copy is bound in vellum.

This volume was formerly in the Stewart collection, #4404. At the foot of the title page are two former ownership marks in ink: "Noel Baulonge (?)" and "Ex Bibl. P. de Carodomel 1645."

BM STC German, p. 471; VD 16, K 986; OCLC: 23300254.

Naogeorg was born in Bavaria and educated at Tübingen. His Protestant ideas were considered suspect by Melanchthon and most other Lutheran theologians. This work on the Kingdom of the Pope enjoyed wide circulation during the author's lifetime. The present volume also includes some of Naogeorg's poems.

1559
Naog

Staphylus, Friedrich, 1512?-1564.

Defensio PRO TRIMEMBRI THEOLOGIA. M. LVTHERI, CONTRA AEDIFICA-
TORES BABYLONICAE TVRRIS. *Phil. Melanthonem. Shvvenckfeldianum Longinum. And. Musculum. Mat. Flacc. Illyricum. Iacobum Andream Shmidelinum.*

DILLINGAE Apud Sebaldum Mayer Anno D[omi]ni M.D.LIX.

[231] p. ; 20 cm. (4to) Signatures: A-Z, a-f^4; [A] unsigned, A1b, f4b blank.

This volume was formerly in the Stewart collection, #6188. There are bibliographical notes on F. Staphylus in ink on the the recto and verso of the upper flyleaf.

BM STC German, p. 829;   Klaiber, 2942;   VD 16, S 8581;   OCLC: 23898399.

In 1558, F. Staphylus wrote an *Epitome in Three Parts on the Theology of Martin Luther*. The book was soundly criticized by various Protestant authors. In this present pamphlet Staphylus replies to the comments of Melanchthon, Schwenckfeld, Musculus, Flacius Illyricus, and Andreae. Some of Schwenckfeld's and Melanchthon's contributions to this controversy are included in this bibliography.

1559
Stap A

Defénſio

PRO TRIMEM-
BRI THEOLOGIA. M. LV-
THERI, CONTRA ÆDIFICATORES
BABYLONICÆ TVRRIS.

Phil. Melanthonem.
Shvvenckfeldianum Longinum.
And. Muſculum.
Mat. Flacc. Illyricum.
Iacobum Andream Shmidelinum.

Authore Friderico Staphylo.

Conſtitue Domine legislatorem ſuper eos, vt ſciant gentes quoniam homines ſunt. Pſal. 9. Quoniam non eſt in ore eorum
veritas, cor eorum vanum eſt, Pſal. 5.
Non reddetis malum pro malo, nec maledictum pro maledicto:
ſed contrà benedicetis, ſcientes quòd in hoc vocati eſtis, vt be-
nedictionem hæreditate poſsideatis. 1. Pet. 3. Si probris affi-
cimini propter nomen Chriſti, beati eſtis. 1 Pet. 4.

Cum Gratia & Priuilegio Cæſ. Maieſt.

Anno Dñi   M. D. L. IX.

Staphylus, Friedrich, 1512?-1564.

HISTORIA DE VITA, MORTE, ET IVSTIS CAROLI V. MAximi, Imperatoris Rom. &c. nunc recens edita, & varijs illustrata virtutu[m] fortun[a]eq[ue] exemplis.

AVGVSTAE VINDELICORVM Philippus Vlhardus excudebat. ANNO Sal. 1559. Calend. Iunij.

[243] p. ; 21 cm. (4to) Signatures: A-Z, a-f^4, g^6; [a] unsigned, g6b blank.

This volume was formerly in the Stewart collection, #6188. There are some manuscript marginalia in the text.

BM STC German, p. 829; Klaiber, 2941;   VD 16, S 8584;   OCLC: 23896285.

A biography of Holy Roman Emperor Charles V, written by Staphylus shortly after the emperor's death in 1558.

1559
Stap

Vergerio, Pietro Paolo, 1498-1565.

*DIALOGI QVATVOR DE LIBRO, QVEM STANISLAVS OSIVS, GERMANO
POLONVS, EPISCOPVS VARMIENsis, proximo superiore anno, contra Brentium &
Vergerium Coloniae edidit.*

[S.l. : s.n.] ANNO DOMINI M.D.LIX. Mense Martio.

104 leaves ; 21 cm. (4to) Signatures: A-Z, a-c⁴; [A] unsigned, A1b, c4b blank; b2 missigned "B2".

This volume was formerly in the Stewart collection, #6635.

Adams, V-418; OCLC: *22781080.*

The attacks of Catholic polemicists against P. Vergerio continued through the 1550's. One of Vergerio's later critics was
the Bishop of Ermland, Stanislaw Hozyusz. He condemned Vergerio and Brenz for their misunderstanding of the Church
and the Sacraments. This is Vergerio's reply.

1559
Verg

❧ DIALOGI QVATVOR ❧

DE LIBRO, QVEM

STANISLAVS OSIVS, GERMA=
NO POLONVS, EPISCOPVS VARMIEN-
fis, proximo fuperiore anno, contra
Brentium & Vergerium
Coloniæ edi=
dit.

DEQVE ALIIS DVOBVS EIVSDEM
Ofij libellis Dilingæ impreßis, quorum alteri eft titulus
de expreßo uerbo Dei, alteri uerò, num
calicem Laicis.cjc.

AVTORE VERGERIO.

ANNO DOMINI M. D. LIX.
Menfe Martio.

1560

Bekanntnus vnnd Bericht der Theologen vnd Kirchendiener im Fürstenthumb Würtemberg, von der warhafftige[n] gegenwertigkeit des Leibs vnnd Bluots Jesu Christi im heiligen Nachtmal.

Getruckt zuo Tüwingen [s.n.] im Jar. M.D.LX.

[11] p. ; 31 cm. (fol. in 6s) Signatures: A^6; [A] unsigned, A6b blank.

This volume was formerly in the Stewart collection, #7141.

VD 16, B 1558 (under Bekenntnis...); OCLC: *15178664.*

In 1559 J. Brenz completed the new Church Ordinance for the Duchy of Württemberg. The present volume is an addendum to that ordinance, a report on the real presence, issued in 1560. Because it was issued by committee, the work is not usually recognized as being by J. Brenz. W. Köhler, however, includes it in his Brenz bibliography.

1560
Beke

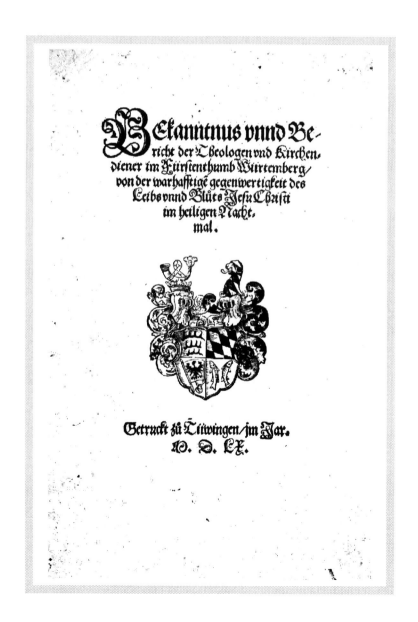

BREVIS NARRATIO EXPONENS. QVO FINE VITAM IN TERRIS SVAM CLAVSERIT REVERENDVS VIR D. PHILIPPVS MELANTHON, Vna cum prae-cedentium proxime dierum & totius morbi, quo confectus est breui descriptione. *CON-SCRIPTA A PROFESSORIBVS ACADEMIAE VVITEBERGENSIS,* qui omnibus quae exponuntur interfuerunt.

EXPRESSVM VITTEBERGAE (EXCVDEBAT PETRVS SEITZ) ANNO 1560.

[68] p. ; 21 cm. (4to) Signatures: A-H^4, I^2; [A] unsigned, G3 missigned "G4".

There is a former ownership mark at the foot of the title page, and some manuscript marginalia in the text.

BM STC German, p. 921; *Jackson, 2130; Pegg, Bibliotheca, 2049; VD 16, B 8245;* OCLC: *12791352.*

Melanchthon died on April 19, 1560. This tract was written by professors at Wittenberg. It details the last days of his life. This is the first printing.

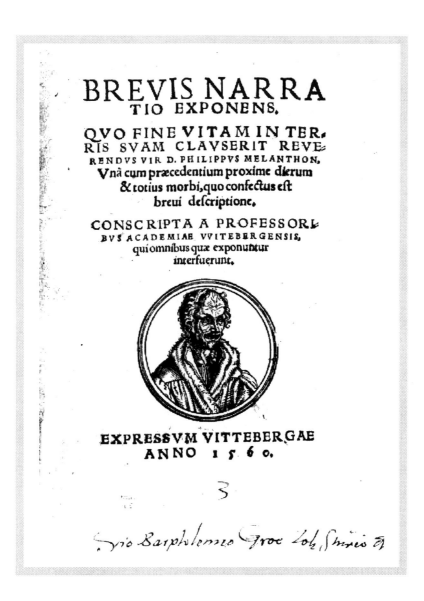

1560
Univ A

Flacius Illyricus, Matthias, 1520-1575.

INDVLGENTIA PLENARIA PRO PACE CONSERvanda, Haeresibus extirpandis, ac sacro generali consilio prosequendo.

[S.l. : s.n., after 25 March 1560.]

[7] p. ; 20 cm. (4to) Signature: unsigned.

Hohenemser, 3689; Preger, II, 559-560; VD 16, K 472; OCLC: 17738387.

Flacius here satirizes the most recent plenary indulgence, granted to help stamp out Protestant heresy and further the work of the Council of Trent.

1560
Cath

Luther, Martin, 1483-1546.

ENCHIRIDION PIARVM PRECATIONVM, cum Calendario & Passionali, ut uocant &c.

VVITEBERGAE. (excudebat Laurentius Schuuenck), 1560.

> [504] p. : ill., port. ; 14 cm. (12mo) Signatures:)(^{12} A-V^{12}; [A] unsigned, [)(]1b, V12b blank,A4, 7, C6, H7, I6 unsigned, K3 missigned "k3".

> This volume is bound in blind-stamped bleached pigskin over paper boards, dated "1560" with the initials "C.C."

> This volume was formerly in the Beck Lutherana collection, #379. On the upper flyleaf is a manuscript note that is a Latin annotation, "Erasmi de Luthero," and at the foot of the title page is a former ownership mark reading, "Sum Christo. Cyri. W."

> *VD 16, L 4125; WA 10, 2, p. 363; OCLC: 18114914.*

> Luther began work on his prayer book (Betbüchlein) in 1522, shortly after completing the Christmas Postil. The Latin edition was produced by G. Rörer in 1529. This particular volume has two noteworthy features. On the upper flyleaf is a short passage in Latin comparing positions of Erasmus and Luther. At the end of the book, from leaf Pi onwards are a series of woodcuts illustrating scenes from the Bible.

1560
Luth

Melanchthon, Philipp, 1497-1560.

EXPLICATIO SENTENTIARVM THEOGNIDIS, IN SCOLA VVITEBERGENSI.

VVITEBERGAE EXCVDEBAT LAVRENTIVS Schuenck. 1560.

[16], 137 leaves; 17 cm. (8vo) Signatures: A-S^8, T^3; [A] unsigned.

This is the second item in a bound collection, bound with Theognis' *THEOGNIDIS MEGARENSIS SENTENTIAE CVM VERSIONE LATIna,...*; VVITEBERGAE EXCVDEBAT LAVRENTIVS Schuenck. 1561.

There are scattered manuscript marginalia in the text.

BM STC German, p. 612; OCLC: 20772068.

In addition to the dual-language text of Theognis' elegiac poetry, Melanchthon also wrote a commentary on his works. These two works are frequently (as here) found bound together.

1561
Theo: 2

EXPLICA‑
TIO SENTENTIA‑
RVM THEOGNIDIS, IN
SCOLA VVITEBERGENSI
VCTORE REVERENDO ET CLA‑
riſſimo uiro, Philippo Melanthone,
Anno 1551. die 27. Maij:

COLLECTA

à

IOHANNE MAIORE
DOCTORE, ET IN
publicum commodum
ædita.

CVM PRIVILEGIO
ad ſexennium.

VVITEBERGAE EXCV‑
DEBAT LAVRENTIVS
Schuenck.

1560.

Melanchthon, Philipp, 1497-1560.

IVDICIVM D. Philippi MeLANCHTHONIS DE controuersia Coenae Domini.
BASILEAE, [s.n.] 1560.

[13] p. ; 16 cm. (8vo) Signatures: a^8; [a] unsigned, a7b, a8 blank.

This is the first item in a bound collection.

This volume was formerly in the Stewart collection, #4057. There is a table of contents in manuscript for the bound collection on the upper flyleaf that lists 9 items: one being a continuation of item 6, though Pitts Library has only 7 items, and one being the continuation of item 5.

VD 16, M 3529; OCLC: 12686795.

Count Palatine Friedrich III was an ardent Lutheran. In 1557, he inherited his father's lands and introduced the Reformation into the Simmerian Palatinate. Friedrich tried to make religious peace within the quarreling Lutheran ranks and appealed to Melanchthon for encouragement. In this tract Melanchthon gives his approval to Friedrich's efforts.

1560
Mela A: 1

Melanchthon, Philipp, 1497-1560.

PHILIPPI MELANTHONIS EPIGRAMMATVM LIBRI TRES.

VITEBERGAE EXCVDEBAT PETRVS SEITZ. ANNO M.D.LX.

[200] p. ; 15 cm. (8vo) Signatures: A-M^8, N^4; [A] unsigned, L3 missigned "L2", leaf "N" unprinted in this copy.

This volume was formerly in the Stewart collection, #4057. A missing leaf has been supplied in manuscript, though it is now faded and illegible. There is a manuscript note to that effect on the upper flyleaf.

BM STC German, p. 611; VD 16, M 3176; OCLC: 12657015.

This is a collection of Melanchthon's poetry edited by Hildebrand Granthaus. The volume, a fairly uncritical gathering of unrelated works, is incomplete.

1560
Mela

SCRIPTORVM PVBLICE PROPOSITORVM A PROFESSORIBVS IN *Academia VVitebergensi, Ab anno 1540. usq[ue] ad annum 1553. TOMVS PRIMVS.*

VVITEBERGAE EXCVSVS AB HAEredibus Georgij Rhaw. Anno 1560.

[976] p. ; 17 cm. (8vo) Signatures: A-Z^8, a-z^8, 2A-2P^8; [A] unsigned, 2P7b, 2P8 blank. Some pages numbered as leaves.

This volume is bound in blind-stamped, bleached pigskin over wooden boards, clasps missing.

On the inside, upper cover in ink is a note: "Henricus Vagetius Anno 1637. Septemb. 2," followed by a Latin inscription. The upper left-hand corner of the title page has been cut away, with a slight loss of text, and at the foot is a former ownership mark of "David Vagetius Hamburg. Anno 1611. Mense Maio." There is a former ownership stamp on the verso of the title page reading, "Ex Bibliotheca Gymnasii Altonani," with another stamp inside this one reading, "Ungültig."

BM, 259, col. 902; BM STC German, p. 921; OCLC: 12796328.

First volume of a large and comprehensive collection of academic dissertations defended at the University of Wittenberg. This volume covers the years 1540-1553.

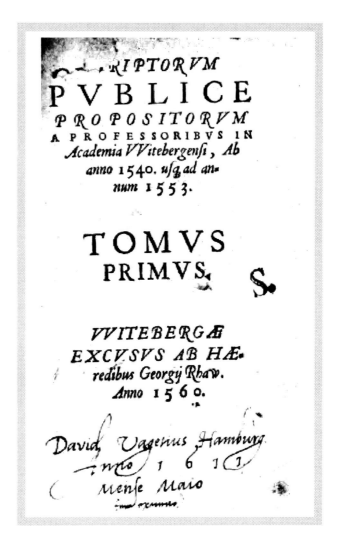

1560
Univ

SCRIPTVM PVBLICE PROPOSITVM IN ACAdemia *Vuitebergensi, de ordine aliquot lectionum publicarum constituto post pium & foelicem obitum Domini PHILIPPI MELANTHONIS, Die 23. Aprilis.*

VVITEBERGAE EXCVDEbat Vitus Creutzer. ANNO. 1560.

[14] p. ; 20 cm. (4to) Signatures: A-B^4; [A] unsigned, B4 blank.

This copy was formerly in the J.K.F. Knaake collection.

BM STC, German, p. 921;   VD 16, S 5157;   OCLC: 12791004.

This tract is the official notification by the University of Wittenberg of the death of Melanchthon. It served as both an obituary and as an advertisement for the now vacant position in the university. This is the second printing of the work.

1560
Univ B

SCRIPTVM
PVBLICE PROPOSITVM IN ACA-
demia Vuitebergenſi, de ordine aliquot lectionum publicarum conſtituto poſt pium &
fœlicem obitum Domini PHILIP-
PI MELANTHONIS,
Die 23. Aprilis.

VVITEBERGAE EXCVDE-
bat Vitus Creutzer.

ANNO.
1560.

Staphylus, Friedrich, 1512?-1564.

Von dem rechten vorstandt dess Göttliche[n] Worts, Dolmetschungk der Heiligen Bibel, vnnd wegen seiner eigenen Person vorantwortung wieder Philippum Melanthonem vnd andcre dergleichen.

Gedruckt zur Neyss, auff dem Kaldenstein, durch Johan. Creutziger. Anno etc. LX.

[107] p. ; 20 cm. (4to) Signatures: A-M⁴, N⁶; [A], A3, B3, I3 unsigned, N6b blank.

BM STC German, p. 829;   *Kuczynski, 2552;   VD 16, S 8606;   OCLC: 21105781.*

F. Staphylus belonged at first to the circle of Melanchthon, but later converted to Catholicism. This book deals with biblical interpretation and translation.

1560
Stap

THESES, QVAE VERAM DE COENA DOM. SENTENTIAM IVXTA PROPHETICA ET APOSTOlica Scripta, eruditae ac piae antiquitatis consensum ...

[S.l. : s.n.] Anno M.D.LX.

[23] p. ; 16 cm. (8vo) Signatures: A^8, B^4; [A] unsigned, B4b blank.

This is the fifth item bound with Philipp Melanchthon's *IVDICIVM D. philippi MeLANCHTHONIS DE controuersia Coenae Domini*, BASILEAE, [s.n.] 1560.

Adams, H-157;   OCLC: 12691329.

This is an anonymous series of theses presented for formal disputation on June 3 and 4, 1560, on doctrines concerning the Lord's Supper according to the Augsburg Confession.

1560
Mela A: 6

1561

CATALOGVS *oder Register der bücher Herren Caspar Schwenckfelds, die er mehr dann von XXX jaren her geschriben, vnd was durch ihn inn truck ist khommen.*

[Frankfurt am Main? : s.n.] 1561.

[70] p. ; 21 cm. (4to) Signatures: a-h^4, i^3; [a] unsigned, a1b blank.

This volume was formerly in the Stewart collection, #8295.

BM STC German, p. 804; Corpus Schwenckfeldianorum 17, Doc. 1160; Kuczynski, 2459; Pegg, Bibliotheca, 915; OCLC: 22669780.

In the closing months of Schwenckfeld's life, his friends and literary executors (notably Johann Heid von Daun) prepared and printed a bibliography of his works. The finished catalogue was printed in August 1561, four months before his death. Although not a complete bibliography, the work is of historical value because it attributes many anonymously published works to Schwenckfeld.

1561
Cata

Luther, Martin, 1483-1546.

ALLEGOriarum, typorum, ET EXEMPLORVM VEteris & noui Testamenti Libri duo.

BASILEAE, IN OFFICIna Arnoldi Gymnici, sumptibus Ioannis Oporini, Ano Salutis humanae M.D.LXI. Mense Augusto.

[16], 566, [2] p. ; 15 cm. (8vo) Signatures: [alpha]^8, a-z^8, A-M^8, N^4; [A] unsigned, A1b, N4b blank, D3 missigned "D5", M5 missigned "M2."

This copy is bound in vellum.

This volume was formerly in the Stewart collection, #3956. There are some manuscript marginalia in the text.

VD 16, L 3496; OCLC: 21465719.

The works in this volume were collected from Luther's Latin writings. They seek to show how Luther used allegories, types, and exempla in his biblical commentaries. Such collections were valuable for the theological training of future clergymen.

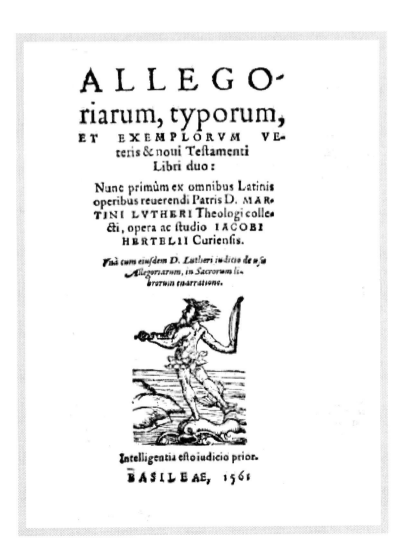

1561
Luth

Luther, Martin, 1483-1546.

Corpus LIBRORVM D. MARtini Lutheri Sanctae Memoriae, de uerbis Domini, HOC EST CORPVS MEVM etc. Das ist, Die Bücher D. Martini Luthers, Gottseliger gedechtnus, vom rechten vnd waren verstand der wort des Herrn, DAS IST MEIN LEIB etc.

Gedruckt zu Vrsel, durch Nicolaum Heinricum, vnd Sigmund Feyerabend, Anno 1561.

[30], 784 [i.e. 800] p. ; 16 cm. (8vo) Signatures:)(^{8}, A-Z^8, a-z^8, Aa-Dd^8; [)(]unsigned, A8 blank, S5, Z5, o5 Dd5 unsigned.

This copy is bound in blind-stamped pigskin over wooden boards, clasps missing.

This volume was formerly in the Stewart collection, #3956. There are former ownership marks on the title page, and one on the inside lower flyleaf reading, "Paulus Hayder, 1662."

VD 16, B 2487 (a 1563 Ursel ed., under "Beyer, Hartmann");   OCLC: 21429477.

This volume collects all of Luther's major statements on the Lord's Supper in German prepared for easy reference. This is an excellent specimen of a sixteenth century binding of a small book made in imitation of a large folio volume.

1561
Luth A

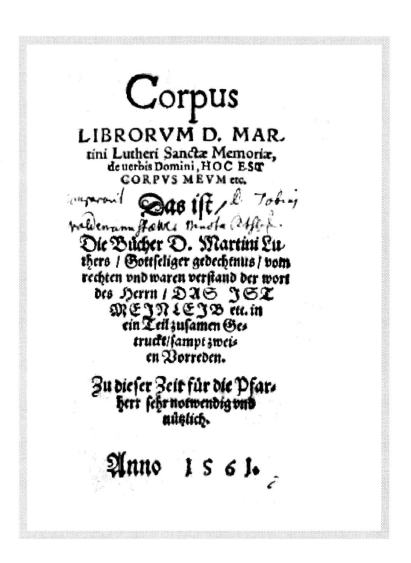

Luther, Martin, 1483-1546.

Warhafftige vnd bestendige meinung vnd zeugnis, Von der Erbsünde vnd dem freien willen. Des Ehrwirdigen tewren Mans Gottes D. Martin Luthers. Aus allen seinen schrifften trewlich vnd mit vleis zusamen gezogen, zu nottürfftigem vnd hochnützlichem vnterricht in itzt schwebenden zwispalten.

Gedruckt zu Jhena, durch Thomam Rebart. 1.5.6 1.

[154] p. ; 20 cm. (4to) Signatures: A⁴, *⁶, B-T⁴; [A], O3 unsigned, Q4 missigned "P4", the 4th leaf is usually signed.

This volume was formerly in the Beck Lutherana collection, #755 and in the W. H. Stifel collection, #672. There is a fore-edge shelf mark.

VD 16, L 3498;   OCLC: 18697422.

Another collection of Luther's statements on theological issues, in this case on Free Will. This particular collection was prepared by Flacius Illyricus, possibly in an attempt to show that his own positions were more in line with Luther's original intent than the writings of Flacius' opponents.

1561
Luth B

Melanchthon, Philipp, 1497-1560.

BREVIS ET VTILIS COMMENTARIVS IN PRIOREM EPIstolam Pauli ad Corinthios, & in aliquot capita secundae.

Vitebergae (Excudebat Iohannes Crato) ANNO. M.D.LXI.

[12], 163, [3] leaves ; 17 cm. (8vo) Signatures: [aleph]^8, [beth]^4, B-X, Y^6; [aleph] unsigned.

This is the third item bound with P. Melanchthon's *IN DANIELEM PROPHETAM Commentarius,* VITEBERGAE (Per Iohannem Lufft), Anno 1543.

Hartfelder, 672;   VD 16, M 2618;   OCLC: 06105481.

Melanchthon's commentary on First Corinthians and on several chapters from Second Corinthians was written by 1551 but edited posthumously by P. Eber, a friend and colleague of Melanchthon. This is the first printing of the work; it includes two portraits of Melanchthon and two epitaphs on him.

1543
Mela B: 3

Novicampianus, Albertus.

DE CORRVPTISSIMIS SECVLI HVIVS MORIBVS, VARIISQVE ATQVE TVRBVLENTIS IN religione Christiana doctrinis.

COLONIAE Apud Maternum Cholinum M.D.LXI.

[279] p. ; 16 cm. (8vo) Signatures: A-R^8, S^4; [A] unsigned, I8 missigned "I3", S4b blank.

This volume was formerly in the Stewart collection, #4459. There is a bookplate of a former owner on the inside upper pastedown that reads: "Ex libris Henrici Vandem Block, P[res]b[y]tri & insignis Collegiatae Ecclesiae DD. Michaelis & Gudelae Bruxellis Capellani." On the first blank page there is an inscription that has been inked out.

VD 16, N 1934 (under Nowopolski, Wojciech);   OCLC: 12939955.

A. Novicampianus was doctor and professor of theology at the University of Cracow. He had been the tutor of Johann Sigismund, King of Poland. This volume discusses the internal divisions of Christianity and includes two letters by Erasmus condemning the "false evangelicals," i.e. Protestants.

1561
Novi

Ochino, Bernardino, 1487-1564.

Prediche di M. BERNARDINO OCHINO SENESE, NOMATE LABERINTI del libero, o uer seruo Arbitrio, Prescienza, Predestinatione, & Libertà diuina, & del modo per vscirne.

IN BASILEA [s.n., 1561?]

[6], 260 p. ; 16 cm. (8vo) Signatures: A-Q^8; [A] unsigned, C4 missigned "B5", K5 missigned "L5", N5 missigned "N4", Q5 missigned "P5".

This volume was formerly in the Stewart collection, #4470. There is a manuscript bibliographical note on the upper flyleaf in French.

BM, v. 174, col. 311 (that gives date as [1569]);   Benrath, p. 322, Nr. 42, (that gives date as 1561);   VD 16, O 217; OCLC: 19878172.

B. Ochino began his public career as a preacher in the Observant Franciscan Order before becoming a Capuchian in 1534. Cited to Rome to answer for his Protestant opinions in 1542, he fled to Geneva, thence to England where he wrote this series of sermons some time between 1547 and 1553. These works constitute a critique of the doctrine of predestination.

1561
Ochi

Schwenckfeld, Caspar, 1489-1561.

Kurtze grundliche verantwortung Caspar Schwenckfelds, deren Artickell, mit welchen ihn seine wid[er] wertigen vnwarhafftig belegen. Auch von Caluini Lehre im Artickel des Herren Nachtmals.

[S.l. : s.n.] 1561.

[41] p. ; 21 cm. (4to) Signatures: a-d^4, e^5; [a] unsigned, e5b blank.

There are extensive marginalia throughout this volume, including notes on the title page referring to parts of the text. There is a table of contexts on the verso of the title page, that is expanded with page numbers, and additional topics added in a sixteenth century hand.

BM STC German, p. 802; *Corpus Schwenckfeldianorum, 16, Doc. 1087;* Hohenemser, 3694; VD 16, S 4941; OCLC: 20699624.

A former Bishop wrote to Schwenckfeld asking about his teachings and beliefs. This is Schwenckfeld's reply. The Bishop's letter is also included, but his name is not mentioned hence his real identity is unknown. Of note is Schwenckfeld's reply to J. Calvin.

1561
Schwe

Schwenckfeld, Caspar, 1489-1561.

Unterricht, Von Caspar Schwenckfeldts Streitschrifften, die er zur beschirmu[n]g der warheit vnd verantwortung sein vnd seiner lere, mit benamung der widerwertigen, hat lassen aussgehen, das sie mit nutz vnnd frucht seindt zuo lesen.

[S.l. : s.n.] 1561.

[11] p. ; 20 cm. (4to) Signatures: a^6; [a] unsigned, a1b, a6b blank.

Corpus Schwenckfeldianorum, 17, Doc. 1163; Stickelberger-Folger, 700; VD 16, S 4992-4993; OCLC: 25489304.

Near the end of his life, Schwenckfeld felt compelled to justify the tone of his controversialist writings. In this tract he defends these works, arguing that he avoided scurrilous language and ad hominem attacks and instead concentrated on exposing the theological errors of his opponents.

1561
Schwe A

Theognis.

THEOGNIDIS MEGARENSIS SENTENTIAE CVM VERSIONE LATIna, ita ut uerbum uerbo conferri possit, addita earundem explicatione.

VVITEBERGAE EXCVDEBAT LAVRENTIVS Schuenck. 1561.

[1], 46 leaves ; 17 cm. (8vo) Signatures: A-F^8; [A] unsigned, F8b blank.

This is the first item in a bound collection.

There are manuscript marginalia in the text.

OCLC: 20771712.

Theognis wrote over half of all the Greek elegiac poetry that has survived. Mastery of Theognis was crucial for students planning to pursue higher degrees at Wittenberg during Melanchthon's tenure in the Greek faculty. This particular example is a dual language edition.

1561
Theo: 1

1562

Flacius Illyricus, Matthias, 1520-1575.

DISPVTATIO DE ORIGINALI PECCATO ET LIBERO ARBITRIO, INTER
MAthiam Flacium Illyricum & Victorinum Strigelium.

[S.l. : s.n.] Anno M.D.LXII.

[20], 395, [48] p. ; 22 cm. (4to) Signatures: [alpha]⁴, [beta]⁶, a-z, A-Z, Aa-Hh⁴, Ii⁶; [alpha] unsigned; [alpha]1b, [beta]6, Ii6b blank.

This is the first item in a bound collection, bound in blind-stamped pigskin over wooden boards, clasps missing.

There are manuscript contents notes on the verso of the upper flyleaf, as well as manuscript former ownership marks and notes on the title page.

Adams, F-563 (with conjectural imprint, "either Cologne: Heirs of Birkmann or Basel: J. Oporinus"); OCLC: *28004181.*

The Weimar Disputation on original sin took place in August 1560, between V. Strigel and M. Flacius Illyricus. Flacius held that original sin is the substance of human nature, hence human action cannot lead to salvation. Strigel held the opposing, Melanchthonian, view. The outcome of the disputation was inconclusive. This copy of the report on the Weimar Disputation is especially noteworthy because of the author's presentation inscription on the title page. Flacius presented the work to Wilhelm Jechholtz, an otherwise unknown figure.

1562
Flac A: 1

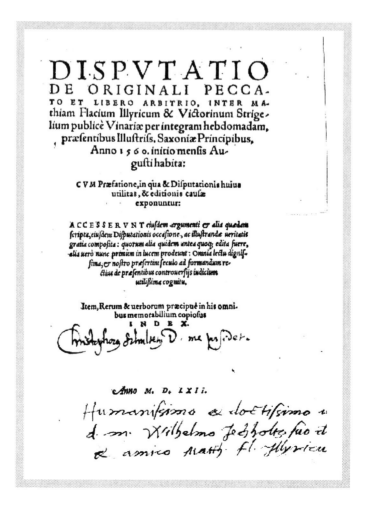

Luther, Martin, 1483-1546.

Kirchen Postilla das ist: Auslegung der Episteln vnd Euangelien, von Ostern bis auff das Advent.

Wittemberg. Gedruckt durch Hans Lufft. 1562.

2 pts. bd. as 1 v. ; ill. ; 34 cm. (fol. in 6s) Signatures (Part I): A^6, [clover]^6, [circle]^6, [gothic]A-Z^6, a-z^6, 2A-2P^6, 2Q^8; (Part II): a-l^6, m ; [A] unsigned, A6, [circle]5b, 6 blanks.

This volume is bound in blind-stamped, bleached pigskin over wooden boards, clasps missing.

This volume was formerly in the Beck Lutherana collection, #436.

VD 16, L 5631 and L 5632; OCLC: 19864588.

Luther's Church postils continued to be published throughout the sixteenth century up to the present day. The sermons were preached in German, recorded in macaronic shorthand and then edited for publication.

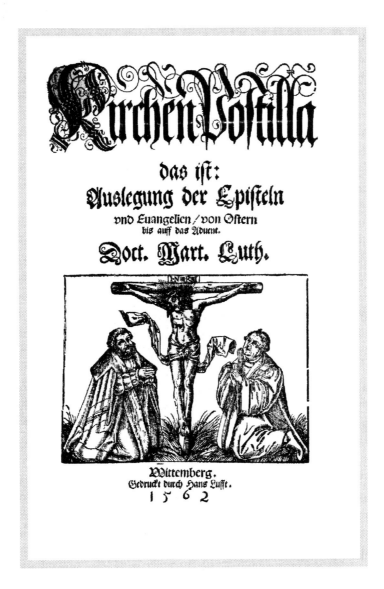

1562
Luth
(OS)

Major, Georg, 1502-1574.

VITAE PATRVM, IN VSVM MINISTRORVM VERBI, QVOAD EIVS fieri potuit repurgatae.

IMPRESSVM VVIttebergae per Vitum Creutzer. ANNO 1562.

[28], 255, [125] leaves : port. ; 17 cm. (8vo) Signatures: A-2S^8, 2T^4; [A] unsigned, A1b, 2T4b blank.

This volume is bound in blind-stamped pigskin over wooden boards.

This volume was formerly in the Stewart collection, #3985. There is an old ownership mark in ink on the upper pastedown that is only partly legible. There are also manuscript notes on both the recto and the verso of the upper flyleaf. The note on the upper flyleaf is a commentary on Luther, and the note on the verso is a two line Latin epigram.

Adams, M-226; Jackson, 2038; VD 16, M 2209; OCLC: 21569224.

This is a later printing of G. Major's Protestant version of the *Lives of the Fathers*.

1562
Majo

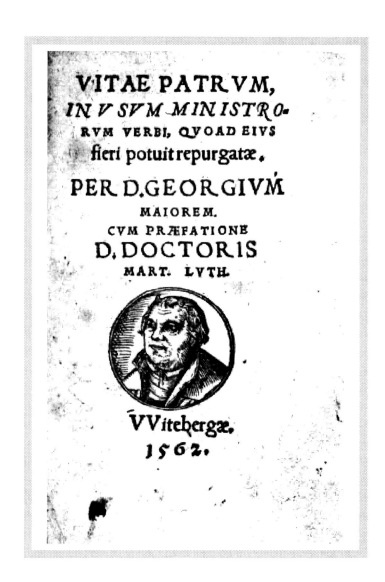

Melanchthon, Philipp, 1497-1560.

ADVERSVS ANABAPTISTAS.

FRANCOFORTI EXCVDEBAT PETRVS Brubachius. M.D.LXII.

[105] p. ; 16 cm. (8vo) Signatures: A-F^8, G^4.

This is the fourth item bound with Philipp Melanchthon's *IVDICIVM D. Philippi MeLANCHTHONIS DE controuersia Coenae Domini.* BASILEAE, [s.n.] 1560.

Adams, M-1095;   BM STC German, p. 609;   Hillerbrand, 3633;   VD 16, M 2425;   OCLC: 08196697.

Common legal opinion held that because Anabaptists repudiated their first baptism, they were guilty of treason and ought to be put to death. Melanchthon and Brenz did not share these views but sought rather to convert the Anabaptist rather than execute them. This is apparently only the second printing of the original Latin version of these two essays, first printed in 1528.

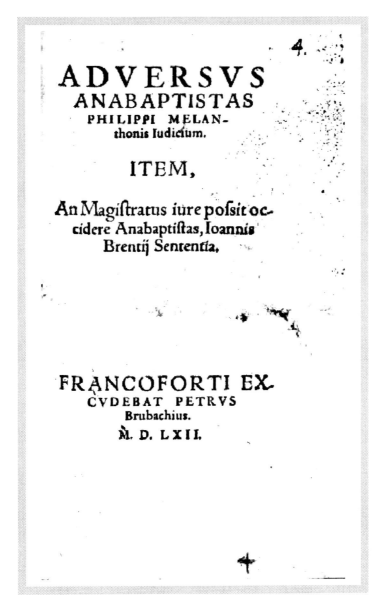

1560
Mela A: 4

Melanchthon, Philipp, 1497-1560.

OMNIVM OPERVM.

[Wittenberg : Johannes Crato, 1562-1564; see below for details.]

4 v. ; 37 cm. Edited by Kaspar Peucer. Vol. 3, 1563; v. 4, 1577. Vol. 4 previously published in 1564.

All four volumes are bound blind-stamped, bleached pigskin over wooden boards, with the portraits of Luther and Melanchthon on the front and back covers. The clasps on all four volumes are missing.

The woodcut portrait of Melanchthon on the title page of volume one has been meticulously hand-colored. There are bookplates of Dea[con]. Sam[ue]l Stone in each volume, and these volumes mark the beginning of Hartford Seminary's rare book collection. There are manuscript marginalia in all the volumes.

Adams, M-1068; BM STC German, p. 608; Hartfelder, 680; Jackson, 2050; VD 16, M 2331-36; OCLC: 04835607.

Kaspar Peucer (1525-1602), Melanchthon's son-in-law, served as his literary executor and spiritual heir in the Wittenberg Arts Faculty. He edited and published his father-in-law's collected works in the years 1562-1564. This is the first successful attempt to issue a complete collected edition of the works of Melanchthon. Indeed, the popularity of Peucer's version ensured that a second edition was required in the 1570's. The full page, full-figure portraits of Melanchthon were drawn by Lucas Cranach the Younger and were executed by Jacob Lucius. The printing information for each volume is as follows: Vol. I: VVITTEBERGAE EXCVDEBAT IOHANNES CRATO. ANNO M.D.LXII. Vol. II: VVITTEBERGAE EX-CVDEBAT IOHANNES CRATO. ANNO M.D.LXII. Vol. III: VVITTEBERGAE EXCVDEBAT IOHANNES CRATO. ANNO M.D.LXIII. Vol. IV: VVITEBERGAE EXCVDEBAT IOHANNES CRATO. ANNO M.D.LXIIII.

1562
Mela
(OS)

NOMINA, COGNOMINA, PATRIAE, DIGNITATES, ET PROMOTIONES ILLVSTRISS. ET REVERENDISS. PATRVM, *Qui conuenerunt ad Concilium TRI-DENTINVM. Vsque in diem ordinat. Iuxta promotionem Cuiusque ad suas dignitates.*

Brixiae Apud Damianum Turlinum. Anno. MDLXII.

[15] p. ; 21 cm. (4to) Signatures: A-B^4; [A] unsigned, A1b, B3b, B4b blank.

This volume is bound in vellum.

This volume was formerly in the Stewart collection, #6597. There is an armorial bookplate pasted onto the inside, upper cover.

OCLC: 29763864.

The third and final phase of the Council of Trent met on Jan. 18, 1562. This pamphlet lists the names and titles of 113 bishop and theologians present at this session. The volume, of which this pamphlet forms the first part, also includes speeches by Italian and Spanish prelates on the items discussed at the last sessions of the Council. This last session issued the final decrees of the council, and hence constitutes a key moment for the history of the Counter-Reformation.

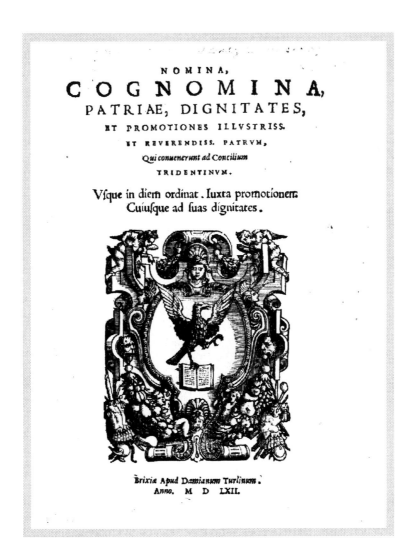

1562
Nomi: 1

Pole, Reginald, 1500-1558.

DE CONCILIO LIBER.

ROMAE, Apud Paulum Manutium Aldi F. M.D.LXII.

[8], 64 leaves ; 20 cm. (4to) Signatures: A-S^4; [A] unsigned, A1b, B4, R2b blank.

This is the first item bound in a collected volume. It is bound in limp vellum.

There is a manuscript note on the title page that has been inked out, and a manuscript note on the first page of text.

Renouard, II, p. 21, no. 3;   Brunet, IV, col. 787;   OCLC: 09226951.

Reginald Pole had remained true to the Catholic faith despite pressure from Henry VIII. He returned to England under Mary Tudor as the Cardinal Legate and led the English Counter-Reformation. This volume contains a series of eighty-six questions and answers dealing with General Councils. This is the first printing of the work.

1562
Pole: 1

Pole, Reginald, 1500-1558.

REFORMATIO ANGLIAE.

ROMAE, Apud Paulum Manutium Aldi F. M.D.LXII.

27, [1] leaves ; 22 cm. (4to) Signatures: A-G^4; [A] unsigned, A1b, G4a blank, printers device on the title page and repeated on G4b.

This is the second item bound with Reginald Pole's *DE CONCILIO LIBER*, ROMAE, Apud Paulum Manutium Aldi F. M.D.LXII.

OCLC: *15026745.*

It was Cardinal Pole's greatest ambition to bring the English back into the Catholic fold. Under Mary Tudor, he became Archbishop of Canterbury in 1556, and devoted the last year-and-a-half of his life to his reforming activities. This volume includes the decrees he issued as Archbishop. This is the first printing of this work.

1562
Pole: 2

REFORMATIO ANGLIAE

EX DECRETIS REGINALDI
POLI CARDINALIS,
SEDIS APOSTOLICAE LEGATI,
ANNO M. D. LVI.

ROMAE, M. D. LXII.
Apud Paulum Manutium Aldi F.

Rhegius, Urbanus, 1489-1541.

OPERA.

IMPRESSA NORIBERGAE, IN OFFICINA Ioannis Montani & Vlrici Neuberi, M.D.LXII.

3 pts. bd. as 1 v. ([12], CCCCXXXVIII, XCXIX [i.e. XCIX], [1], [6], CXIIII leaves) ; 34 cm. (fol. in 6s) Signatures: [alpha]-[beta]^6, A-4D^6, I-16^6, 17-3,)(^{6}; [alpha], y4, 3C4, BB4, 9 unsigned, 2B2, 2D4, 2O4, 84, AA, HH, II are missigned "B2", "D4", "2P4", "94", "A", "H", "I" respectively, TT6b blank.

This volume was bound in blind-stamped, bleached pigskin over wooden boards; clasps intact. The binding is dated, "1584," and has the initials, "I.I.S."

This volume was formerly in the Stewart collection, #5468.

Adams, R-284; BM STC German, p. 736 (parts I-II only); Liebmann, 142; VD 16, R 1723; OCLC: 01048391.

U. Rhegius was a cautious but committed convert to Lutheranism. He had been a student of Eck and a staunch humanist, as well as a crowned poet laureate and royal orator. In 1530, he became Superintendent in Lüneburg. He wrote the Church Ordinances for Lüneburg (1531) and Hannover (1536). He took part in the negotiations leading to the Wittenberg Concord (1536) and the Schmalkald Agreement (1537). This volume includes his Latin works collected by his son E. Rhegius. They show his concern for pastoral care and the cure of souls.

Schwenckfeld, Caspar, 1489-1561.

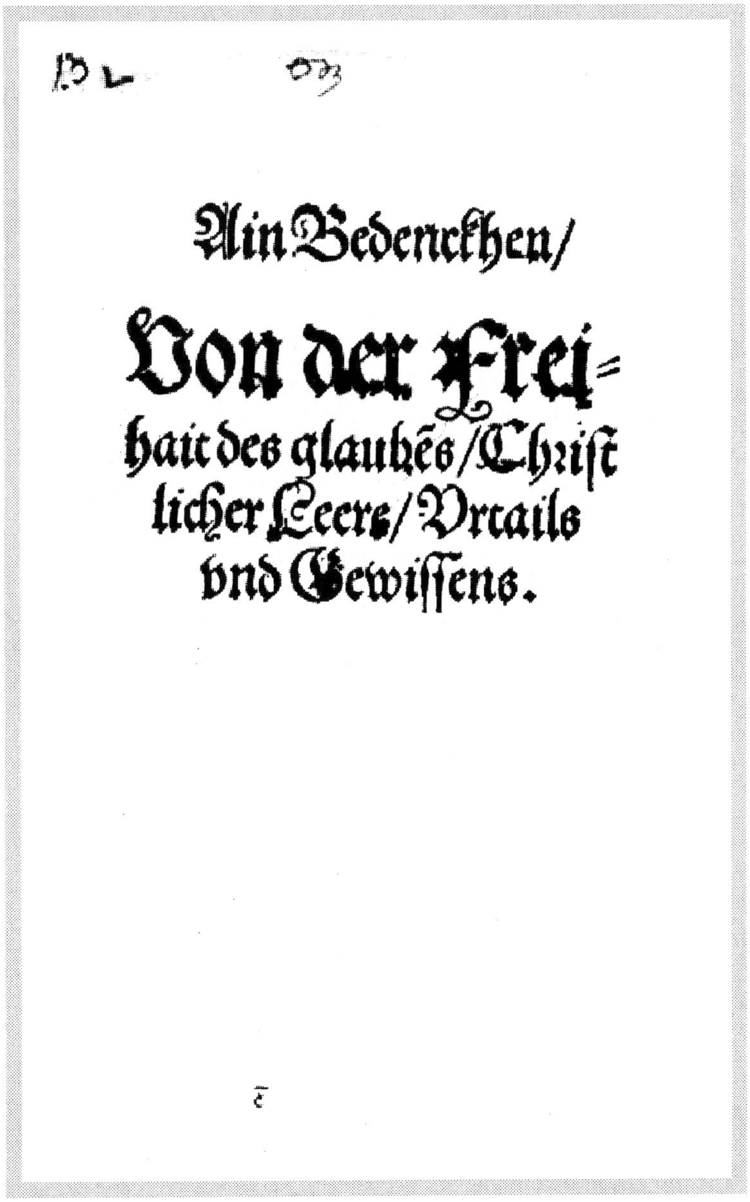

Ain Bedenckhen, Von der Freihait des glaube[n]s, Christlicher Leere, Vrtails vnd Gewissens.

[S.l. : s.n., 1562?]

[39] p. ; 16 cm. (8vo) Signatures: A-B^{8}, C^{4}; [A] unsigned, A1b, C4b blank.

Corpus Schwenckfeldianorum, 17, Doc. 1159; OCLC: *22465545.*

This tract is an expanded extract from Schwenckfeld's commentary on the Augsburg Confession.

Ain Bedenckhen/
Von der Frei-
hait des glaubẽs/Christ
licher Leere/Vrtails
vnd Gewissens.

1562
Schwe A

Schwenckfeld, Caspar, 1489-1561.

Ain Christlich bedencken, Ob Judas, vnnd die vnglaubigen falschen Christen, den leib vnd das bluot Jesu Christi im Nachtmal des Herren etwan[n] entpfangen, oder auch noch heüt empfahen oder niessen mögen.

[S.l. : s.n., 1562?]

[38] p. ; 16 cm. (8vo) Signatures: A-B^8, C^3; [A] unsigned.

BM STC German, p. 464;   Corpus Schwenckfeldianorum, 3, Doc. 87D;   VD 16, S 4903;   OCLC: 22465671.

This is a treatise on the Real Presence of Christ in the eucharist. The participation of Judas in the Last Supper served as proof for Schwenckfeld for his position that Christ could not be physically present in the bread and wine. If Christ had been present, according to Schwenckfeld, then the betrayer and greatest sinner of all time would have partaken of His body.

1562
Schwe

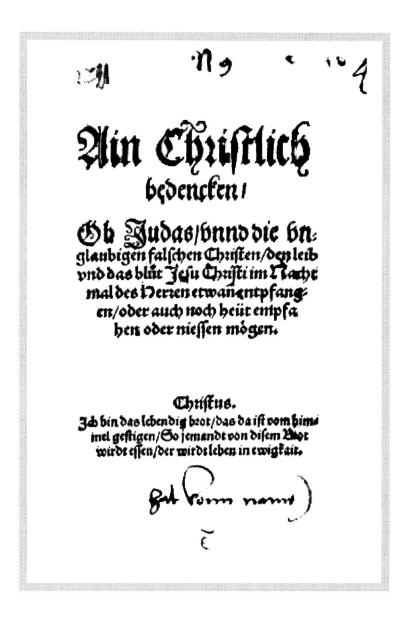

Schwenckfeld, Caspar, 1489-1561.

Vom Artickell vnsers Christlichen glaubens: Das Christus ist auffgestigen gen Him[m]el, Sytzet zur Rechten Gottes dess Allmechtigen Vatters.

[Pfortzheim? : Georg Rab?] 1562.

XXVII leaves ; 21 cm. (4to) Signatures: a-f^4, g^3; [a] unsigned, a1b blank, f3 missigned "3f".

Corpus Schwenckfeldianorum, 3, Doc. 74C; Hohenemser, 3703; VD 16, S 5005; OCLC: 22482808.

The Lutheran doctrine of the Lord's Supper rested on the ubiquity of the flesh of Christ. Schwenckfeld criticizes this doctrine in the present booklet on the *Ascension and Session of Christ at the Right Hand of God*. This is the third edition (the first complete one) of this work. It was originally written as a letter to an unnamed friend, possibly B. Egetius or J. Werner. A copy was sent to Wolfgang Capito, who issued the first edition. This edition was printed in 1557, but reissued with dated title page in 1562.

1562
Schwe B

Staphylus, Friedrich, 1512?-1564.

Historia vnnd Gegenbericht bayder partheyen, der Catholischen vnd Confessionisten, von zertrennung des Colloquiumbs, so am jüngsten zuo Wormbs angestellt worden, an alle des Catholischen Glaubens beschützer.

Getruckt zuo Ingolstat, durch Alexander vnd Samuel Weyssenhorn gebrüder. ANNO M.D.LXII.

[87] p. ; 20 cm. (4to) Signatures: A-L^4; [A], E^2 unsigned, A^{1}b, L^{4}b blank.

VD 16, S 8586;   OCLC: 29516204.

The colloquy of Worms was an official attempt by Ferdinand and the princes to bring about a religious peace through negotiation. It met from August 24-November 28, 1557. Each side was to have six colloquists, six adjuncts, six auditors, and two notaries. The president was to be J. von Pfug, Bishop of Merseburg and one of the Catholic colloquists. P. Melanchthon headed the Protestant delegation, made up of Philippists and Gnesio-Lutherans. The colloquy was supposed to be oral, but the Catholics began presenting position papers to which the Protestants replied. The Catholics, noting the Protestants' disunity, played on this causing rifts between the two factions. This caused the colloquy to break up, to the delight of the Catholics who put their trust in the Council of Trent, and to the discomfiture of the Protestants. The only result of the colloquy was that the Protestants agreed among themselves to the condemnation of C. Schwenckfeld.

1562
Stap

1563

Flacius Illyricus, Matthias, 1520-1575.

PROTESTATIO CONCIONATORVM ALIQVOT AVGVstan[a]e Confessionis, *aduersus conuentum Tridentinum, perniciem uerae Religioni & Ecclesiae molientem: & aduersus eius Conuentus autorem Antichristum Romanum. . .*

[S.l. : s.n.] Anno 1563. Mense Martio.

[8], 176 p. ; 22 cm. (4to) Signatures: [alpha]^4, a-y^4; [alpha] unsigned, M3 missigned "l3", p3 unsigned.

This is the second item bound with Matthias Flacius Illyricus' *DISPVTATIO DE ORIGINALI PECCATO ET LIBERO ARBITRIO,* [S.l. : s.n.] Anno M.D.LXII.

Adams, A-2148 (under "Augsburg, Confession [Appendix]"); OCLC: 28004241.

M. Flacius Illyricus here writes in the name of "Several Pastors of the Augsburg Confession" to protest the actions taken by the Council of Trent. Some scholars think that N. Gallus may have helped write this work, but his name does not appear on it. As with previous work, this copy includes Flacius' inscription on the title page.

1562
Flac A: 2

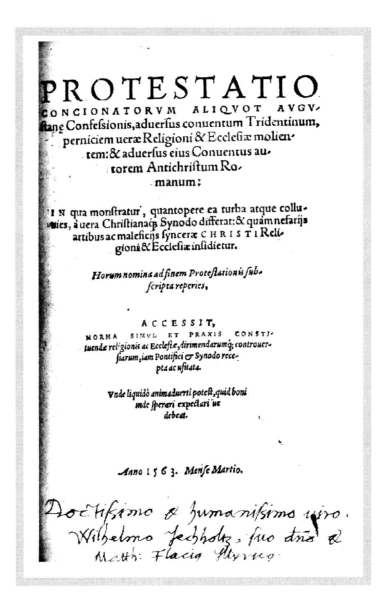

Luther, Martin, 1483-1546.

IN EPISTOLAM S. PAVLI AD GALATAS COMMENTARIVS, Ex praelectione D. Martini Lutheri collectus, diligenter recognitus, castigatus, &c.

FRANCOFVRTI EX OFFicina Petri Brubachi, Anno Salutis humanae M.D.LXIII. mense Aprili.

954 [i.e. 960], [15] p. ; 17 cm. (8vo) Signatures: A-Z, a-z, Aa-Pp^8; [A] unsigned, A1b, Pp8b blank, Cc4 missigned "c4".

This volume is bound in blind-stamped pigskin over wooden boards, one clasp intact.

This volume was formerly in the Beck Lutherana collection, #333. There is a top-edge and a fore-edge shelf mark.

Adams, L-1793; VD 16, B 5088; WA 40, 1, 14; OCLC: 22549589.

Luther's Galatians commentary was read and reprinted after his death. This is the work's first posthumous Latin printing. No separate German edition appeared before the eighteenth century.

1563
Luth

IN EPISTO
LAM S▸ PAVLI AD
GALATAS COMMENTARIVS,
Ex prælectione D. Martini Luthe
ri collectus, diligenter recogni‑
tus, castigatus, &c.

Adiecto etiam Indice rerum scitu
necessariarum.

Virtus mea per infirmitatem
perficitur.

FRANCOFVRTI,

1563.

Strigel, Victorinus, 1524-1569.

[UPOMNEMATA (romanized form)] In omnes Psalmos Dauidis, ita SCRIPTA, VT A PIIS AMANTIBVS consensum expressum in scriptis Propheticis, Apostolicis, Symbolis, & Scriptoribus vetustis ac purioribus vtiliter legi possint.

LIPSIAE. IN OFFICINA ERNESTI VOEGELINI CONSTANTIENSIS. [1563?]

[17], 726, 62, [24] p; 34 cm. (fol. in 6s) Signatures: [alpha]6, [beta]4, A-Z⁶, a-z⁶, 2A, 2O⁶, 2P⁴, 3A-3F⁶, 3G⁷; [alpha] unsigned, O5 missigned "02"; [beta]1b, 4a-b blank.

This volume is bound in blind stamped, bleached pigskin over wooden boards; dated "1563," with the initials, "H.T.M."

This volume was formerly in the Stewart collection, #6283. There is a former ownership stamp on the title page, as well as a manuscript mark, dated "1643."

Adams, S-1932; OCLC: 19494648.

V. Strigel was a staunch disciple of Melanchthon at the University of Jena from 1549-1562. In Jena he taught according to synergistic doctrine. When M. Flacius Illyricus came to Jena the two men came into conflict over this issue and Flacius was able to have Strigel arrested. When a colloquy was finally held, Strigel prevailed and Flacius Illyricus was banished. Strigel later adopted the Reformed position regarding the Lord's Supper.

1563
Stri

Suevus, Sigismundus, 1526-1596.

INDEX OMNIVM SCRIPTORVM REVERENDI PATRIS D. MARTINI Lutheri:
accommodatus & ad 19. Tomos Vitebergenses & 12. Ihenenses, tum veteris tum
recentioris Editionis: omnibus Studiosis Librorum Lutheri perutilis.

VRATISLAVIAE Ex Officina Crispini Scharffenberg. ANNO. 1563.

[95] p. ; 22 cm. (4to) Signatures: [alpha]-[beta]^4, A-K^4; [alpha], B2 unsigned, K4b blank.

This is the second item bound with Sigismundus Suevus' *Register aller Schrifften des Ehrwirdigen Herrn D. Martini Lutheri ...*, Gedruckt zu Bresslaw, durch Crispinum Scharffenberg. M.D.LXIII.

BM STC German, p. 804;   VD 16, L 3453 (under: "[Luther, Martin. Opera. Indices]." There is no separate entry for the Latin index.);   OCLC: 23898491.

S. Suevus or Schwabe was a popular preacher and biblical interpreter whose life was marked by many changes of occupation and residence because of religious disputes. This is the Latin edition of his index to both the Wittenberg and Jena editions of Luther's collected works.

1563
Suev: 2

INDEX OMNI-
VM SCRIPTORVM REVE-
RENDI PATRIS D. MARTINI
Lutheri: accommodatus & ad 19. Tomos
Vitebergenses & 12. Ihenenses, tum
veteris tum recentioris Editionis:
omnibus Studiosis Librorum
Lutheri perutilis.

Per

SIGISMVNDVM SVEVVM
Freistadiensem.

Qui cupit ingenii, cognoscere scripta LVTHERI,
Quælibet & quo sint inuenienda Tomo,
Comparet, exiguo, quem condidit, ære, libellum,
SVEVVS, & hunc animo candidiore legat.
M. H. S.

VRATISLAVIAE
Ex Officina Crispini
Scharffenberg.

ANNO,
1 5 6 3.

Suevus, Sigismundus, 1526-1596.

Register aller Schrifften des Ehrwirdigen Herrn D. Martini Lutheri, gerichtet zugleich auff die XIX. Wittenbergischen, vnd XII. Jhenischen Tomos, beyders des Alten vnnd Newen Drucks, allen Liebhabern der Bücher Lutheri gantz nützlich zu gebrauchen.

Gedruckt zu Bresslaw, durch Crispinum Scharffenberg. M.D.LXIII.

[177] p. ; 22 cm. (4to) Signatures: [asterisk]^4, [chi]^1, A-X^4; [A], G2, X3 unsigned, X4b blank.

This is the first item in a bound collection, bound in blind-stamped pigskin over wooden boards, one clasp intact.

BM STC German, p. 804; VD 16, L 3453 (under: "[Luther, Martin. Opera. Indices]"); OCLC: 24033696.

This is a very rare example of the index prepared to help students find specific works by Luther. Since Luther's writings had been collected in two different sets--the nineteen volume Wittenberg edition, and the twelve volume Jena edition--such an index was necessary.

1563
Suev: 1

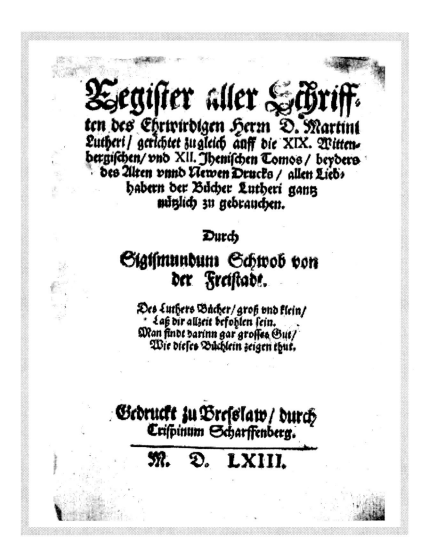

Unicornius, Paulus.

INTERPRETATIO LEGITIMA Responsionis PHILIPPI MELANCHTONIS post mortem ipsius, ...

VRSELLIS, [s.n.] Anno 1563.

[16], 190 p. ; 16 cm. (8vo) Signatures: A-N^8; [A] unsigned, N8 blank.

This is the second item bound with Philipp Melanchthon's *IVDICIVM D. Philippi MeLANCHTHONIS DE controuersia Coenae Domini*, BASILEAE, [s.n.] 1560.

Kuczynski, 2652;   OCLC: 12686850.

P. Unicornius (Einhorn?) was a Swiss theologian originally from Oberursel. This posthumous attack on Melanchthon apparently gave its author qualms of conscience, for he justifies himself in the title by calling his interpretation "legitimate."

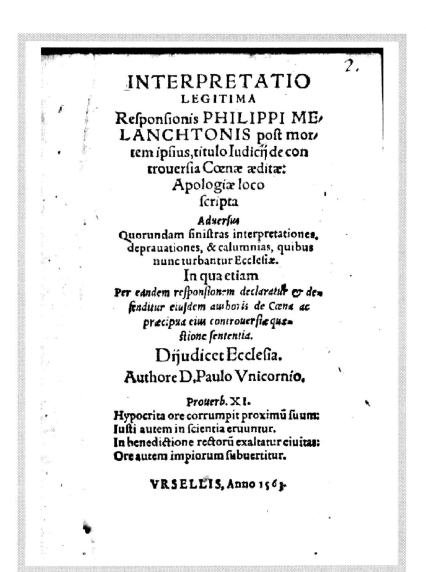

1560
Mela A: 2

1564

CANONES, ET DECRETA SACROSANCTI OECVMENICI GENERALIS CON-
CILII TRIDENTINI, SVB PAVLO III, IVLIO III, ET PIO IIII, PONTIFICIBVS
MAX. *Index Dogmatum, & Reformationis.*

ROMAE, Apud Paulum Manutium, Aldi F. IN AEDIBVS POPVLI ROMANI. MDLXIIII.

33 [i.e. 337], [48] p. ; 17 cm. (8vo) Signatures: A-Z^8, AA^7; [A] unsigned, A1b blank.

This volume was formerly in the Stewart collection, #6433.

Adams, C-2801; BM, v. 241, col. 185; OCLC: 22836975.

This is the second, revised printing by Paulus Manutius of the Canons and decrees of the Council of Trent.

1564
Coun

DEFENSIO ECCLESIASTICAE LITVRGIAE, QVA SCISMATICOrum quorundam eruditorum confutationes summa breuitate refutantur.

COLONIAE Apud Haeredes Arnoldi Birckmanni. ANNO DOMINI 1564.

[14], [168] p. ; 17 cm. (8vo) Signatures: A^7, B-L^8, M^3. Only the rectos are numbered.

There are manuscript marginalia in the text.

Klaiber, 3441 (entered under Georg Witzel as author without mention of the anonymous nature of the piece); OCLC: *12226536.*

This is a defense of the Catholic liturgy, probably written by Georg Witzel.

1564
SGV

DEFENSIO
ECCLESIASTICAE
LITVRGIAE, QVA SCISMATICO,
rum quorundam eruditorum
confutationes fumma bre,
uitate refutan,
tur,

Auctore S. G. V.

COLONIAE
Apud Hæredes Arnoldi Birckmanni,

ANNO DOMINI
1 5 6 4.

Erasmus, Desiderius, 1466?-1536.

COLLOQVIORVM FAMILIARVM OPVS.

ANTVERPIAE, Excudebat Christophorus Plantinus. M.D.LXIIII.

782, [2] p. ; 11 cm. (16mo) Signatures: A-Z^8, a-z^8, 2A-2C^8; [A] unsigned, z4 missigned "Z4".

Haeghen, I, p. 38;   OCLC: 12939882.

This is a later printing of Erasmus' Colloquies.

1564
Eras

COLLOQVIORVM

FAMILIARVM OPVS,

DES. ERASMO ROT.

AVCTORE.

*Nunc denuo ad auctoris ἀντίγραφα diligenter collatum,
vigilantissimé que excusum, appositis ad locos diffi-
ciliores Annotatiunibus.*

ANTVERPIAE,
Excudebat Christophorus Plantinus.
M. D. LXIIII.

CVM PRIVILEGIO.

p

Hemmingsen, Niels, 1513-1600.

Commentarius IN VTRAMQVE EPISTOLAM PAVLI APOSTOLI AD CORIN-THIOS.

[Leipzig : Voegelin, 1564?]

2 pts. bd. as 1 v. ([16], 325, [2], 212 p.) ; 17 cm. (8vo) Signatures: [Pars I]: A-X[8], Y[4], [Pars II]: a-n[8], o[3]; [A], [a] unsigned, b2 missigned "q2".

There are manuscript marginalia in the text, and a stamp on the verso of the last leaf reading "SB."

OCLC: 20772127.

N. Hemmingsen was a Danish pupil of Melanchthon in the 1530's. After returning home he became a professor of theology at Copenhagen. His later life was clouded by charges of Crypto-Calvinism brought against him by more "orthodox" Lutherans on the faculty. He was forced to resign and spent the last twenty years of his life in active academic retirement. This is his commentary on St. Paul's two Epistles to the Corinthians.

1564
Hemm

Schiess, Abraham.

Kurtze verzaichnus Der Fürnembsten Historien, vom M.D. Jar biss in dises gegenwerttig M.D. Lxiiij. Das ist was sich beyleuffig bey Manssgedechtnuss zugetragen hab.

Getruckt zuo Laugingen, durch Emanuel Saltzer. M.D.Lxiiij.

[87] p.; 20 cm. (4to) Signatures: A-L⁴; [A] unsigned, L4b blank.

At the foot of the title page is an old library stamp: "Bibliotheca Ponickaviana."

BM STC German, p. 788;   VD 16, S 2844;   OCLC: 18479489.

A. Schiess was a schoolmaster in Augsburg. His verse-chronology of the Reformation is among the first histories of the movement. The verse form may have been chosen as a mnemonic aid for students. The work is unlisted in most Reformation bibliographies.

1564
Schie

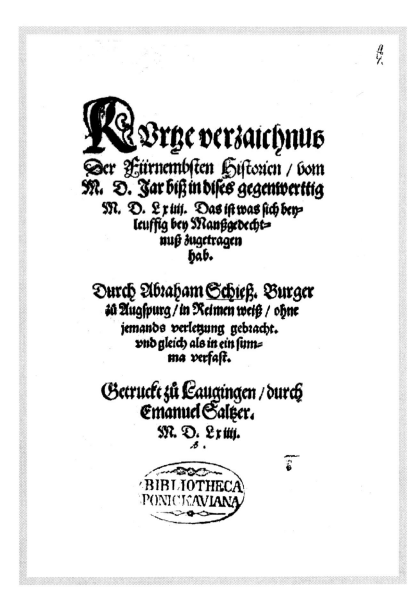

Schwenckfeld, Caspar, 1489-1561.

Der Erste Theil Der Christlichen Orthodoxischen bücher und schrifften, des Edlen, theuren, von Gott hoch begnadeten vnd gottseligen Man[n]s, ...

[S.l. : s.n.] Anno M.D.LXIIII.

[46], 974 p. ; 36 cm. (fol. in 6s) Signatures: a⁵, b-d⁶, A-4M⁶; [a] unsigned, a2 missed in signing, 2P4 unsigned.

This volume is bound in blind-stamped, bleached pigskin over wooden boards, clasps missing.

There is a book stamp of a former library on the title page, as well as the manuscript mark reading, "Conssistorium." There is also a stamp on the verso of the title page.

Corpus Schwenckfeldianorum, 2, p. 182; VD 16, S 4830; OCLC: 05010171.

After Schwenckfeld's death in 1561, his followers in southern Germany decided to issue an edition of his works designed to demonstrate his orthodoxy. The printing was stopped after only four volumes had appeared as the Schwenckfelder communities around Frankfurt am Main were broken up and dispersed.

1564
Schw

Spangenberg, Cyriacus, 1528-1604.

Ware vnd Gewisse Contrafet, Vnd abmalung des gantzen Antichristischen Reichs des Bapsthumbs. Geschrieben zur Antwort wider die Gifftigen Lügenschrifften des Albern Hansen zu Jngolstad, vnd Doct. Grünfelds, desgleichen anderer Papistischen Lesterer.

Gedruckt zü Eisleben bey Vrban Gaubisch. M. D. LXIIII.

[128], 346 [i.e. 340], [5] leaves ; 17 cm. (8vo) Signatures: pi^8, A^4, B-Z^8, a-z^8, Aa-Ll^8, Mm^7; p4, Ll4, 5, Mm2 unsigned, pi1b blank; pi are numbered ij-v.

This volume is bound in blind-stamped, polished calf over wooden boards, clasps intact.

There are former ownership marks on the inside, upper cover and title page. The latter are dated 1572 and 1721 but unfortunately are either faded or incomplete. There is a bottom-edge shelf mark.

VD 16, S 7719;   OCLC: 29585361.

C. Spangenberg was a Gnesio-Lutheran who sided with Flacius Illyricus against Melanchthon. In this work he lashes out against J. Alberti and F. Grünfeld of Ingolstadt University, two of his Catholic opponents who had just recently written books attacking him.

1564
Span

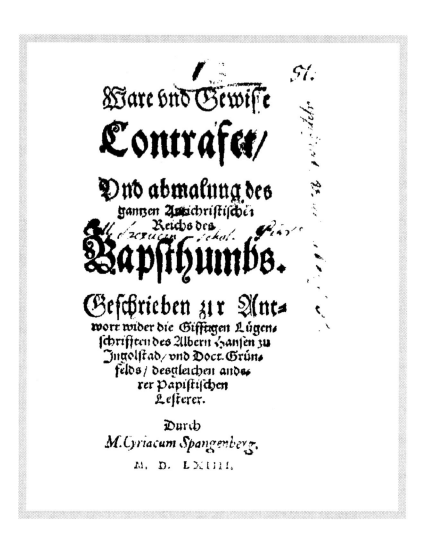

1565

Brunus, Conradus, 1491?-1563.

ADVERSVS NOVAM HISTORIAM ECCLESIASTICAM, QVAM MATHIAS IL-
LYricus & eius collegae Magdeburgici per centurias nuper ediderunt, ne quisq[am] illis
malae fidei historicis nouis fidat, admonitio Catholica.

DILINGAE APVD SEBALDVM MAYER. M.D.LXV.

[333] p. ; 16 cm. (8vo) Signatures: *^{8}, A-T^8,V^7; [A], V5 unsigned, A1b, V7b blank.

This is the first item bound in a bound collection, and bound in blind-stamped calf over wooden boards, clasps
missing.

There is a former ownership mark on the inside upper cover dated 1594, and a bibliographical note at the
head of the title page. On the verso of the title page are the stamps reading, "Ad Bibli. Acad. Land." and "U
B M abgegeben."

Adams, B-2960;   BM STC German, p. 158;   VD 16, B 7194;   OCLC: 06154622.

Brunus was a former professor at the University of Tübingen and served as a chancellor to several cardinals, including
Albert of Mainz and Otto v. Truchsess. In 1563 he became the Recording Secretary of the Imperial Commission on
Religion. In this work Brunus attacks the Church History of M. Flacius Illyricus.

1565
Brun: 1

Eisengrein, Wilhelm, 1542/1544-1584.

CATALOGVS TESTIVM VERITATIS LOCVPLETISSIMVS, OMNIVM ORTHO-
DOXAE MATRIS ECCLESIAE DOctorum, extantium & non extantium, publica-
torum & in Bibliothecis latentium, qui adulterina Ecclesiae dogmata, impuram,
impudentem & impiam haeresum vaniloquentiam, in hunc vsque diem firmissimis
demonstrationum rationibus impugnarunt, variaq[ue] scriptorum monumenta re-
liquerunt, seriem complectens.

DILINGAE EXCVDEBAT SEBALDVS MAYER. Anno D[omi]ni M.D.LXV.

[4], 211, [12] leaves ; 20 cm. (4to) Signatures: A-Z, a-z, Aa-Kk^4, Ll^3; [A], Hh3 unsigned, Hh4b blank.

This volume was formerly in the Stewart collection, #2560. At the head of the title page in ink is a former
ownership mark reading, "Ad usum Monachorum S. Magni in Giessen."

BM STC German, p. 263;   Klaiber, 953;   VD 16, E 831;   OCLC: 06214403.

Wilhelm Eisengrein was a Catholic scholar and church historian from Speyer. Two volumes of his proposed sixteen
volume history of the Church were printed between 1566 and 1568. This volume is Eisengrein's reply to Flacius Illyricus'
Catalogue of Witnesses of 1556 (see, in this bibliography under 1562). Eisengrein emphasized the orthodoxy of the
ancients even as Flacius had emphasizes their heterodoxy.

1565
Else

Jerome, Saint, 340?-420.

OMNES QVAE EXTANT D. HIERONYMI STRIDONENSIS LVCVBRATIONES, ADDITIS VNA PSEVDEPIGRAPHIS ET ALIENIS, SCRIPTIS IPSIVS ADMIXTIS, IN NOVEM TOMOS, PER DES. ERASMVM ROTERODAMVM digesta, ...

BASILEAE, EX OFFICINA EPISCOPIANA, PER NICOLAVM ET EVSEBIVM EPISCOPIOS FRATRES. ANNO M.D.LXV.

9 v. bound in 3 ; 40 cm. (fol in 6s).

Volumes 1-3 are bound in one volume and volumes 4-7 are bound in another. These two volumes are bound in blind-stamped bleached pigskin over wooden boards, clasps intact. Pitts Theology Library does not have volume 8-9.

On inside upper flyleaf of volume one and two is an old ownership inscription in ink of "Balthasar Poltzman[us]...." One of the former ownership mark on the title page of volume one reads: "Est conventus Viennensis FF. Eremitorum Discalceatorum S.C. Augustini." The other which is inscribed on the title page of both volume one and two reads: "Ex dono admodum Re[veren]di D[o]mi[ni] Melchizedech Plengl Parochi in maiori Enserstorff ad Conuentum Eremtarum S. Augustini Viennensem A. MDCXXIII 20 Juli."

Adams, J-119; VD 16, H 3486 (under Hieronymus, Eusebius Sophronius); OCLC: 13139416.

This is a later printing of Erasmus' 1516 edition of the works of St. Jerome.

1565
Jero

Melanchthon, Philipp, 1497-1560.

EPISTOLAE SELECTIORES ALIQVOT.

VVITEBERGAE EXCVDEBAT IOHANNES CRATO. ANNO M.D.LXV.

[16], 559, [13] p. ; 15 cm. (8vo) Signatures: A-Z^8, Aa-Nn^8, Oo^6; [A] unsigned, A1b blank.

This is the first item in a bound collection.

This volume was formerly in the Beck Lutherana collection, #694. On the inside, upper cover is the inscription, "Ktema [romanized form] Joh: Henr: Zorn P. 1736."

VD 16, M 3222 (v.1);   OCLC: 01888685.

This is a collection of selected letters of Melanchthon issued in Wittenberg.

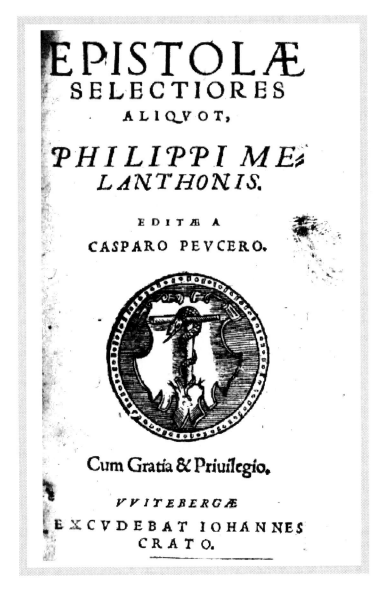

1565
Mela B: 1

Melanchthon, Philipp, 1497-1560.

EPISTOLAE SELECTIORES ALIQVOT.

[Wittemberg : Johannes Crato, 1565-1574; see below for details.]

2 v.; 17 cm. (4to).

There is a manuscript note on the upper flyleaf of volume one, as well as manuscript marginalia in the text. On the title page of volume two is a library Stamp of "Aalborg Skole" in Denmark.

Adams, M-1211;   BM STC German, p. 608;   VD 16, M 3222, 3224;   OCLC: 17965146.

The second collected edition of Melanchthon's correspondence was edited by his son-in-law Kaspar Peucer. It is a more complete collection and offers better texts of the material included than did the first collected edition of J. Manlius in Basel also printed in 1565. The printing information for these volumes is as follows:Vol. I: VVITEBERGAE EXCVDE-BAT IOHANNES CRATO. ANNO M.D.LXV. Vol. II: VVITEBERGAE EXCVDEBAT IOHANNES CRATO, ANNO M.D.LXXIIII.

1565
Mela

Melanchthon, Philipp, 1497-1560.

EPISTOLARVM.

BASILEAE, PER PAVLVM Queckum: M.D.LXV.

[16], 550 [i.e. 592], 1 p. ; 15 cm. (8vo) Signatures: [alpha]⁸, a-z⁸, A-O⁸; [a], p4 unsigned, B3 missigned "B4", a8b, O8b blank.

This is the second item bound with P. Melanchthon's *EPISTOLAE SELECTIORES ALIQUOT, VVITE-BERGAE EXCVDEBAT IOHANNES CRATO, ANNO M.D.LXV.*

A possible former ownership mark on the title page has been erased.

Adams, M-1210; BM STC German, p. 608; Jackson, 2184; VD 16, M 3220; OCLC: 17369375.

J. Manlius was born in Ansbach, studied in Wittenberg, and admired Melanchthon greatly. In addition to this collection of Melanchthon's letters, Manlius also issued a volume of selections from his writings.

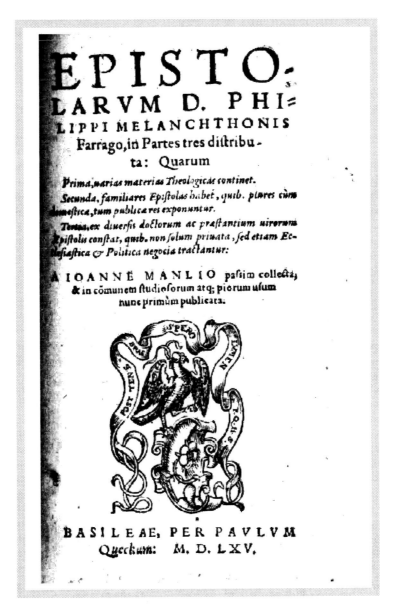

1565
Mela B: 2

Melanchthon, Philipp, 1497-1560.

ORATIONES POSTREMAE.

VVITEBERGAE. [Johannes Crato] ANNO M.D.LXV.

[14], 1056 p. ; 18 cm. (8vo) Signatures: A-3X^8; [A] unsigned, A8 blank.

This volume is bound in blind-stamped, bleached pigskin over wooden boards. The binding dated, "1566," with the owner's initials, "D.F.N.," for Daniel Fugman Newkyrchensis.

There is a bottom-edge shelf mark reading, "DF.NK. 1587." There is an inscription on the inside, upper cover reading, "Daniel Fugman. Newkyrchensis. 1582..." and relating bibliographical information. There is a similar inscription on the lower inside cover. There is another former ownership mark on the title page.

BM STC German, p. 608;   VD 16, M 379 (under J. Maius);   OCLC: 17975987.

This is a collection of Melanchthon's academic orations from roughly 1550-60. The collection also includes the eulogies delivered in the University of Wittenberg at Melanchthon's death.

1565
Mela A

ORATIONES
POSTREMÆ
SCRIPTAE A REVE-
RENDO VIRO PHILIPPO ME-
LANTHONE, proximis annis
ante obitum.

HIS ADIVNCTÆ SVNT ALIÆ
Orationes ab illius obitu recitatæ publicè
in Academia VVitebergensi.

Cum Gratia & Priuilegio ad
annos quindecim.

VVITEBERGÆ.
ANNO   M. D. LXV.

1566

Brenz, Johannes, 1499-1570.

IN SCRIPTVM APOSTOLI ET EVANGELISTAE MATTHAEI. DE REBVS GESTIS Domini nostri Jesu Christi. Commentarius.

TVBINGAE, Apud viduam Vlrici Morhardi. M.D.LXVI.

[12], 749 p. ; 32 cm. (fol. in 6s) Signatures: *, A-Z, Aa-Zz, Aaa-Qqq^6, Rrr^3; [*] unsigned, *1b, *6b blank, Bb4 missigned "4Bb", Gg4, Zz4 unsigned.

At the foot of the title page is a former owner's donation inscription to the, "Templo Tenobachiensi (?) ad SS. Trinit," signed "L. Georgius Weissius, Leucopetra'us" and dated, "Cal. Jan. A[nn]o 1692."

VD 16, B 7773; OCLC: 28912340.

J. Brenz spent the last years of his life as a Lutheran pastor in Württemberg, advising the count in religious policy and writing Biblical commentaries. This commentary on the Gospel of Matthew was printed four years before Brenz's death. This is the first printing of the work.

1566
Bren

Camerarius, Joachim, 1500-1574.

DE PHILIPPI MELANCHTHONIS ORTV, TOTIVS VITAE CVRRICVLO ET
MORTE, IMPLICATA RERVM MEMORABILIVM TEMPORIS ILLIVS
HOminumque mentione atque indicio, cum expositionis serie cohaerentium: ...
LIPSIAE, Excudebat Ernestus Voegelin Constantiensis. ANNO 1566.

10 leaves., 419, [1], 420-423, [17] p. ; 20 cm. (8vo) Signatures: A-Z^8, a-e^8, f^7; [A] unsigned, F7b blank.

Pitts Theology Library owns two copies of this book. The second copy is bound in blind-stamped bleached pigskin over paper boards.

In the first copy are two bookplates of former owners: "Bibl. Hammer Stockholm," and "D.G.V-B" in geometric design suggesting an arrow and the letters Z W. There are some manuscript marginalia in the text. The second copy was formerly in the Stewart collection, #4057. There is also a bookplate of Charles James Blomfield, Bishop of London.

Adams, C-420; BM STC German, p. 176; VD 16, C 502; OCLC: 06166618.

Camerarius was the first biographer of Melanchthon. He had been Melanchthon's personal friend and theological companion for thirty-eight years, and it is from this intimate concord that he was to write with authority and conviction about his friend.

1566
Came

Flacius Illyricus, Matthias, 1520-1575.

DE TRANSLATIONE IMPERII ROMANI AD GERMANOS. Item DE ELEC-
TIONE EPISCOPOrum, quòd aequè ad plebem pertineat.

BASILEAE [Petrum Pernam] 1566.

2 pts. bd. as 1 v. ([64], 271, [1], [8], 17-398] p.) ; 17 cm. (8vo).

This volume was bound in blind-stamped, bleached pigskin over paper boards and is signed by Frobenius Hempel, a Wittenberg binder. This copy also includes L. Valla's *De falso credito et ementita Constantini danatio Declamatio* with U. von Hutten's preface. The cover is dated 1582 and has the initials "I.Z.C."

There is a faded former ownership mark on the inside, upper cover, "Johan Murin?" dated 1628, as well as a bibliographical note on the upper flyleaf above a faded stamp. On the recto of the upper flyleaf is a manuscript index. There is an old ownership entry on the title page in ink, only partly legible, and dated 1687.

Adams, F-561;   BM STC German, p. 305;   Preger, II, p. 564;   VD 16, F 1503 and L 1249;   OCLC: 25489443.

In this volume Flacius details how secular authority was transferred from the declining Roman Empire to the Germans. He takes pains to show that the claims of popes and bishops to temporal power were unfounded and unjustified. He quotes extensively from earlier historians and source materials. Included as Part II of this work are reprints of Lupold von Bebenberg's "On Roman Laws," and Ulrich von Hutten's edition of Lorenzo Valla's work on the false Donation of Constantine, together with other source materials on the same subjects. This is the first printing of the work.

1566
Flac A

Flacius Illyricus, Matthias, 1520-1575.

REFVTATIO INVECTIVAE BRVNI CONTRA CENturias Historica Ecclesiasticae: in qua simul recitantur amplius 100 Historiae, maximiq[ue] momenti Papistarum mendacia.

BASILEAE, EX OFFICINA IOANnem Oporinum, Anno Salutis M.D.LXVI, Mense Iunio.

280, [19] p. ; 23 cm. (4to) Signatures: a-z^4, A-N^4, O^6; [a] unsigned; O6b blank.

There is a former ownership signature of "Stephanus Baluzius Tutelensis." on the title page.

Pegg, Bibliotheca, 465; Preger, II, p. 564; VD 16, F 1475; OCLC: 18697347.

The ecclesiastical history of Flacius Illyricus aroused a strong Catholic response. C. Brunus, a Catholic lawyer, wrote an especially harsh criticism of it. Flacius here points out over one hundred errors in Brunus' work.

1566
Flac

REFVTATIO
INVECTIVÆ BRVNI CONTRA CEN-
turias Hiftoriæ Ecclefiafticæ: in qua fimul recitantur amplius 100 Hiftorica, maximiǫ momenti Papiftarum mendacia:
Authore

MATTHIA FLACIO
ILLYRICO.

ACCESSERVNT & alij Libelli diuerforum Scriptorum, tum ad confirmationem illarum narrationum,
tum alioqui præfens inftitutum comprimis fa-
cientes: Quorum Catalogum poft Præfa-
tionem reperies.

BASILEAE, PER IOAN-
nem Oporinum.

Stephanus Baluzius Tutelensis.

Mathesius, Johann, 1504-1565.

Historien, Von des Ehrwirdigen in Gott Seligen thewren Manns Gottes, Doctoris Martini Luthers, anfang, lehr, leben vnd sterben.

Nürnberg, [Ulrich Neuber] M.D.LXVI.

[8], ccxxv, [1] leaves ; 22 cm. (4to) Signatures: [Roman] A-B^4, [Gothic] A-3K^4, 3L^2; [Roman[A]] unsigned, [Roman] A1b, [Gothic] 3L2b blank.

There is a former ownership mark on the inside upper cover dated, "A. Heusinger, 1772," as well as one on the title page, "Joh: Schnabell Mahler..." dated "a[nn]o [17?]69."

VD 16, M 1490 (under Matthesius, Johannes); OCLC: 11992322.

J. Mathesius was the Reformer of Joachimsthal and a powerful Lutheran preacher. In this series of sermons he presents the first full-length biography of Luther. This is the first printing of the work.

1566
Math

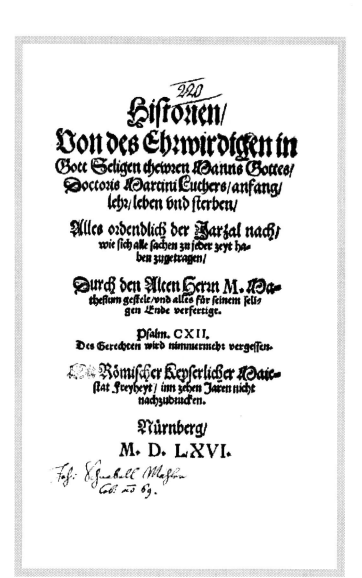

Melanchthon, Philipp, 1497-1560.

ETHICAE DOCTRINAE ELEMENTA, ET ENARRATIO LIBRI QVINTI ETHI-
CORVM. ADDITAE SVNT QVAESTIONES de Iuramentis, de Excommunicatione,
& de alijs quibusdam materijs.

VITEBERGAE [Johannes Crato] ANNO M.D.LXVI.

[16], 302 p. ; 17 cm. (8vo) Signatures: A-T^8, V^7; [A] unsigned.

This is the first item in a bound collection, bound in blind-stamped, bleached pigskin over wooden boards, clasps intact.

There is an inscription on the recto of the upper flyleaf in Greek which are quotes from Gregory of Nazianus, Ep. 60, and Socrates in a sixteenth or seventeenth century hand. There are also manuscript marginalia in the text.

VD 16, M 3299; OCLC: 12791230.

Melanchthon wrote, translated, and commented on the Ethics and Physics of Aristotle in his capacity as Greek professor at Wittenberg. Both volumes included here were standard Wittenberg textbooks and were printed many times after his death, their texts remaining for the most part exactly as he had left them. The coat-of-arms on the title page is that of Melanchthon.

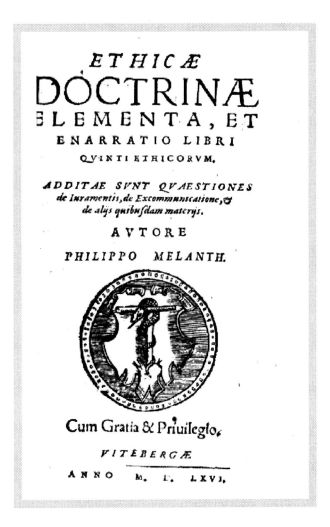

1566
Mela: 1

Schwenckfeld, Caspar, 1489-1561.

Epistolar, Des Edlen, von Gott hochbegnadete[n] theuwren Man[n]s Caspar Schwenck-feldts von Ossing.

[Frankfurt am Main, s.n.] 1566.

[8], XXVII, [1], 880, [82] p. ; 34 cm. (fol. in 6s) Signatures: A^4, B^6, C^8, 2A-2C^6, D-Z^6, a-z^6, 2A-3K^6, 3L^8; [A] unsigned, P3 missigned "O3", C8b, 3L7b, 3L8a-b blanks.

This copy is bound in blind-stamped, bleached pigskin over wooden boards, clasps missing.

There is a former ownership stamp on the title page reading, "Dupl. E Bibl. Reg. Regio(?)," as well as "Consistorium" written in ink. On the verso of the title page is a former ownership stamp reading, "Bibliotheca Regiomo...(?)."

The title page is printed in red and black.

Adams, S-746; Corpus Schwenckfeldianorum, 2, p. 183; VD 16, S 4831; OCLC: 13798395.

After the first volume of Schwenckfeld's collected works had appeared, A. Reissner and J. Heid von Duan joined J. Held von Tieffenau in the project. This is the first volume of the correspondence series produced by this group of editors.

1566
Schw
(OS)

Stössel, Johann.

APOLOGIA.

IENAE, Ex Officina Donati Ritzenhaini, Anno Christi, M.D.LXVI.

[22] p. ; 22 cm. (4to) Signatures: A-B^4, C^3; [A] unsigned, A1b blank.

This is the third item bound with Matthias Flacius Illyricus' *DISPVTATIO DE ORIGINALI PECCATO ET LIBERO ARBITRIO*, [S.l. : s.n.] Anno M.D.LXII.

OCLC: 28005595.

J. Stössel was a student at Wittenberg where he earned the M.A. in 1549. He became a Gnesio-Lutheran during his time as Court Preacher in Weimar. He defended his stern orthodoxy in this Apology. Later, however, he tried to bring about reconciliation with those theologians he had earlier opposed. He later was forced to resign his post on the theology faculty at Jena in 1567 on account of his views.

1562
Flac A: 3

APOLOGIA
D. IOANNIS STOSSELII,
OPPOSITA SOPHISTICIS ET FRI-
uolis cauillationibus quorundam censorum , in Comitatu
Mansfeldensi, qui ambitione & odio accensi, potentiam &
autoritatem reformandi alienas Ecclesias arroganter si-
bi sumunt, & prætextu puritatis doctrinæ, & glo-
riæ Dei, ad nouas seditiones, aut distractio-
nes sæuiores in Ecclesia Christi
clasßicum canunt.

1. Corinth. 4.
Ego verò nihil facio à vobis iudicari, vel ab humano die,
Dominus est, qui verè & iustè de me sententiam laturus
est.

Esaie 9.
Vnusquisq, deuorat carnem brachij sui, Manasse Ephra-
im, & Ephraim Manassen.

Galat. 5.
Qui conturbat vos, iudicium portabit, quisquis est.

Prouerb. 18.
Iustus in principio accusator est sui, postea inquirit in alios,
I E N Æ, Ex Officina Donati Ritzenhaini,
Anno Christi, M. D. LXVI.

Westphal, Joachim, 1510?-1574.

ANNOTATIONES IN IOHANNIS STOSSELII MODVM AGENDI, ET BREVIS CONFVTATIO Calumniarum, quibus falso nominatam Apologiam suam repleuit.

ISLEBII. Excudebat Vrbanus Gubisius. ANNO M.D.LXVI.

[52] p. ; 22 cm. (4to) Signatures: A-F⁴, G²; [A] unsigned.

This is the fourth item bound with Matthias Flacius Illyricus' *DISPVTATIO DE ORIGINALI PECCATO ET LIBERO ARBITRIO*, [S.l. : s.n.] Anno M.D.LXII.

OCLC: 28006948.

In this work Westphal criticizes Stössel's Apologia. Both men were Gnesio-Lutherans, so their conflict was over details and method rather than broad theological positions.

1562
Flac A: 4

ANNOTATIONES

IN IOHANNIS

STOSSELII MODVM AGENDI,
ET BREVIS CONFVTATIO
Calumniarum, quibus falso nominatam Apologiam suam
repleuit.

*Per Theologum quendam in Saxo-
nia inferiori.*

PSAL: XCIIII.

*Non derelinquet IEHOVA populum suum, & haere-
ditatem suam non derelinquet.
Nam tandem vsq; ad iustitiam, reuertetur iudicium, &
post illam omnes recti corde.*

*ISLEBII.
Excudebat Vrbanus Gubisius.*

ANNO M. D. LXVI

1567

Irenaeus, Saint, 130?-200?

OPVS ERVDITISSIMVM DIVI IRENAEI EPISCOPI LVGDVNENSIS, IN QVIN-QVE libros digestum ...

PARISIIS, Apud Audoënum Paruum, sub intersignio Lilij aurei, via ad diuum Iacobum. 1567.

[577] p. ; 18 cm. (8vo) Signatures: *^{8}, A-2M^8; [*] unsigned, *8b blank.

There are old ownership marks in ink on the title page which read, "F(?). Laur.," "Silv. Phelan," and "J. Pmor. (?)"

Haeghen, II, p. 32; OCLC: 13020513.

St. Irenaeus was born in Asia Minor and served as Bishop of Lyons from 177 until his death. He wrote extensively against various heresies, especially Gnosticism. This work in five parts, or books, is Ireneaus' refutation of the heresies of his time. It was written in Greek and early translated into Latin. This edition was prepared by Erasmus of Rotterdam.

1567
Iren

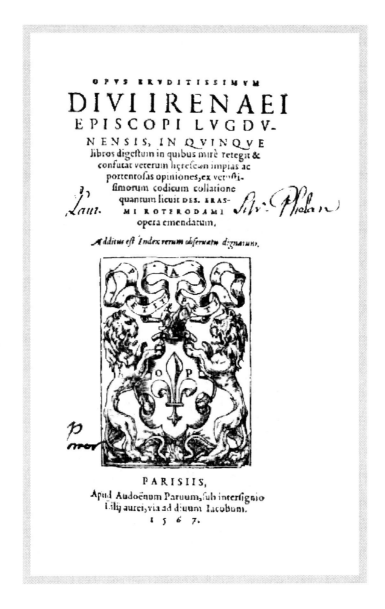

Luther, Martin, 1483-1546.

COLLOQVIA *Oder Tischreden Doctor Martini Lutheri, so er in vielen jaren, die Zeyt seines Lebens, gegen Gelehrten Leuchen, Auch hin und wider bey frembden Gesten, vnd seinen Tischgesellen geführet, ...*

Gedruckt zu Franckfurt am Mayn, &c. durch Peter Schmid [1567].

[12], 582 p., [18] leaves ; 35 cm. (fol in 6s) Signatures:)6,)(6, A-5H^6; M3 missigned iijM; 2K4 missigned K4, 3Y4 unsigned; C3 may have been in error, corrected in ink, 5E3, 4 missigned 4E3, 4, 5H6b blank.

This volume is bound in blind-stamped pigskin over wooden boards, clasps intact.

There is a former ownership mark of "Erika Meyer" on the inside, upper cover dated, "April 4, 1936." Also on the upper pastedown is the signature of "Pasche Stampeel Ao. 1570." There is a long manuscript note on the upper flyleaf the "Spruche von Luthern," as well as a former ownership mark which has been cut away leaving only a "Dr."

VD 16, L 6751; OCLC: 01825785.

J. Aurifaber became a secretary to Luther in 1545 and was with him when he died. He edited Luther's *Table Talk* for edifying purposes: he combined similar texts and took other liberties with the texts as well. The first printing appeared in 1566.

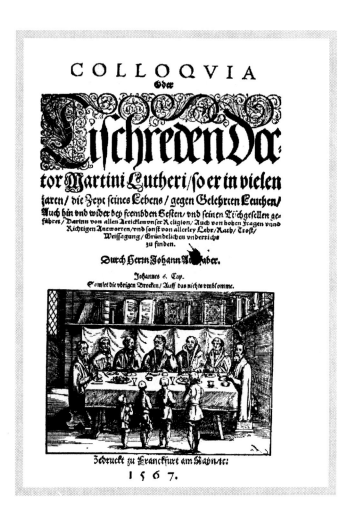

1567
Luth
(OS)

Sleidanus, Johannes, 1506-1556.

Ein bescheidener, historischer, vnschmälicher Bericht, an alle Churfürsten, Fürsten vnd Stende dess Reichs. Von des Bapstumbs auff vnd abnemen, desselben geschicklichheit, Vnd was endtlich darauss folgen mag.

[Strasbourg : J. Rihel] Getruckt im Jar 1567.

[76] p. ; 20 cm. (4to) Signatures: A-J^4, K^2; [A] unsigned, A1b blank, E3 missigned "iijE."

There are manuscript notes on the title page.

VD 16, S 6649 *(with place and printer as above);*   BM STC German, p. 639 *(no place indicated);*   OCLC: 30491487.

J. Sleidanus was a German historian whose history of the Protestant Reformation was so unbiased that it pleased neither side. This work is Sleidanus' call to the German princes to look to their own affairs and interests before concerning themselves with the affairs of the papacy. This work was first printed in 1542.

1567
Slei

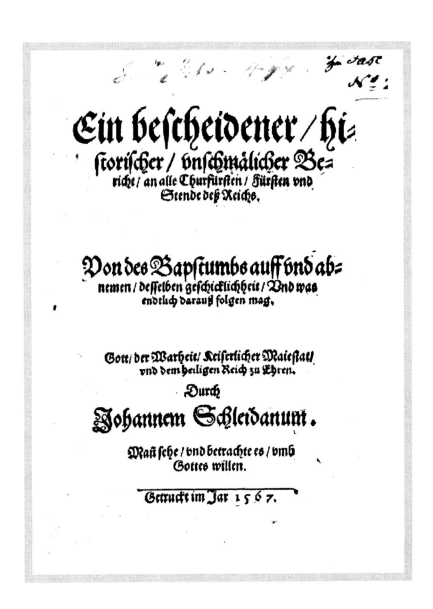

1568

Cochlaeus, Johannes, 1479-1552.

HISTORIA IOANNIS COCHLAEI DE ACTIS ET SCRIPTIS *Martini Lutheri Saxonis, Chronographice ex ordine ab Anno Domini M.D.XVII. usq[ue] ad Annum M.D.XLVI inclusiue, fideliter descripta, & ad posteros denarrata.*

COLONIAE Apud Theodorum Baumium, sub Sole aureo, M.D LXVIII.

[24], 363 [i.e. 339], [1] leaves ; 17 cm. (8vo) Signatures: [alpha]-[gamma]8, A-Z^8, a-t^8, v^4; [alpha]2 missigned "[alpha]3", [alpha]5 unsigned, [gamma]8b blank, M4 missigned, "M3."

This volume is bound in blind-stamped, bleached pigskin over paper boards and is dated 1570. The leather ties are missing.

There is a manuscript bibliographical note on the upper flyleaf. At the head of the title page there is a manuscript note, and at the foot is a note which reads, "Sum M. Under Öchsli Cenobite Partisan Friburgi Brogue Emptus anno 1570." On the verso of title page is an old ownership stamp, "Monsateri Petri Dom[us]" of the, "Monastery of Petershausen."

Adams, C-2271; BM STC German, p. 247; VD 16, C 4279; OCLC: 17022781.

J. Cochlaeus was one of Luther's most virulent critics. Although certainly not historically accurate, this biography set the tone for Catholic thought on Luther for many decades.

1568
Coch

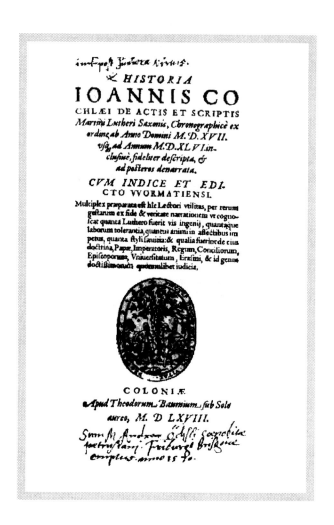

Gamerius, Hannard van, d. 1580.

SATYRAE DVAE: ILLOS, QVOS PAPISTAE LVTHERANOS APPELLANT, VERE ESSE ET SEMper fuisse CACHOLICOS: In quibus ostenditur, qualiter mundus uelit, falliq[ue] debeat: ...

[Munich : Adam Berg] M.D.LXVIII.

[38] p. ; 21 cm. (4to) Signatures: A-D⁴, E³; [A] unsigned, B4 signed, A1b blank.

Klaiber, 1274 (with place as:" [Antwerpen?]"); Kuczynski, 875; VD 16, G 352; OCLC: 29585503.

H. van Gamerius was born in Maastricht, The Netherlands. He became a poet laureate and professor in Ingolstadt University. He closed his life as Rector in Tongren, The Netherlands. He wrote several works against the Reformers, including these two satires against J. Andreae and on doctrinal controversies in the Lutheran community. This is the first printing of the work.

1568
Game

SATYRAE DVAE:

ILLOS, QVOS
PAPISTÆ LVTHERANOS
APPELLANT, VERE ESSE ET SEM-
per fuisse CACHOLICOS: In quibus ostenditur, qualiter mundus uelit, fallitq
debeat:

Item.

QVOMODO LVTHERA-
ni inter se de fidei & Augustanæ Confessionis articulis conueniant: con-
scriptæ, & in Pathmo
editæ.

Authore

HANNARDO GAMERIO Mosæo, Poëta
Laureato, Et Comite Palatino Cæsareo, olim in Academia Ingolstadiensi Profeßore, nunc autem veræ
Religionis, & verbi Dei pro-
motore.

M. D. LXVIII.

Pelt, Théodore Antoine, 1511-1584.

DISPVTATIO *De Sanctorum origine, canonizatione, cultu, inuocatione, reliquiis &
imaginibus, Anno sexagesimo octauo in Academia Ingolstadiana proposita, publice
q[ue] defensa.*

Ingolstadij ex Officina Vueissenhorniana. Anno 1568.

[56] p. ; 20 cm. (4to) Signatures: A-G⁴; G4b blank.

VD 16, P 1269 (under Pelt, Théodore Antoine); OCLC: 09420558.

Pelt was a Jesuit from the town of Pelte in the diocese of Liege. He taught theology at Ingolstadt from 1557 to 1574,
receiving his doctorate in 1562. He later retired to the Collegium at Augsburg, where he died in 1584. This work is an
academic dissertation on the cult of the saints.

1568
Pelt

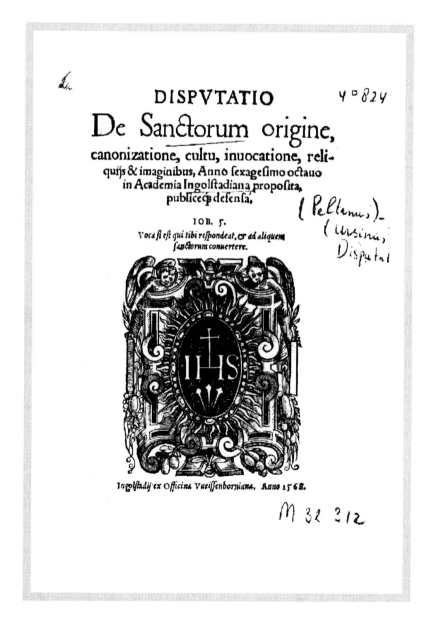

Ravesteyn, Josse, 1506?-1571?

CATHOLICAE CONFVTATIONIS PROPHANAE ILLIVS ET PESTILENTIS
CONFESSIONIS, *(quam Antuerpiensem Confessionem appellant Pseudoministri qui-
dam) contra varias & inanes cauillationes Mat. Flacci Illyrici,* APOLOGIA *seu
defensio.*

LOVANII, Apud Petrum Zangrium Tiletanum. 1568.

438, [1] leaves ; 17 cm. (8vo) Signatures: A-3H^8, 3I^7; [A] unsigned, M5 missigned "N5".

There is an old ownership mark in ink at the head of the title page which is partly broken away and illegible.

BM, v. 199, col. 192; Klaiber, 2654; OCLC: 23826255.

Ravesteyn was a Flemish Catholic theologian and Rector of the University of Louvain. This work condemns Flacius'
adaptation of the Augsburg Confession for the Protestants of Antwerp.

1568
Rave

1569

Bekentnis. Von der Rechtfertigung für Gott. vnd Von guten Wercken.

Gedruckt zu Jhena, durch Christian Rödinger. M.D.LXIX.

[43] p. ; 21 cm. (4to) Signatures: A-E^4, F^2; [A] unsigned, A1b blank.

This is the fifth item bound with *Gründtlicher, warhafftiger vnd bestendiger...*, Gedruckt zu Wolffenbüttel, durch Conradt Horn. M.D.LXX.

OCLC: 28833927.

Johann Wigand was a Gnesio-Lutheran professor at Jena with Flacius Illyricus. He also worked on the Magdeburg Centuries. This tract is on justification and good works.

1569
Etli: 5

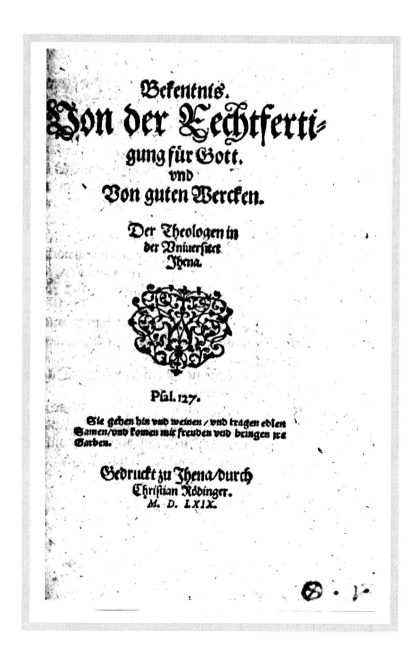

Braunschweig-Wolfenbüttel. Sovereigns (1568-1589 : Julius).

Kirchenordnung.

Gedruckt zu Wolffenbüttel , durch Cunrad Horn. M.D.LXIX.

[128], 442 [i.e. 448], [7] p., [1] p. of plates ; 22 cm. (4to) Signatures:)(^{4}, ()^4, A-O^4, a-z, Aa-Zz, Aaa-Lll^4; [)(], c2 unsigned, Aa2b, Lll4b blank.

This volume is bound in blind-stamped pigskin over wooden boards, clasps missing.

This volume was formerly in the Stewart collection, #7908. There are manuscript notes on the upper flyleaf, the inside lower cover, and manuscript marginalia in the text.

VD 16, B 7331;   OCLC: 26816927.

Julius of Braunschweig-Wolfenbüttel (1568-89) effected the Reformation in his territories. This church ordinance, prepared by Martin Chemnitz and Jacob Andreae, provided the foundation for the territorial church in the duchy. This is a rare example of the first printing. The text is defective: part of the Apostles' Creed is missing.

1569
Brau

Braunschweig-Wolfenbüttel. Sovereigns (1568-1589 : Julius).

Kirchenordnung.

Gedruckt zu Wulffenbüttel, durch Cunradt Horn. M.D.LXIX.

[136], 451 [464], [7] p. [1] p. of plates ; 21 cm. (4to) Signatures:)(^{4}, ()^4, A-P^4, a-z^4, Aa-Zz^4, Aaa-Mmm^4; a2 missigned "A2", b3 missigned "B2", X2 Mm2, Vv3, Eee3 unsigned.

This volume is bound in blind-stamped, bleached pigskin over paper boards.

This volume was formerly in the Stewart collection, #3723. There is a manuscript note on the upper flyleaf, at the foot of the title page, manuscript marginalia in the text, and manuscript notes on the verso of the last page and the inside lower cover.

BM STC German, p. 518; OCLC: 04154777.

This is the second printing of the church ordinance issued by Julius, Duke of Braunschweig-Wolfenbüttel. Like the earlier printing, this version also lacks a complete text of the Apostles' Creed.

1569
Brau A

Kirche[n] Gesäng, Aus dem Wittenbergischen, vnd allen andern den besten Gesang-büchern, so biss an hero hin vnd wider aussgangen, colligirt vnd gesamlet ...

Gedruckt zu Franckfurt am Mayn bey Joan. Wolffen. M.D.LXIX.

[4] leaves, 353 leaves of music, [7] leaves : ill. ; 40 cm.

This volume is bound in blind-stamped pigskin over wooden boards. The corner bosses are intact and the clasps have been repaired.

There are manuscript notes on both the inside upper and lower covers, the former having the Latin title and bibliographic notes. There are also twenty-five pages of manuscripts bound at the end containing hymns in Latin and German with notations, mostly from the sixteenth and seventeenth centuries.

VD 16, K 924-925;   OCLC: 11429315.

This hymn book sums up the first generation of Protestant hymnology; it also presents a beautiful specimen both of typography and book design.

1569
Kirc

Melanchthon, Philipp, 1497-1560.

LIBER CONTINENS CONTINVA SERIE EPISTOLAS PHILIPPI MELANCH-
THONIS SCRIPTAS ANNIS XXXVIII. AD Ioach. Camerar. Pabep[erg].

LIPSIAE, [s.n.] Absoluebantur haec Mense Octobri anno Christi Jesu, M.D.LXIX.

[40], 821, [3] p. ; 21 cm. (8vo) Signatures: [alpha]-[beta]8, [gamma]4, A-3D^8, 3E^4, 3F^8; [alpha] unsigned, 3F8 blank.

This volume is bound in blind-stamped, bleached pigskin over wooden boards. There are portraits of Melanchthon and Camerarius on the covers.

Adams, M-1213;   BM STC German, p. 608;   Jackson, 2136;   VD 16, M 3553;   OCLC: 06300795.

This is an edited collection of texts include 912 letters written by Melanchthon between 1522-60. The letters are not complete and may have been abridged or even censored.

1569
Mela

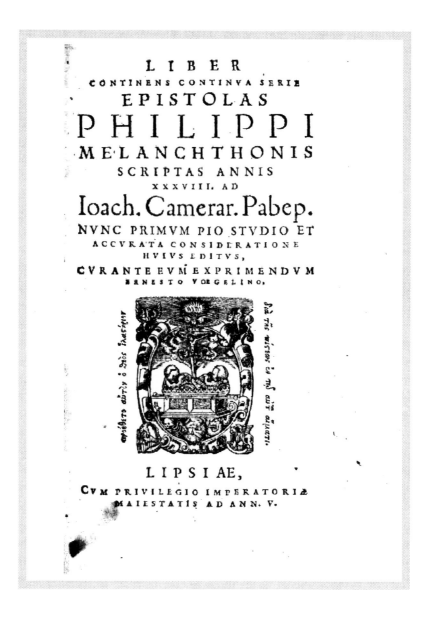

Saccus, Siegfridus, 1527-1596.

DE ACADEMICA PONTIFICIORVM DVBITATIONE IN NEGOCIO IVSTIFICA-TIONIS, quae omnem evertit FIDVCIAM nitentem certissima promissione diuina & meritis Iesu Christi. CAPITA LIBELLI VERSA PAGINA INVENIET pius Lector.

EXCVSVM A MATTHAEO GISEKEN TYPOGRAPHO MAGDEburgensi. ANNO 1569.

[414] p. ; 17 cm. (8vo) Signatures: A-Z^8, Aa-Bb^8, Cc^7; [A], R2 unsigned.

This volume is bound in blind-stamped, bleached pigskin over paper boards. The binding is by Frobenius Hempel for "H.W.G." and is dated, "1569."

There are manuscript notes on the inside upper cover and the upper flyleaf as well as the lower cover.

Adams, S-43; VD 16, S 1152; OCLC: 30339333.

S. Saccus was the first Lutheran cathedral preacher in Magdeburg. He took the position in 1567 after the Cathedral Chapter adopted the Augsburg Confession. Saccus had been a student in Magdeburg, then at Wittenberg and finally graduated from Jena. In 1554 he became co-rector of the School in Magdeburg, becoming the Rector in 1557 when Praetorius left. This volume refutes Catholic objections to the Lutheran tenet of Justification by Faith alone. This volume was bound in 1569 in Wittenberg by Frobenius Hempel for "H.W.G." Hempel's initials are in the front cover stamp on the right-hand side. Such well-preserved dated contemporary bindings are quite rare.

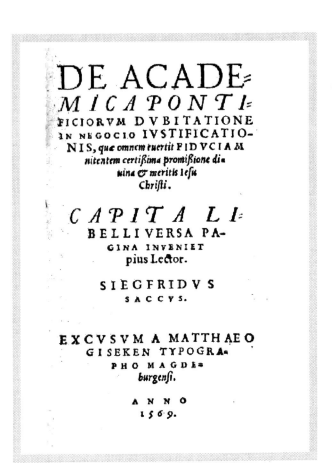

1569
Sacc

1570

BEKENTNIS Vom Freien Willen. So im Colloquio zu Altenburg, hat sollen vorbracht werden, von Fürstlichen Sechsischen Theologen.

Gedruckt zu Jhena, [Donat Richtzenhan] Anno 1570.

[103] p. ; 21 cm. (4to) Signatures: A-N^4; [A] unsigned, A1b, N4b blank: the 4th leaf is signed except for "N4," which is not.

This is the third item bound with *Gründtlicher, warhafftiger vnd bestendiger...*, Gedruckt zu Wolffenbüttel, durch Conradt Horn. M.D.LXX.

VD 16, B 1565; OCLC: 03963182.

The electoral Saxon theologians were supposed to present this *Confession on Free Will* at the Colloquy of Altenburg, but apparently did not do so, hence its publication as a separate tract here.

1570
Etli: 3

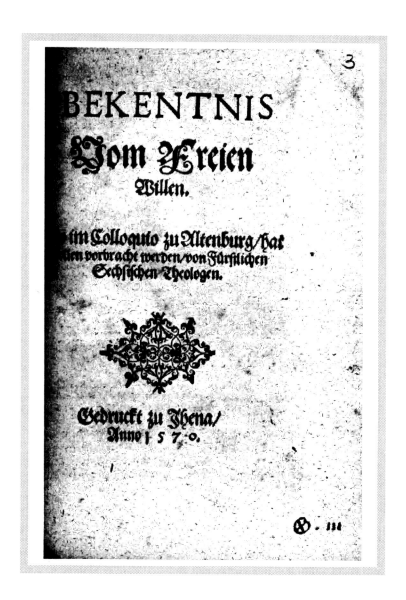

Bekentnis Von Fünff Streittigen Religions Artickeln.

Gedruckt zu Jhena, [Christian Rödinger] M.D.LXX.

[46] p. ; 20 cm. (4to) Signatures: A-E^4, F^3; [A] unsigned; A1b blank.

This is the sixth item bound with *Gründtlicher, warhafftiger vnd bestendiger...*, Gedruckt zu Wolffenbüttel, durch Conradt Horn. M.D.LXX.

VD 16, B 1571-1573 *(no further specification possible, but all 3 printings are attributed to "[Christian Rödinger]")*; OCLC: 18170358.

This tract is the University of Jena's adjudication against M. Flacius Illyricus' position on justification, among other things. Flacius and J. Wigand had been friends, but fell out over this issue.

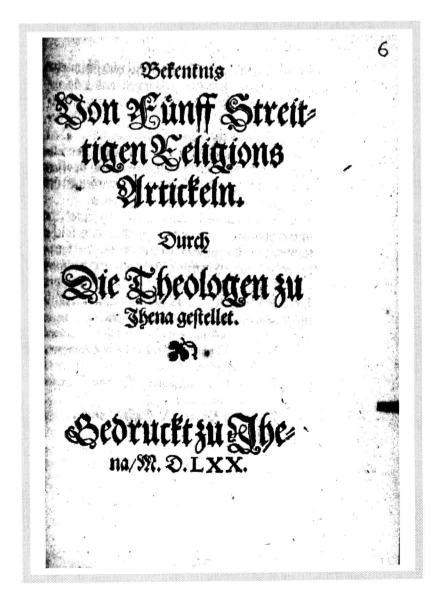

1570
Etli: 6

Coelestin, Johann Friedrich.

Von D. Johan Pfeffingers Vorrede, jtzt newlich ausgangen, die gegenwertigen streitigen Hendel, in der Religion belangend.

[Jena, Donat Richtzenhan] Gedruckt, Anno 1570.

[36] p. ; 21 cm. (4to) Signatures: A-D^4, E^2; [A] unsigned, A1b blank.

This is the fourth item bound with *Gründtlicher, warhafftiger vnd bestendiger...*, Gedruckt zu Wolffenbüttel, durch Conradt Horn. M.D.LXX.

OCLC: 28833906.

J. F. Coelestin was a Gnesio-Lutheran professor at Jena. This tract was written in opposition to J. Pfeffinger's preface to an edition of Luther's "Admonition to the Delegates at the Diet of Augsburg."

1570
Etli: 4

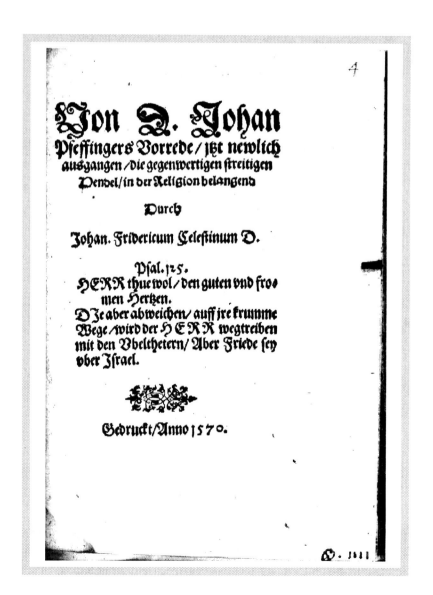

Crell, Paul, 1531-1579.

PROPOSITIONES THEOLOGICAE OPPOSITAE PRAESTIGIIS D. IOACHIMI MORLINI E.S. quibus deformare Ecclesias & Scholas harum regionum conatus est.
VVITEBERGAE Iohannes Schvvertell excudebat. 1570.

[31] p. ; 21 cm. (4to) Signatures: A-D⁴; [A], A2 unsigned, A1b, D4b blank.

This is the seventh item bound with *Gründtlicher, warhafftiger vnd bestendiger* ..., Gedruckt zu Wolffenbüttel, durch Conradt Horn. M.D.LXX.

Pegg, Bibliotheca, 224;   VD 16, C 5775;   OCLC: 28833969.

P. Crell was a professor of theology at Wittenberg. These theses are in opposition to positions taken by J. Mörlin, a one-time Wittenberg professor and controversialist. These theses attempt to explain the correct meaning of the proposition that good works are necessary in the process of repentance.

1570
Etli: 7

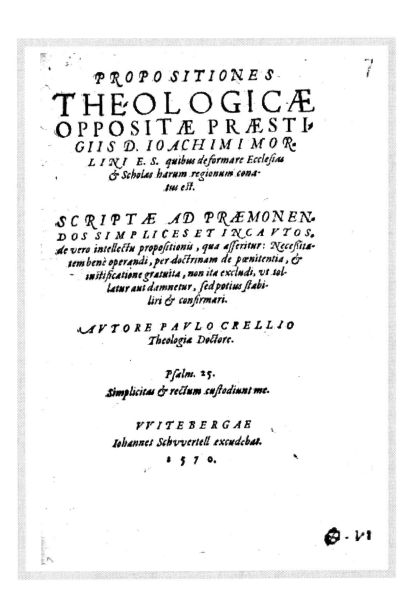

Der Psalter mit den Summarien.

Leipzig. Bey M. Ernesto Vögelin. 1570.

[590] p. ; 21 cm. (8vo) Signatures: A-2N^8, 2O^7; [A] unsigned, A1b blank, 2A3 missigned "A3".

This volume is bound in blind-stamped, bleached pigskin over wooden boards, clasp missing. It is dated, "1573." This copy is incomplete. All after p. [590] is wanting; which is apparently only the leaf with the colophon. This is supplied in facsimile from the copy in the Colgate-Rochester Theological Seminary Library.

This volume was formerly in the Beck Lutherana collection, #319. At the foot of the title page is a former ownership mark in ink: "Johann Albrecht Majer." and a faded manuscript note in the margin on the title page. There is a manuscript note on the inside lower cover referring to Penitential Psalms, 6, 36, 38, 51, 102, 130, and 143.

VD 16, B 333; OCLC: *18145941.*

This is a later printing of Luther's German Psalter. Of note are the page borders. Each page is enclosed in a frame. These are repeated in each gathering. Summaries of the Psalms are presented in smaller type at the beginning of each Psalm.

1570
Bibl

Gründtlicher, warhafftiger vnd bestendiger bericht: Von Christlicher Einigkeit der Theologen vnd Predicanten, so sich in einhelligem, rechtem, warhafftigem, vnd eigentlichem verstand, zu der Augspurgischen Confession, in Ober vnd Niedersachssen, sampt den Oberlendischen vnnd Schwebischen Kirchen bekennen.

Gedruckt zu Wolffenbüttel, durch Conradt Horn. M.D.LXX.

[178] p.; 21 cm. (4to) Signatures: a⁶, A-V⁴, X³; [A] unsigned, A1b blank; the fourth leaf is occasionally signed; S3-4 missigned "s3-4" respectively.

The first item in a bound collection, bound in blind-stamped, bleached pigskin over paper boards.

This was formerly in the Stewart collection, #2127. There is a manuscript table of contents for the bound collection on the verso of the upper flyleaf. There are manuscript marginalia in the text.

VD 16, A 2641 (under: "Andreae, Jakob, d.Ä.); OCLC: 28005825.

In 1569, a gathering of Saxon Lutheran theologians met in Zerbst to try to work out their theological differences. This book contains the report of their deliberations. This was a major step towards the Formula of Concord.

1570
Etli: 1

Heshusius, Tilemann.

EPISTOLA. D. TILEMANI HESHVSII Ad M. MATTHIAM FIACIVM ILLYRICVM De controuersia An peccatum Originis sit substantia.
IENAE IN OFFICINA HAEREDVM CHRISTIANI RHODII. Anno M.D.LXX.

[64] p. ; 21 cm. (4to) Signatures: A-G^4, H^3; [A] unsigned, A1b blank.

This is the ninth item bound with *Gründtlicher, warhafftiger vnd bestendiger...*, Gedruckt zu Wolffenbüttel, durch Conradt Horn. M.D.LXX.

VD 16, H 3034;   OCLC: 01224179.

T. Heshusius was an orthodox Lutheran theologian. He was a student of Melanchthon and taught rhetoric and dogmatics in Wittenberg for a time. This tract contains a Letter by Heshusius to Flacius on the issue of Original Sin.

1570
Etli: 9

Major, Georg, 1502-1574.

TESTAMENTVM.

Wittemberg. Gedruckt durch Hans Lufft. Anno M.D.LXX.

[15] p. ; 20 cm. (4to) Signatures: A-B⁴; [A] unsigned; A1b, B4b blank.

This is the eighth item bound with *Gründtlicher, warhafftiger vnd bestendiger ...*, Gedruckt zu Wolffenbüttel, durch Conradt Horn. M.D.LXX.

BM STC German, p. 606;   VD 16, M 2190-2192;   OCLC: 12299027.

In this *Testament*, the Wittenberg Dean Georg Major declares his adherence to the Augsburg Confession.

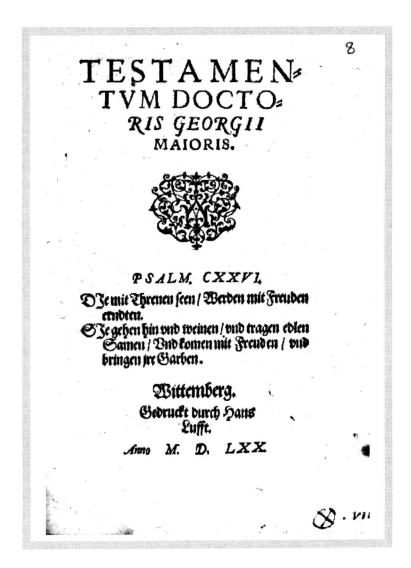

1570
Etli: 8

Melanchthon, Philipp, 1497-1560.

EPISTOLARVM.

VVITEBERGAE. Excvdebant Clemens Schleich & Anthonius Schöne. ANNO M.D.LXX.

2 v. bd. as 1 ([16], 524, [1], [12], [4], 590, [2] p.) ; 17 cm. (8vo) Signatures: Liber primus: A-Z^8, Aa-Kk^8, Ll^7; [A] unsigned, Ee4 missigned "EC4." Alter libelus: A-Z8, Aa-Pp8; [A] unsigned, A1b, Pp8b blank.

This volume is bound in blind-stamped, bleached pigskin over wooden boards, clasps missing.

This volume was formerly in the Stewart collection, #4056. There is a former ownership mark in ink on the front pastedown that is only partly legible. There are manuscript marginalia in the text and missigned leaves have been corrected in ink.

BM STC German, p. 608;   VD 16, M 3223-3224;   OCLC: 12243873.

This volume includes the second edition of the first volume of Melanchthon's collected letters, published in 1570, and the first edition of the second volume, published in 1574. K. Peucer, Melanchthon's son-in-law, edited this collection.

1570
Mela A

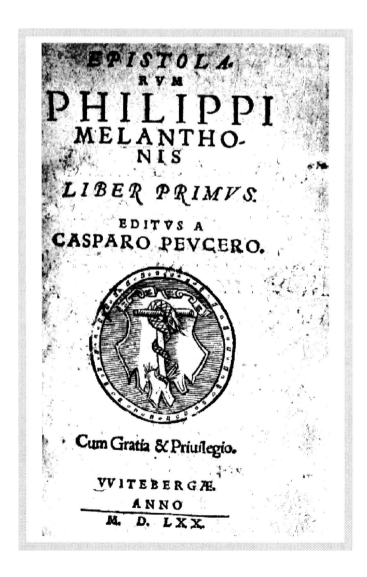

Melanchthon, Philipp, 1497-1560.

INITIA DOCTRINAE PHYSICAE, DICTATA IN ACADEMIA VVITEBERGENSI.

VITEBERGAE EXCVDEBAT IOHANNES CRATO, ANNO M.D.LXX.

[12], 363 [i.e. 393], [10] p. ; 17 cm. (8vo) Signatures: A-2C^8; [A] unsigned, O4 missigned "O3", 2C4 missigned "C4", 2C8 blank.

This is the second item bound with Philipp Melanchthon's *ETHICAE DOCTRINAE ELEMENTA ...,* VITEBERGAE [Johannes Crato] ANNO M.D.LXVI.

Hartfelder, 242; VD 16, M 3480; OCLC: 12791258.

This is Melanchthon's commentary on the Physics of Aristotle.

1566
Mela: 2

Melanchthon, Philipp, 1497-1560.

PHILIPPI MELANTHONIS ELEmentorum Rhetorices Libri duo.

BASILEAE, EX OFFIcina Oporiniana. Anno salutis humanae M.D.LXX, mense Augusto.

663 [i.e 664], [66] p. ; 18 cm. (8vo) Signatures: a-z^8, A-Y^8, Z^4; [a], l2, T4 unsigned, V2 missigned "V".

This volume was formerly in the Sunderland collection, #8333. There are manuscript former ownership marks on the title page.

Adams, M-1137 (Pitts copy lacks the folded table);   VD 16, M 3127;   OCLC: 25605705.

Martin Crusius was a Lutheran professor of Greek at the University of Tübingen. He translated the Augsburg Confession into Greek and sent a copy to the Patriarch of Constantinople. For a while he was also professor of rhetoric and poetry, during which time he issued this edition of the "Rhetoric" of Melanchthon. The work also includes letters and poems for study and a copious index.

1570
Mela

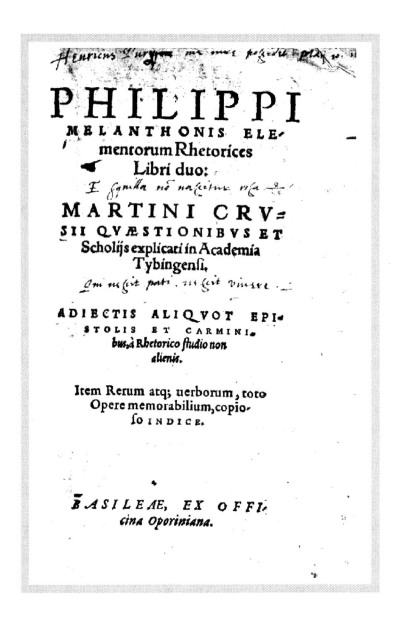

[Tes tou Huiou Theou Kaines Diathekes hapanta (romanized form)] = NOVVM TESTAMENTVM IESV CHRISTI FILII DEI, EX VERSIONE ERASMI, INNVMERIS IN LOCIS *ad Graecam veritatem, genuinumque sensum emendata.* GLOSSA COMPENDIARIA M. MATTHIAE *Flacii Illyrici Albonensis in nouum Testamentum.*

IMPRESSUM BASILEAE PER PETRVM PERNAM ET Theobaldum Dietrich, ANNO M.D.LXX.

[46], 1394 [i.e. 1398], [41] p. ; 36 cm. (fol. in 6s & 8s) Signatures: $*$-3$*^6$, 4$*^4$, A-Q^6, R^8, S-Z^6, 2A- 2Z^6, ^{2}2A-^{2}2D^6, ^{2}2E^5, a-z^6, 2A-2Z^6, 32A-32E^6, 22F-22S^6, 22T^8, 22V-22X^6, 22Y^8; 2D4, 2E2, 2E3 missigned "D4," "2E3", "E3," respectively; [$*$] unsigned.

This copy is bound in blind-stamped pigskin over wooden boards, dated, "1570," and has the initials, "C.B.M." The clasps are missing.

On the inside front flyleaf is the former ownership mark that reads, "Fr. H. Geissler I. Class: Gymn: Zittav: April 1821." On the title page the former ownership mark, "Ex Libris Scherbarti," has been crossed out, and at the foot is the inscription reading, "Ionasium. Northuso-Cheniseus (?) est h[uj]us L[ibri] p[osessor] a[nn]o 1626 past[or] in Capellendorff." There are manuscript marginalia in the text.

Darlow-Moule, 4636; VD 16, B 4214; OCLC: 08872219.

One of the areas in which M. Flacius Illyricus made a significant contribution to Christian scholarship is that of hermeneutics. He emphasized study of the original biblical languages to facilitate the interpretation of texts. This edition of the New Testament includes his own commentaries as well as Erasmus' amended Greek testament and Latin translation.

ΤΗΣ ΤΟΥ ΥΙΟΥ ΘΕΟΥ
ΚΑΙΝΗΣ ΔΙΑΘΗΚΗΣ ΑΠΑΝΤΑ.

NOVVM TESTAMENTVM
IESV CHRISTI FILII DEI, EX VERSIO-
NE ERASMI, INNVMERIS IN LOCIS
ad Græcam veritatem, genuinumque
sensum emendata.

GLOSSA COMPENDIARIA M. MATTHIAE
Flacij Illyrici Albonensis in nouum Testamentum.

Cum multiplici indice tum ipsius sacri Textus, tum etiam glossæ.

Quid prætereafit in commodum Lectoris in hac editione præstitum,
sequens nuncupatoria præfatio indicabit.

BASILEAE
ANNO M. D. LXX.

Thomas Aquinas, Saint, 1225?-1274.

D. THOMAE AQVINATIS DOCTORIS ANGELICI, COMPLECTENS Primam partem Summae Theologiae Cum Commentarijs R.D.D. Thomae de Vio, Caietani, Cardinalis. S. Sixti. Et expositionem eiusdem D. Tho. in librum Beati Dionysii de Divinis Nominibus.

Romae [Apud Iulium Accoltum], M.D.LXX.

[16] 363, 47 leaves ; 38 cm. (fol. in 8s) Signatures: [dagger]^6, [*]^8, A-2Y^8, 2Z^4, ^{2}A-^{2}f^8; [dagger] unsigned, 2Z4, 2Fb blank.

This volume is bound in blind-stamped pigskin over wooden boards, clasps missing.

This volume was formerly in the Stewart collection, #6667. There is a former ownership mark on the title page.

Adams, A-1395;   OCLC: 28006128.

T. de Vio Cajetan became Apostolic Delegate to Germany in 1517. He helped get Charles V elected Holy Roman Emperor in 1519. He tried unsuccessfully to obtain Luther's obedience to the Catholic Church. This volume includes Part I of the Summa Theologica and was annotated in 1511.

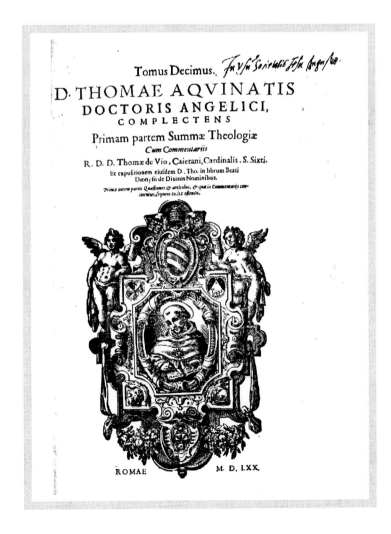

Vergil, Polydore, 1470?-1555.

An abridgemente of the Notable worke of Polidore Virgile.

Imprinted at London by Ihon Tisdale dwelling in Knightriders streate, neare to the Quenes wardrop. [ca. 1570].

[8], CLII, [14] + leaves ; 14 cm. (8vo) Signatures: A^8, a-v^8, x^6+ ; [A], e5, f5, k4, 5, l5, m3, n4, q5, s5, t5, v5 unsigned, A1b, A8b, t8b blank, i1-4 missigned "I1-4" respectively, l1-4 missigned "L1-4" respectively.

There are errors in foliation: LXV for LXIII, LXXXIII for LXXXVIII, CXXIX for XCCCIII, CXXXV for CLI and CLII.

Pasted onto the inside upper cover is an old armorial bookplate with a library shelf number, but without a name of the former owner. However, according to a penciled note on the lower inside cover, it is possibly that of the "late Duke of Sussex." Also on the inside upper cover is a bookseller's label, "Sold by Thomas Baker 1 Soho Square, 1 London."

OCLC: 06365599.

This work of P. Vergil, *De inventoribus rerum*, was translated into English by Thomas Langley in 1545.

1570
Verg A

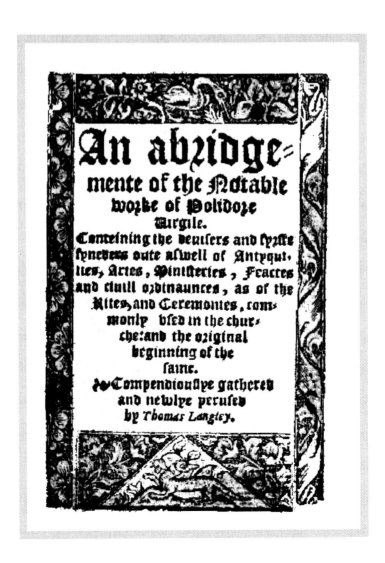

Vergil, Polydore, 1470?-1555.

*POLYDORI VERGILII VRBINATIS ANGLICAE HISTORIAE LIBRI VIGIN-
TISEPTEM. Ab ipso autore postremum iam recogniti, adq; amussim, salua tamen
historiae veritate, expoliti.*

BASILEAE, APVD THOMAM GVARINVM, ANNO M.D.LXX.

1 p. of leaves 691, [39] p. ; 33 cm. (fol. in 6s) Signatures: a-z^6, A-2L^6, 2M^4, [alpha]-[gamma]^6, chi^2.

This volume is bound in vellum, blind-stamped and with the initials "E G."

This volume was formerly in the Stewart collection, #7077.

Adams, V-452; BM STC German, p. 889; OCLC: 04284263.

P. Vergil was an English antiquary and historian of Italian descent, born in Urbino and educated in Bologna. His book on the discoverers, or originators, of things is the second work he published. It was first printed in Latin in 1499 and was translated into German, Italian, and English. In 1502, he came to England as Deputy Collector of Peter's pence, a church tax, for Cardinal Guido Ubaldo. From 1505-1533 he worked on his History of England. His book of Latin proverbs, or Adagia, was the first of its kind to be printed.

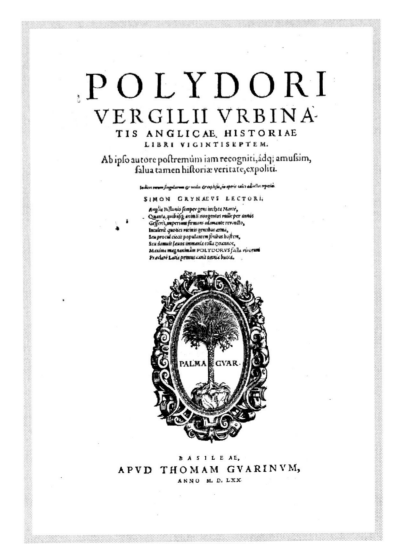

1570
Verg

Warhafftiger bericht vnd kurtze Warnung.

Gedruckt zu Wittemberg, durch Peter Seitz. 1570.

[46] p. ; 21 cm. (4to) Signatures: A-E⁴, F³; [A] unsigned, A1b blank.

This is the second item bound with *Gründtlicher, warhafftiger vnd bestendiger...*, Gedruckt zu Wolffenbüttel, durch Conradt Horn. M.D.LXX.

Hohenemser, 3732; OCLC: 28006900.

The Colloquy of Altenburg (1568-1569) was an unsuccessful attempt to reconcile the differences between Philippist and Gnesio-Lutherans. This tract is an attack on the recently published "acts" of the Colloquy of Altenburg. The tract is by theologians from the Philippist Universities of Wittenberg and Leipzig.

1570
Etli: 2

1571

Contarini, Gasparo, 1484-1542.

GASPARIS CONTARENI CARDINALIS OPERA.

PARISIIS. Apud Sebastianum Niuellium, sub Ciconiis in via Iacobaea. 1571.

[39], 627, [23] p. ; 39 cm. (fol. in 6s) Signatures: a^4, b-c^6, d^4, A-2Z^6, ^{2}2A- ^{2}2H^6, ^{2}2I^4; [a] unsigned, a4b, d4b, H4, I1b, V5b, Z1b, 2Y5b, ^{2}2I4b blank, d2 missigned "p2."

Adams, C-2560;   OCLC: 14084383.

This volume includes the complete works of G. Contarini. He was picked by Pope Paul III to head the Reform Committee in 1536. In 1537, they presented a frank report to the Pope that was widely circulated in both Protestant and Catholic circles. In 1541, Contarini tried unsuccessfully at the Colloquy of Regensburg to effect a Protestant-Catholic compromise on religious matters.

1571
Cont

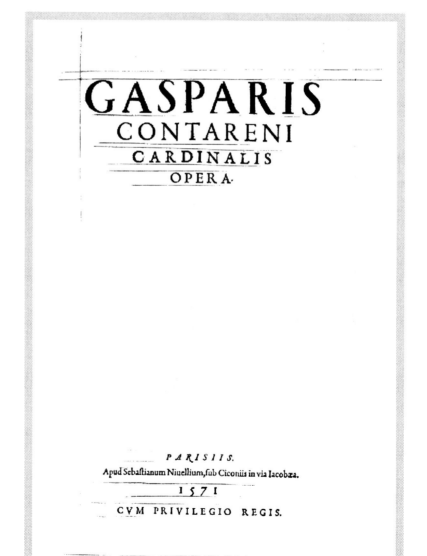

GASPARIS
CONTARENI
CARDINALIS
OPERA.

PARISIIS.
Apud Sebastianum Niuellium, sub Ciconiis in via Iacobæa.
1571
CVM PRIVILEGIO REGIS.

DE PECCATO ORIGINIS SCRIPTA QVAEDAM contra Manichaeorum delirium.
Quod Peccatum Originis sit Substantia.

Ienae Donatus Ritzenhan typis excussit, Anno reparatae salutis 1571.

[232] p. ; 17 cm. (8vo) Signatures: A-O^8, P^4; [A], B2, K3 unsigned, A1b blank.

This is the fourth item bound with P. Melanchthon's *IN DANIELEM PROPHETAM Commentarius.* VITEBERGAE. (Per Iohannem Lufft), Anno 1543.

VD 16, P 1093; OCLC: *28905704.*

A collection of tracts on original sin by J. Wigand, T. Heshusius, J. Mörlin, and M. Chemnitz. The focus of most of the work is the teachings of M. Flacius Illyricus on this subject. This is the first printing of the work.

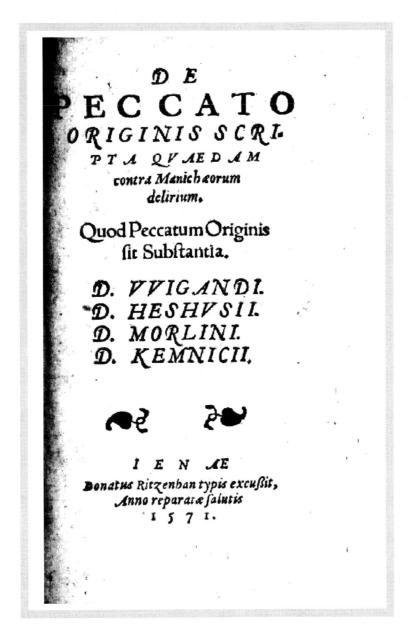

1543
Mela B: 4

Flacius Illyricus, Matthias, 1520-1575.

ORTHODOXA CONFESSIO.

[S.l. : s.n.] Anno M.D.LXXI.

599 p.; 18 cm. (8vo) Signatures: -8, a-z^8, A-O^8, p^4.

This copy is bound in blind-stamped pigskin over wooden boards, one clasp intact.

There is a small note on the inside upper cover, and scattered marginalia in the text.

Pegg, Bibliotheca, 464;   Preger, II, p. 568;   VD 16, F 1463;   OCLC: 18801326.

In 1567, Flacius Illyricus added a tract on original sin to the current edition of his *Clavis Scripturae Sacrae* ("Key to the Holy Scriptures"). This tract aroused the enmity of several of his former friends, notably J. Mörlin, T. Heshusius, and J. Wigand, and re-ignited the controversy over original sin that ultimately led Flacius to write this *Orthodox confession on original sin*. The prioress Catharina von Meerfeld had taken him into her cloister in Frankfurt-am-Main, and there he ended his days in 1575, as a hunted theologian, nearly friendless.

1571
Flac

Polygranus, Franciscus.

ASSERTIONES QVORVNDAM ECCLESIAE DOGMATVM, CVM AB ALIIS
quondam, tum a Lutherana factione denuo in dubium reuocatorum.

COLONIAE AGRIPPINAE Apud Ioannem Birckmannum. Anno M.D.LXXI.

[12], 283 [i.e. 282], [33] p. ; 16 cm. (8vo) Signatures: $*^8$, $2*^4$, A-Z, Aa-Qq^8, Rr^3; * unsigned, *1b, 2*4b, Rr3b blank, C3 missigned "B3".

This volume was formerly in the Stewart collection, #4854. Pasted onto the upper pastedown is the former owner's label: "Charles Goddard, D.D. Archdeacon of Lincoln." There is a possible former ownership mark that has been inked out.

Adams, P-1818; Klaiber, 2588; VD 16, P 4105; OCLC: 29768563.

F. Polygranus was a Franciscan who wrote several books of sermons. Here he presents a refutation of old errors that the Lutherans have resurrected.

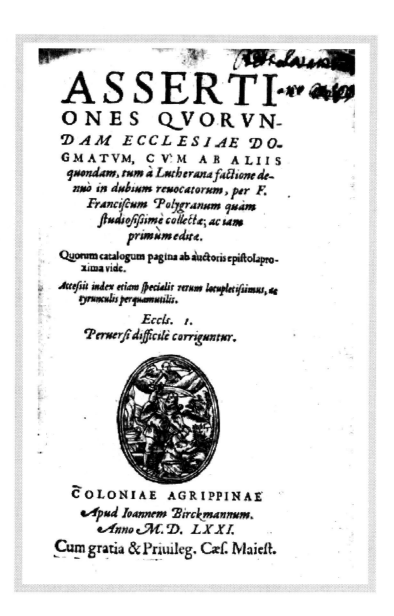

1571
Poly

1572

Erasmus, Desiderius, 1466?-1536.

ADAGIORVM DES. ERASMI ROTERODAMI.

PARISIIS, Apud Michaelem Sonnium, via Iacobaea, sub Scuto Basiliensi. M.D.LXXII.

[48] p., 1360 columns ; 35 cm. (fol. in 6s) Signatures: a[6], e[6], i[6], o[6], u[5], a-z[6], Aa-Zz[6], 2A-2I[6], 2K[5]; [a], d4, Qq4 unsigned, h2 missigned "g2", r4 missigned g4.

The colophon is bound before the title page in this copy.

There is a long manuscript bibliographical note on the verso of the title page.

Haeghen, I, p. 5-6, (which says it was printed in 1570, following colophon, whereas the title page has 1572);   OCLC: 12982851.

This is another edition of Erasmus' proverbs, expurgated in accordance with the decrees of the Council of Trent. It also contains material gathered from other sources.

1572
Eras
(OS)

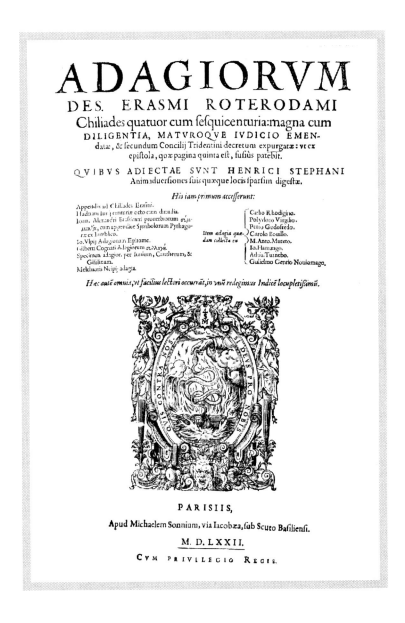

Luther, Martin, 1483-1546.

Reuerendi Viri D. MARTINI LVTERI, MISSA AD THEOLOGOS NORIMBER-GENSES (orta quadam inter ipsos dissensione) PIA ET VERE Apostolica EPISTOLA: QVEMADMODVM TVM AD exemplum illius eo tempore, Vir dignitate & autoritate & studio pietatis excellens ascripsit.

EXPRESSA LIPSIAE CHAracteribus VOEGELIANIS. 1572.

[23] p. ; 16 cm. (8vo) Signatures: A-C^8; [A] unsigned, A1b, C8b blank.

VD 16, L 5464; WA Br, 6, 98, Nr. 1818; OCLC: 21465607.

Luther's letter to J. Brenz and the theologians at Nuremberg is actually a postscript to a letter of Melanchthon written in the middle of May 1531.

1572
Luth

Reuerendi Viri
D. M A R T I N I.
L·V T E R I,
MISSA AD THEOLOGOS
NORIMBERGENSES (orta
quadam inter ipsos diſſenſione)
PIA ET VERE
Apoſtolica
EPISTOLA:

QVEMADMODVM TVM AD·
exemplum illius eo tempore , Vir dignitate & autoritate & ſtudio pietatis
excellens aſcripſit.

CVM APPENDICE
NON SPERNEN-
DA.

EXPRESSA LIPSIÆ CHA-
racteribus VOEGELIANIS.

1 5 7 2.

1574

Barschamp, Ivo.

Sterbens Kunst, Disputatio oder Gesprech, zwischen einem krancken Menschen, vnd dem Versucher. Sampt etlichen Christlichen Gebetlein, Gesunden vnd Krancken, nützlich vnd tröstlich zu lesen.

Bresslaw. [durch Crispinum Scharffenberg] M.D.LXXV.

[62] p. ; 15 cm. (8vo) Signatures: A-C^8, D^4; [A] unsigned, A1b blank, only the first leaf in each gathering is signed.

This volume is bound in blind-stamped calf over paper boards.

There is a manuscript note on the inside lower cover reading, "C.C.C.C.C. G. L. Cheminicensis."

OCLC: 28005961.

I. Barschamp was a professor in the University of Jena in 1561, when the first printing of this "Disputation or Dialogue between a sick man and the tempter" took place. This "Art of Dying" was quite popular. There were at least ten printings in German before 1600. This book also includes prayers and meditations for sick persons and healthy ones.

1574
Savo: 3

Kurtz Bekentnis vnd Artickel vom heiligen Abendmal des Leibs vnd Bluts Christi.
Gedruckt zu Wittenberg, durch Hans Lufft. 1574.

[84] p. ; 19 cm. (4to) Signatures: A-K^4, L^2.

BM STC German, p. 864 (under: "Torgau. Landtag"); Hohenemser, 3739; VD 16, K 2821 or 2822 (no further specification possible); OCLC: 08291340.

The struggle to reunite the Lutheran factions was long and fierce. Through various means, compromises were achieved. This volume forms part of a compromise document, concerning the Lord's Supper. Included are lists of the theologians who signed it.

1574
Torg

1582

Luther, Martin, 1483-1546.

TOMVS PRIMVS [-SEPTIMUS] OMNIVM OPERVM REVERENDI DOMINI MARTINI LVTHERI ...

Wittebergae : 1545-1583. [See annotation below.]

7 v. ; 31 cm. (fol. in 6s).

There is a stamp on the last flyleaf of all seven volumes reading, "Disposed of by the Royal institution."

Aland, p. 562; OCLC: *16187859.*

The Wittenberg edition of Luther's Latin works. The first volume appeared in 1545 and had a preface by Luther himself. In this preface Luther tried to see himself in historical perspective. This set is an artificially created set with no apparent reason for the inclusion of each of the volumes. Possibly it represents what a theology student could find and afford. The texts are all here, only the printings are not uniform as we have the last printing of each volume:Vol. I: VVITEBERGAE Typis Zachariae Lehmani, M.D.LXXXII. Vol. II: [Wittenberg: Lorenz Schwenck, 1562.]Vol. III: VVITEBERGAE Typis Zachariae Lehmani, M.D.LXXXIII. Vol. IV: VVITEBERGAE EXCVDEBAT IOHANNES LVFFT ANNO M.D.LXXIIII. Vol. V: VVITEBERGEE PER Ioannen Lufft. 1554. Vol. VI: UUITEBERGAE, Excudebat Matthaeus UUelack. Anno M.D.LXXX. Vol. VII: VVITEBERGAE, Per Thomam Klug. 1558. Kurt Aland's *Hilfsbuch zum Lutherstudium* has a concise printing history of this work.

1582
Luth

Index of Authors and Contributors

A

C

Cajetan, Tommaso de Vio, 1469-1534. 1-64, 1-240, 3-810, 3-1049

Camerarius, Joachim, 1500-1574. 4-1269, 4-1288, 4-1347, 4-1436

Capella, Galeazzo Flavio, 1487-1537. 3-947

Capito, Wolfgang, 1478-1541. 2-652

Carion, Johannes. 3-1113

Carranza, Bartolomé, 1503-1576. 3-1114, 4-1289

Castellense, Adriano, b. 1458? 3-831

Catharinus Politus, Ambrosius, 1483?-1553. 1-241, 3-1071

Charlemagne, 742-814. 3-1194

Charles V, Holy Roman Emperor, 1500-1558. 3-1087

Chytraeus, David, 1531-1600. 4-1308

Civilius, pseudonym. 4-1216

Clamanges, Nicolas de, 1355?-1437. 1-164

Clichtove, Josse, d. 1543. 2-411, 2-514, 2-653

Cochlaeus, Johannes, 1479-1552. 2-412, 2-515, 2-598 - 2-600, 2-706, 2-722, 2-723, 2-744, 3-833, 3-857, 3-948, 3-949, 3-1072 - 3-1074, 3- 1115, 3-1195, 4-1447

Coelestin, Johann Friedrich. 4-1459

Cogelerus, Johannes, fl. 1558-1588. 4-1349

Cologne (Ecclesiastical Province). Council (1536). 3-950, 3-1020

Contarini, Gasparo, 1484-1542. 4-1473

Cortesi, Paolo, 1465-1510. 1-43

Corvinus, Antonius, 1501-1553. 3-903, 3-997

Cragius, Tilemann, fl. 1546-1577. 3-1196

Crautwald, Valentin. 3-1036

Crell, Paul, 1531-1579. 4-1460

Cruciger, Caspar, 1504-1548. 3-1174

Culmann, Leonhard, 1498?-1562. 2-724

Cymber, Udelo, pseudonym 1-243

Cyprian, Saint, Bishop of Carthage, d. 258. 1-244

Cyril, Saint, Patriarch of Alexandria, 370?-444. 2-707

D

Demosthenes, 385?-322 B.C. 2-516, 3-811

Denck, Hans, 1498?-1527. 2-682

Diepold, Johannes 1-326, 2-415

Dietenberger, Johannes, d. 1537. 2-517

Dietrich, Veit, 1506-1549. 3-1050 - 3-1053, 3-1089, 3-1177

Dölsch, Johann, d. 1523. 1-168

Dungersheim, Hieronymus, 1465-1540. 2-783 - 2-785

Durand, Guillaume, 1230?-1296. 1-18

E

Eberlin von Günzburg, Johann, 1470?-1533. 1-247, 1-327, 2-601

Eck, Johann, 1486-1543. 1-105, 1-113, 1-129, 2-654, 2-683 - 2-684, 2-746 - 2-747, 2-786, 3-812 - 3-814, 3-835, 3-904, 3-1021 - 3-1022, 3-1054, 3-1090, 4-1322

Eisengrein, Wilhelm, 1542/1544-1584. 4-1429

Eitzen, Paulus de. 4-1323

Emser, Hieronymus, 1477?-1527. 1-130 - 1-131, 1-248, 2-519

Erasmus, Desiderius, 1466?-1536. 1-89, 1-96, 1-328, 2-520 - 2-522, 2-655, 2-726 - 2-727, 2-787 - 2-788, 3-837, 3-859, 3-951, 3-1001- 3-1004, 3-1120, 4-1351 - 4-1352, 4-1369, 4-1423, 4-1477

I

J

K

L

Schwenckfeld, Caspar, 1489-1561. 2-742, 3-878, 3-995, 3-1145, 3-1164 · 3-1166, 4-1266, 4-1277 · 4-1278, 4-1300 · 4-1301, 4-1315 · 4-1316, 4-1363 · 4-1364, 4-1399 · 4-1400, 4-1411 · 4-1413, 4-1426, 4-1441

Sleidanus, Johannes, 1506-1556. 4-1317, 4-1333, 4-1343, 4-1365, 4-1446

Soto, Pedro de, 1495/1500-1563. 4-1318, 4-1344, 4-1366

Spalatin, Georg, 1484-1545. 1-7 · 1-8

Spangenberg, Cyriacus, 1528-1604. 4-1427

Spangenberg, Johann, 1484-1550. 3-1146, 4-1285

Spengler, Lazarus, 1479-1534. 1-232, 1-319, 2-774, 3-898

Stadion, Christoph von. 3-943

Staphylus, Friedrich, 1512?-1564. 4-1302, 4-1378 · 4-1379, 4-1390, 4-1414

Staupitz, Johann von, d. 1524. 1-62, 1-111, 1-127

Stigel, Johann, 1515-1562. 3-1147

Stoeffler, Johann, 1452-1531. 1-75

Stoltz, Johann, 1514-1556. 1-12

Stör, Thomas 2-587

Stössel, Johann. 4-1442

Strauss, Jakob, 1480?-1533? 1-405 · 1-407, 2-506 · 2-508, 2-589, 2-680

Strigel, Victorinus, 1524-1569. 4-1417

Suevus, Sigismundus, 1526-1596. 4-1418 · 4-1419

Surgant, Johann Ulrich, d. 1503. 1-39

Sutell, Johannes, 1504-1575. 3-996, 3-1070

T

Tauler, Johannes, 1300?-1361. 1-320, 1-408, 4-1345

Thalassius, Bishop of Caesarea 1-233

Theognis. 4-1401

Thomas Aquinas, Saint, 1225?-1274. 1-15, 4-1469

Trogus, Pompeius. 3-852

U

Ulrich, Duke of Württemberg, 1487-1550. 3-926

Ulrich, Saint, Bishop of Augsburg, 890-973. 1-234

Unicornius, Paulus. 4-1420

V

Valla, Lorenzo, 1405-1457. 1-161

Vegio, Maffeo, 1406/7-1458. 1-51 · 1-52

Velleius Paterculus, 19 B.C.?-30 A.D.? 1-235

Vergerio, Pietro Paolo, 1498-1565. 4-1286, 4-1303, 4-1334, 4-1380

Vergil, Polydore, 1470?-1555. 4-1470 · 4-1471

Virvesius, Alphonsus. 3-1047

Vivaldus, Joannes Ludovicus, d. 1540. 1-37

W

W., J. v. 1-173

Wallser, Hans 1-322

Werner, Johann Sigismund, 1491-1554. 4-1367

Westphal, Joachim, 1510?-1574. 4-1267, 4-1443

Wimpina, Konrad Koch, 1460-1531. 2-775 · 2-776

Witzel, Georg, 1501-1573. 3-854 · 3-855, 3-879 · 3-881, 3-899 · 3-900, 3-973 · 3-974, 3-1106, 3-1186 · 3-1188, 4-1209 · 4-1210

Z

Index of Titles

A

B

C

D

E

H

I

J

K

N

O

P

Q

R

S

V

W

X

Z

Index of Printers and Publishers

A

Accolti, Giulio 4-1469
Aich, Arnd von 2-421
Alantsee, Leonhard 1-76
Alantsee, Lukas 1-76
Alopecius, see Fuchs
Andreae, Hieronymus 2-627
Anshelm, Thomas 1-25, 1-30, 1-33, 1-54, 1-61, 1-66, 1-83, 1-85, 1-87 · 1-88, 1-108, 1-115, 1-126, 1-171, 1-218, 1-270
Apianus, Georg 2-692, 2-731
Apianus, Peter 2-692, 2-731
Arrivabene, Andrea 3-1068

B

Bade, Josse 1-330, 3-810
Bapst, Valentin 3-1122, 3-1181, 4-1258, 4-1269, 4-1284, 4-1290, 4-1330, 4-1347
Bär, Hans 2-749, 2-754
Barth, Hans 2-695
Baum, Dietrich 4-1447
Beck, Balthasar 2-790
Behem, Franz 3- 1172, 3-1193, 3-1195, 3-1208, 4-1214, 4-1337
Bellère, Jean 4-1289
Berg, Adam 4-1448
Berwaldt, Jacob 3-1146, 4-1321
Besicken, Johann 1-21
Bienewitz, see Apianus
Birckmann, Arnold 4-1422
Birckmann, Franz 2-706
Birckmann, Johann 4-1360, 4-1476
Blum, Michael 2-773, 3-864
Bonhome, Mathias 3-939
Bonnemère, Antoine 1-246
Boucher, Nicolas 3-1086
Braubach, Peter 3-882, 3-910, 3-1005, 3-1067, 3-1113, 3-1133, 4-1213, 4-1263, 4-1267, 4-1292, 4-1295, 4-1307, 4-1320, 4-1336, 4-1359, 4-1405, 4-1416
Brocar, Arnao, Guillen de 1-84
Brylinger, Nikolaus 3-1056
Buchfürer, Michel 2-456, 2-528

C

Calvo, Andrea 1-305
Canova, Joannes a 4-1332
Carbo, Johannes see Kohl
Cartolari, Girolama de 3-1071
Castiglione, Giovanni da 1-305
Cavellat, Guillaume 4-1215
Cephalaeum, Vuolphium see Köpfel, P
Cervicornus, Eucharius 2-409
Cholinus, Maternus 4-1397
Circhis, Jacobum de 1-37

Z

Zangrius, Petrus 4·1450
Zimmermann, Hans 4·1277

Index of Places

M

Magdeburg 2·750, 3·858, 3·905, 3·907, 3·970, 3·1168 · 3·1169, 3·1176, 3·1185, 3·1189 · 3·1191, 3·1196 · 3·1197, 3·1200 · 3·1202, 3·1204 · 3·1205, 4·1211 · 4·1212, 4·1216 · 4·1217, 4·1220 · 4·1228, 4·1230, 4·1232 · 4·1233, 4·1240, 4·1242, 4·1245, 4·1249 · 4·1254, 4·1265, 4·1268, 4·1275, 4·1279 · 4·1280, 4·1297, 4·1456
Mainz 1·39, 1·313, 3·1151, 3·1172, 3·1193, 3·1195, 3·1208, 4·1214, 4·1271, 4·1337
Marburg 3·993, 3·1018, 4·1267, 4·1338
Milan 1·77, 1·305
Monaco 2·585
München 1·127, 2·648 · 2·649, 2·721, 2·776, 4·1448

N

Naples 2·578
Neyss 4·1390
Nürnberg 1·20, 1·22 · 1·23, 1·34, 1·42, 1·62, 1·93, 1·111, 1·128, 1·144, 1·147 · 1·149, 1·204 · 1·205, 1·217, 1·318 · 1·319, 1·333, 1·374, 2·415, 2·419, 2·447, 2·451 · 2·452, 2·455, 2·460, 2·462 · 2·463, 2·465, 2·468 · 2·470, 2·491, 2·512, 2·523, 2·530, 2·544, 2·547, 2·550, 2·556, 2·558 · 2·559, 2·566, 2·571, 2·579, 2·583, 2·596, 2·608 · 2·609, 2·627, 2·629, 2·637, 2·664, 2·666, 2·668 · 2·670, 2·672, 2·679, 2·691, 2·701 · 2·703, 2·713, 2·718, 2·735, 2·737, 2·740, 2·751, 2·755, 2·761 · 2·762, 2·764, 2·767, 2·770, 2·774, 2·778 · 2·779, 2·796, 2·800 · 2·801, 3·816, 3·820, 3·853, 3·884, 3·911, 3·920, 3·925, 3·959, 3·967, 3·984, 3·998, 3·1000, 3·1010, 3·1024, 3·1040 · 3·1041, 3·1045, 3·1050 · 3·1053, 3·1078, 3·1099, 3·1101 · 3·1102, 3·1105, 3·1118, 3·1159 · 3·1160, 3·1171, 3·1177, 3·1183, 4·1237, 4·1241, 4·1299, 4·1302, 4·1311, 4·1314, 4·1340, 4·1354, 4·1374, 4·1410, 4·1439

O

Oberursel 4·1394, 4·1420
Oppenheim 1·75

P

Paris 1·29, 1·50 · 1·52, 1·132, 1·246, 1·330, 2·411, 2·514, 2·577, 2·726 · 2·727, 3·810, 3·895, 3·915, 3·921, 3·930, 3·1013, 3·1019, 3·1049, 3·1075, 3·1086, 3·1091, 3·1100, 3·1194, 4·1215, 4·1248, 4·1261, 4·1444, 4·1473, 4·1477
Pforzheim 1·25, 1·27, 1·30, 1·33, 4·1367, 4·1413

R

Regensburg 1·364 · 1·365, 1·367 · 1·368, 2·658, 4·1305
Rome 1·16, 1·21, 1·41, 1·46 · 1·49, 1·55 · 1·59, 1·64, 1·67 · 1·74, 1·79 · 1·82, 1·99 · 1·100, 1·240, 3·941, 3·1071, 4·1355, 4·1361, 4·1372, 4·1375, 4·1408 · 4·1409, 4·1421, 4·1469

S

Salamanca 4·1332
Saluzzo 1·37
Schlettstadt 1·312, 1·164
Schwäbisch Hall 3·910, 3·1005
Speyer 1·35, 1·286, 2·549
Steinburck 1·372
Strasbourg 1·15, 1·32, 1·63, 1·89, 1·91, 1·103, 1·106, 1·167, 1·172, 1·176, 1·196, 1·227, 1·242, 1·249, 1·254, 1·311, 1·317, 1·362, 1·381, 1·401, 2·412, 2·424, 2·448, 2·471 · 2·472, 2·474, 2·484, 2·492, 2·495, 2·517, 2·519, 2·557, 2·565, 2·591, 2·605 · 2·607, 2·610, 2·622, 2·634, 2·638, 2·640, 2·646, 2·650, 2·652, 2·675, 2·743, 2·790, 3·937, 3·1107, 3·1083, 3·1085, 3·1144, 4·1317, 4·1365, 4·1446

T

Tübingen 1·54, 1·61, 1·66, 1·83, 1·85, 1·87 · 1·88, 2·704, 2·861, 3·926, 3·1173, 4·1303, 4·1381, 4·1435

U

Ulm 2·504, 3·860
Ursel, see Oberursel

V

Venice 1·17 · 1·19, 1·26, 1·65, 1·310, 3·815, 3·851, 3·877, 3·924, 3·1020, 3·1068, 3·1120, 3·1114, 3·1161 · 3·1163, 4·1331
Vienna 1·76, 1·268

W

Wittenberg 1·116, 1·119, 1·122, 1·141, 1·146, 1·165, 1·168, 1·174 · 1·175, 1·177 · 1·179, 1·182 · 1·185, 1·191 · 1·192, 1·195, 1·198, 1·200, 1·202, 1·207 · 1·209, 1·221 · 1·224, 1·226, 1·232, 1·234, 1·251 · 1·252, 1·256 · 1·257, 1·260 · 1·261, 1·263, 1·265 · 1·267, 1·269, 1·271, 1·275, 1·277 · 1·284, 1·289 · 1·293, 1·297 · 1·298, 1·301 · 1·302, 1·306 · 1·309, 1·324, 1·327, 1·329, 1·332, 1·334, 1·336 · 1·337, 1·354 · 1·355, 1·359 · 1·360, 1·371, 1·373, 1·377, 1·382 · 1·383, 1·385 · 1·386, 1·390, 1·394 · 1·395, 1·397 · 1·398, 1·407, 2·413, 2·416, 2·438, 2·440 · 2·445, 2·449 · 2·450, 2·453, 2·458, 2·461, 2·464, 2·466 · 2·467, 2·477, 2·479 · 2·480, 2·482 · 2·483, 2·487, 2·489, 2·497, 2·513, 2·542, 2·546, 2·551 · 2·555, 2·560 · 2·561, 2·563 · 2·564, 2·568, 2·572 · 2·573, 2·584, 2·595 · 2·596, 2·617, 2·620, 2·623 · 2·624, 2·628, 2·631 · 2·632, 2·635 · 2·636, 2·660 · 2·661, 2·673 · 2·674, 2·676, 2·688, 2·695, 2·697, 2·709 · 2·711, 2·714 · 2·717, 2·719, 2·725, 2·732, 2·734, 2·736, 2·738 · 2·739, 2·741, 2·752 · 2·753, 2·757 · 2·760, 2·763, 2·765 · 2·766, 2·768 · 2·769, 2·771 · 2·772, 2·780 · 2·782, 2·789, 2·791 · 2·795, 2·797 · 2·799, 2·802 · 2·805, 3·817 · 3·819, 3·821 · 3·826, 3·828 · 3·829, 3·832, 3·834, 3·836, 3·838 · 3·847, 3·850, 3·865 · 3·876, 3·883, 3·885 · 3·894, 3·896, 3·898, 3·903, 3·906, 3·908 · 3·909, 3·912, 3·914, 3·916 · 3·919, 3·923, 3·927, 3·929, 3·931 · 3·936, 3·938, 3·940, 3·944, 3·947, 3·954 · 3·958, 3·960 · 3·964, 3·969, 3·971, 3·977 · 3·983, 3·985, 3·987 · 3·989, 3·992, 3·994, 3·996 · 3·997, 3·999, 3·1007 · 3·1009, 3·1011 · 3·1012, 3·1015 · 3·1016, 3·1025 · 3·1027, 3·1030 · 3·1032, 3·1034 · 3·1035, 3·1037, 3·1039, 3·1042, 3·1046, 3·1048, 3·1055, 3·1058 · 3·1061, 3·1063 · 3·1064, 3·1070, 3·1077, 3·1079 · 3·1082, 3·1084, 3·1089, 3·1092, 3·1094, 3·1096 · 3·1098, 3·1103, 3·1110 · 3·1112, 3·1116, 3·1119, 3·1124 · 3·1125, 3·1129 · 3·1131, 3·1134, 3·1136 · 3·1141, 3·1147 · 3·1149, 3·1156, 3·1158 · 3·1174, 3·1184, 3·1206, 4·1231, 4·1235, 4·1256 · 4·1257, 4·1259, 4·1262, 4·1264, 4·1273, 4·1283, 4·1285, 4·1291, 4·1293, 4·1298, 4·1308, 4·1323, 4·1327 · 4·1329, 4·1341 · 4·1342, 4·1346, 4·1349 · 4·1350, 4·1353, 4·1356 · 4·1358, 4·1362, 4·1371, 4·1376, 4·1382, 4·1384 · 4·1385, 4·1387 · 4·1389, 4·1396, 4·1401, 4·1403 · 4·1404, 4·1406, 4·1431 · 4·1432, 4·1434, 4·1440, 4·1460, 4·1464 · 4·1466, 4·1472, 4·1480 · 4·1481
Wolfenbüttel 4·1452 · 4·1453, 4·1462
Worms 2·651
Würzburg 2·776

Y

Z

Zell 3·897
Zürich 1·287 · 1·288, 1·387, 1·391, 2·473, 2·678, 2·720, 3·990, 4·1348
Zwickau 1·358, 2·422, 2·532, 2·562, 2·574, 2·630, 2·662 · 2·663, 2·671, 2·696